I0086037

The Fifth Phase of the Iron Age of Liburnia and the Cemetery of the Hillfort of Dragišić

Dunja Glogović

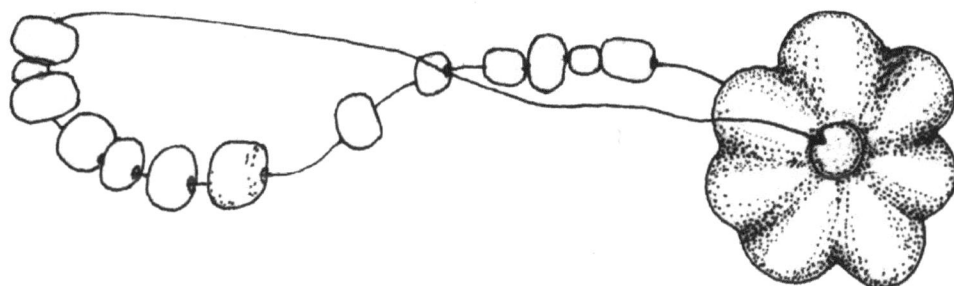

BAR International Series 2689

2014

Published in 2016 by
BAR Publishing, Oxford

BAR International Series 2689

The Fifth Phase of the Iron Age of Liburnia and the Cemetery of the Hillfort of Dragišić

ISBN 978 1 4073 1337 5

© D Glogović and the Publisher 2014

The author's moral rights under the 1988 UK Copyright,
Designs and Patents Act are hereby expressly asserted.

All rights reserved. No part of this work may be copied, reproduced, stored,
sold, distributed, scanned, saved in any form of digital format or transmitted
in any form digitally, without the written permission of the Publisher.

BAR Publishing is the trading name of British Archaeological Reports (Oxford) Ltd.
British Archaeological Reports was first incorporated in 1974 to publish the BAR
Series, International and British. In 1992 Hadrian Books Ltd became part of the BAR
group. This volume was originally published by Archaeopress in conjunction with
British Archaeological Reports (Oxford) Ltd / Hadrian Books Ltd, the Series principal
publisher, in 2014. This present volume is published by BAR Publishing, 2016.

Printed in England

BAR
PUBLISHING

BAR titles are available from:

BAR Publishing
122 Banbury Rd, Oxford, OX2 7BP, UK
EMAIL   info@barpublishing.com
PHONE +44 (0)1865 310431
FAX   +44 (0)1865 316916
www.barpublishing.com

Table of contents

Foreword

This book represents one part of a project that planned for the integral publication of all finds from the excavations of the cemetery at the hillfort of Dragišić. This project was created in the framework of cooperation between the Institute of Archaeology in Zagreb and the Municipal Museum in Šibenik. The analysis of the archaeological finds from Dragišić in fact began while I was still working at the Institute of Archaeology. The cooperation took part with Marko Menđušić, who was a curator in the Šibenik museum in the late 1990s. He was succeeded in this position by Emil Podrug, and I would like to thank both of them for making the archaeological material available for analysis.

They suggested I contact Mario Šlaus, PhD, and Mario Novak, PhD, of the Archaeological Institute of the Croatian Academy of Science and Art in Zagreb, who kindly gave me access to the analysis of osteological remains from the graves at the hillfort of Dragišić that I utilized in the publication, so I would also like to take this opportunity to thank them.

A small selection of photographs of the finds is also published in the book, taken on a volunteer basis by Tomislav Novak, and I thank him sincerely. Thanks also go to my colleagues Andreja Kudelić and Burtol Šiljeg of the Institute of Archaeology for assistance in preparing the illustrative material.

As was true many times before, the archaeological artefacts were drawn for me by Vladimir Glogović, but these were unfortunately his last drawings.

Major encouragement in the publication of this work was given by my esteemed colleagues Kristina Mihovilić and Mitja Guštin in their positive reviews of the text, so I would like to express my special thanks to them, which also extend my colleague Rajka Makjanić, the publisher.

List of figures

List of Plates

THE GEOGRAPHICAL POSITION OF THE LIBURNIANS

The region of the Iron Age Liburnians covered the present Croatian Littoral region, i.e. the Kvarner Bay with its islands, as well as the coast beneath the Velebit Mountains in the northern Adriatic. Northern Dalmatia, the coastal zone of the Ravni Kotari with the Zadar archipelago, and the Bukovica region in the interior represented the central Liburnian territory. The Raša River (Roman: *Arsia fl.*) in the northwestern part of Istria was the northern boundary of Liburnia, while in the south this was the Krka River (Roman: *Titius fl.*) in central Dalmatia.

The Liburnian region ends in Dalmatia to the northwest with the upper course of the Zrmanja River. The Krka River, the southern boundary of the Liburnian area, has its estuary hidden in the deep bay of Šibenik.

Thus, to the north the Liburni shared a boundary with the Histri on the Istrian peninsula, with the Iapodes on the far side of the Velebit Mountains, and with the Delmatae south of the Krka River (Fig. 1).

The above ethnic groups, part of the broader Illyrian nation, are generally considered to have been formed at the beginning of the Iron Age.

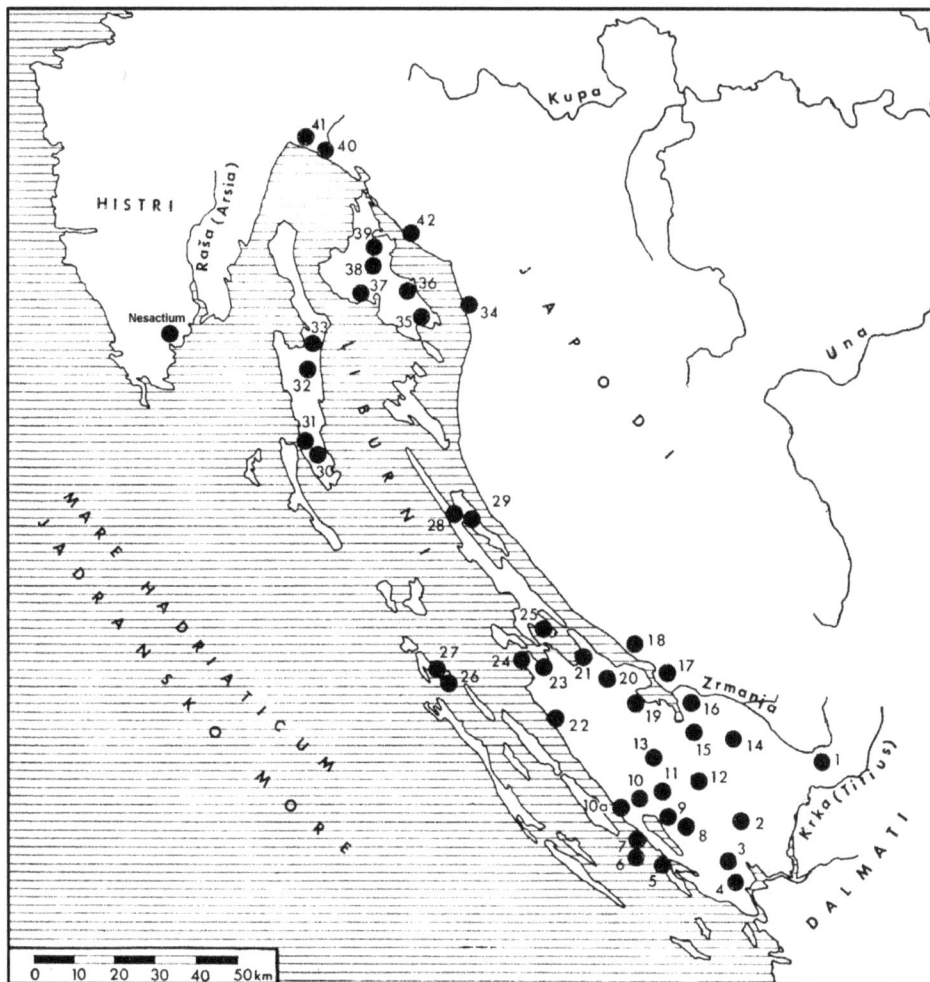

Fig. 1. The map of sites of the last (V) phase of the Liburnian Culture (after Batović 1974). Sites mentioned in the text are in bold. 1. Mokropolje, Đurina gomila; **2. Bribir, Varvaria**; **3. Dragišić, Gradina**; **4. Velika Mrdakovica, Zaton Šibenski**; 5. Murter, Gradina; 6. Vrgada, Gradina; 7. Pakoštane, Školj Veliki; 8. Oton, Vrana Samograd; 9. Vrana, Samograd; 10. Jagodnja Donja, Trojan; 10a. Biograd; **11. Jagodnja Gornja, Gradina**; **12. Podgrađe, Gradina, Asseria**; **13. Nadin, Nedinum**; 14. Medviđa, Gradina, Hadra; 15. Karin, Gradina Miodrag, Corinium; 16. Kruševo; **17. Jesenice, Dračevac**; **18. Starigrad, Argyruntum**; 19. Posedarje, Budim; **20. Radovin, Beretinova Gradina**; **21. Ljubač Kosa, Venac**; **22. Zadar, Iadera**; **23. Nin, Aenona**; 24. Privlaka; 25. Vlašići, Gradac; 26. Molat; 27. Brgulje, Gračina; 28. Novalja, Navalia; 29. Caska, Kissa; 30. Grmozaj kod Osora, Vela Straža; **31. Osor, Apsorus**; 32. Orlec, Skulki; 33. Krčina, Ćuli; 34. Senj, Senia; **35. Baška (island of Krk)**; 36. Vrbnik, Mali grac; 37. Krk, Curicum; 38. Dobrinj, Gračišće; 39. Dobrinj; 40. Rijeka, Tarsatica; **41. Kastav**; 42. Selce

THE LAST OR FIFTH PHASE OF THE LIBURNIAN IRON AGE

The first chronology of the Liburnian cultural group was published in the mid 1960s by Šime Batović. This first periodization encompassed the time from the 11th century BC to the beginning of the new era (Batović Š 1965, 55 ff.). Somewhat later, a transitional phase was added to the Liburnian chronology from the Bronze Age to the Iron Age, so that the beginning, i.e. the first state of the Iron Age was moved to the beginning of the 9th century BC. The first phase continues through the 9th and 8th centuries BC. The second phase of the Liburnian Iron Age has two sub-phases and extends through the 7th and 6th centuries BC. The third and fourth phases cover the 6th and 5th centuries BC, while the last, fifth phase, with sub-phases A and B, extends from the 4th century BC to the beginning of the common era (Batović Š 1987, 349 ff.). The early sub-phase A of the fifth phase encompasses the 4th and 3rd centuries BC, while sub-phase B encompasses the 2nd and 1st centuries BC.

The material that forms the backbone of sub-phase A of the fifth phase of the Liburnian Iron Age consists of a hoard and graves III and IV from **Baška** on the island of Krk. No details are known about the circumstances of discovery of the graves, and the finds from Baška on the island of Krk ended up before the First World War in the Naturhistorisches Museum in Vienna. The hoard, actually a set of silver jewellery, was published first (Vinski 1956, 19 ff.). Somewhat later, the graves and several scattered finds from Baška were also published – all from the museum in Vienna (Lo Schiavo 1970, 426, Pl. 24, 1-10; 11-16).

The next important find from the fifth Liburnian phase is the hoard of silver jewellery from **Jagodnja Gornja**. This hoard contained twenty-some fibulae, necklaces, earrings, and a few pendants. The hoard was found by chance at the hillfort of Ćosina Gradina. This is one of the largest Liburnian hillforts, located near Benkovac. The finders took the hoard to the Archaeological Museum in Zadar (Batović Š 1974, 167, Pl. 14-25; Glogović 2006 b 134).

An important find dated to sub-phase A is grave 80 from **Asseria**. Excavations have been carried out at Roman Asseria (Podgrađe near Benkovac) on several occasions from the end of the 19th century, and were oriented primarily to the remains of the Roman walls. However, many prehistoric graves beyond the walls of the Roman town were also excavated. The exact location of the graves dug up in those earlier excavations remains unknown. According to records in the archives of the Archaeological Museum in Split, grave 80 at Asseria was excavated by Mihovil Abramić in 1911. The material from the grave that was recorded in the inventory book of the Archaeological Museum in Zadar no longer exists in the museum. It definitely disappeared during the Second World War, and supposedly was taken to Italy. An old photograph of the material from grave 80 at Asseria was published (Batović Š 1965, 12.13, Fig. 19a, 19b), as that is all that remains of it. Additionally, the archives of the Archaeological Museum in Split contain old descriptions of the objects from grave 80 at Asseria written by M. Abramić (Batović Š 2011, 23, 24, 35). Several pieces of jewellery from Asseria are in the Archaeological Museum in Split. These objects also come from the above-mentioned excavations of graves carried out at the beginning of the 20th century (Marović 1970, 265 ff., Pl. 1-4). Several of these finds from Split are reproduced on the table of types of sub-phase B of the fifth phase (Fig. 3, 1.15.20.21) Ivan Marović dated these objects to the end of the first century BC and the beginning of the 1st century AD, chronologically somewhat later than the dating by Šime Batović.

Prehistoric cemeteries exist at several sites around **Nin** (Roman *Aenona*), and systematic archaeological excavation has been carried out at some of them. Important graves dated to phase A are graves 17 (Batović Š 1968, Pl. 17) and 76 from Nin (Batović Š 1968, Pl. 18) while grave 82 belongs to sub-phase B of the fifth phase (Batović Š 1965, Pl. 14, Fig. 20).

Much significant archaeological material from the Late Iron Age comes from the site of **Ljubač Kosa** above the village of Ljubač in the western part of the coastal section of the Ravni Kotari Region. This area contains around a hundred tumuli and a large flat Liburnian cemetery. For years, the graves were illegally and unprofessionally dug up by one local inhabitant. A small part of the finds from which grave units could be reconstructed arrived in the Archaeological Museum in Zadar, while the remainder was sold to private collectors and foreign museums (Glogović 1998, 33). The most valuable data remain the photographs of the finds that were published in 2002 and 2010 by Zdenko Brusić (Brusić 2002, 230-239; Brusić a 2010, 243, Pl. 4, 2.3; Pl. 5, 1.3).

The hillfort of **Nadin** (Roman *Nedinum)* near Benkovac in the Ravni Kotari region has been known from as early as the beginning of the 20th century for many chance scattered finds. Excavations took place in the 1980s. The most interesting material relevant to the fifth phase of the Liburnian Iron Age are the objects from Hellenistic grave vaults. This material, however, was gathered without archaeological supervision and brought to the Archaeological Museum in Zadar. Only recently has a complete catalogue been written of all the artefacts from the three graves, or rather three Hellenistic grave vaults, of which grave 1 was the richest (Batović A 2001, 17-63, Pl. 8-56).

The last, fifth phase of the Liburnian Iron Age is marked by a strong Hellenistic influence on the overall material culture of the Liburnians.

The Liburnian settlements on hillforts began to be surrounded at that time by walls made of large worked stone blocks (Cf. Brusić a 2010, 244, Pl. 1: The hillfort of Lergova gradina near Slivnica). This phenomenon is documented at twenty-some hillfort sites in Liburnian territory. The most important hillforts in the central Liburnian region with this type of fortification are Nadin, Asseria and Bribir. The construction of fortresses using the *opus quadratum* technique began in the 3rd century BC (Batović Š 1987, 354).

At the hillforts of Velika Mrdakovica and Dragišić in the southern Liburnian territory, walls of dwellings in the settlement have been documented as also being built from worked stone blocks (Brusić 1976, 116 ff., Pl. 3; Brusić 2000 a, 5 ff., Pl. 24, 1. 2).

The usual burial ritual among the Liburni during the Iron Age was burial in a contracted position in a grave pit lined with four unworked stone slabs and covered with another unworked slab. This manner of burial, which represents a Bronze Age tradition, continued at some Liburnian cemeteries even up to the Roman period, meaning it also continued into the fifth phase of the Liburnian Iron Age (Batović Š 1974, 222).

New elements in terms of burial in the fifth phase of the Liburnian Iron Age are exhibited by the above-mentioned grave vaults at Nadin. They are built of carved slabs and blocks. Several individuals were buried in these grave vaults, hence they were not individual graves. This burial ritual and the grave architecture as documented at Nadin were defined as "a Hellenistic type of grave" (Batović Š 1974, 222). From approximately the same period, walled grave vaults with the deceased placed in an extended position were also documented at the hillfort of Velika Mrdakovica (Brusić 1976, 116, Pl. 4, 2). At the cemetery of the nearby hillfort of Dragišić, the excavated graves contained the extended skeletons of the deceased in grave vaults partly carved into stone and bordered by an oval line of stones (Brusić 2000 a, 1). The dating of such a manner of construction is made difficult by the fact that they were used on several occasions (Brusić 1980, 11).

Excavations were recently started again at Asseria, and again prehistoric graves outside the Roman walls were investigated. These graves had been partially damaged by the construction of the Roman walls. The skeletal remains and the grave goods were scatted around the graves. Nonetheless, they offer an insight into the manner of building the graves of the earlier phase – sub-phase A – of the fifth Liburnian phase. These burials at Asseria were in rectangular pits dug into the bedrock. The pits were lined with stone slabs in the earlier manner. The finds from the graves, which mostly consisted of jewellery, are dated to the fourth phase of the Liburnian Iron Age culture and sub-phase A of the fifth phase of the Liburnian Iron Age. Baška type fibulae predominated. In one of the graves (grave no. 5) they were found together with a fibula of the Certosa type *VII f* according to Teržan (Klarin 2000, 27-30, 33, Pl. 17, 1-5). Only in one grave

was a multiple burial documented, with the deceased in a contracted position. That grave contained six Baška type fibulae and one Certosa fibula (Brusić 2005, 10, 12, Fig. 4, 7).

Judging from the new finds from Asseria, in the earlier sub-phase A of the fifth phase of the Late Iron Age of Liburnia the graves continued the Bronze Age traditions, i.e. grave pits lined with unworked stone slabs. Only in sub-phase B of the fifth phase did Hellenistic type graves appear, such as those as Nadin and Velika Mrdakovica.

In addition to the grave architecture, a new phenomenon in the burial ritual, again a result of Greek influence, was the placement of pottery vessels in the grave, which had not been the custom among the Liburnians until then. Š. Batović noted that the richer graves had more Hellenistic pottery material while the poorer graves contained primarily locally produced pottery, reflecting the social stratification of the Liburnian population.

In the fifth phase of the Liburnian Iron Age many attire items and jewellery go out of fashion, and are replaced by new or imported forms of jewellery and attire accessories (Batović Š 1974, 221-232). New decorative motifs can be found among the locally produced jewellery, such as rosettes, palmettes, masks, and human faces, modelled on Hellenistic and Roman jewellery. The techniques of filigree and gilding silver jewellery are also used. Amber gradually ceases to be used from the beginning of the 4th century BC, to appear again in the Roman period. This phenomenon has been noted throughout a wide area with contemporary cultures featuring a use of amber jewellery (Palavestra 2006, 45).

A table of the types of the material culture of the last phase of the Liburnian Iron Age including both sub-phases – A and B – was published in 1974 in the study of the hoard from Jagodnja Gornja. A table was also published with the forms of imported pottery from southern Italy found at Liburnian sites (Batović Š 1974, 225, Fig. 7, 8, 9).

Newer and modified tables of the types from the last phase of the Liburnian Iron Age were published by Šime Batović at the beginning of the 1980s (Batović Š 1981, 104, Fig. 6, 107, Fig. 7) and they were taken as the final version of the types of the fifth phase.

Sub-phase A of the fifth phase is characterized by the earlier form of silver plate fibulae (Fig. 2, 1.4), fibulae of the Baška type (Fig. 2, 6), Certosa fibulae with a bottle-shaped foot type I variant *c* according to Teržan (Fig. 2, 7), and Certosa fibula (Fig. 2, 5) of type *VII f* (Teržan 1977 a, 319, 328).

Developed forms of spectacle fibulae (Fig. 2, 8) also continue into the beginning sub-phase of the fifth phase. This type of fibula exhibits a long continuity, extending from the second phase of the Liburnian Iron Age (9th-8th centuries BC; Glogović 2003, 23-33).

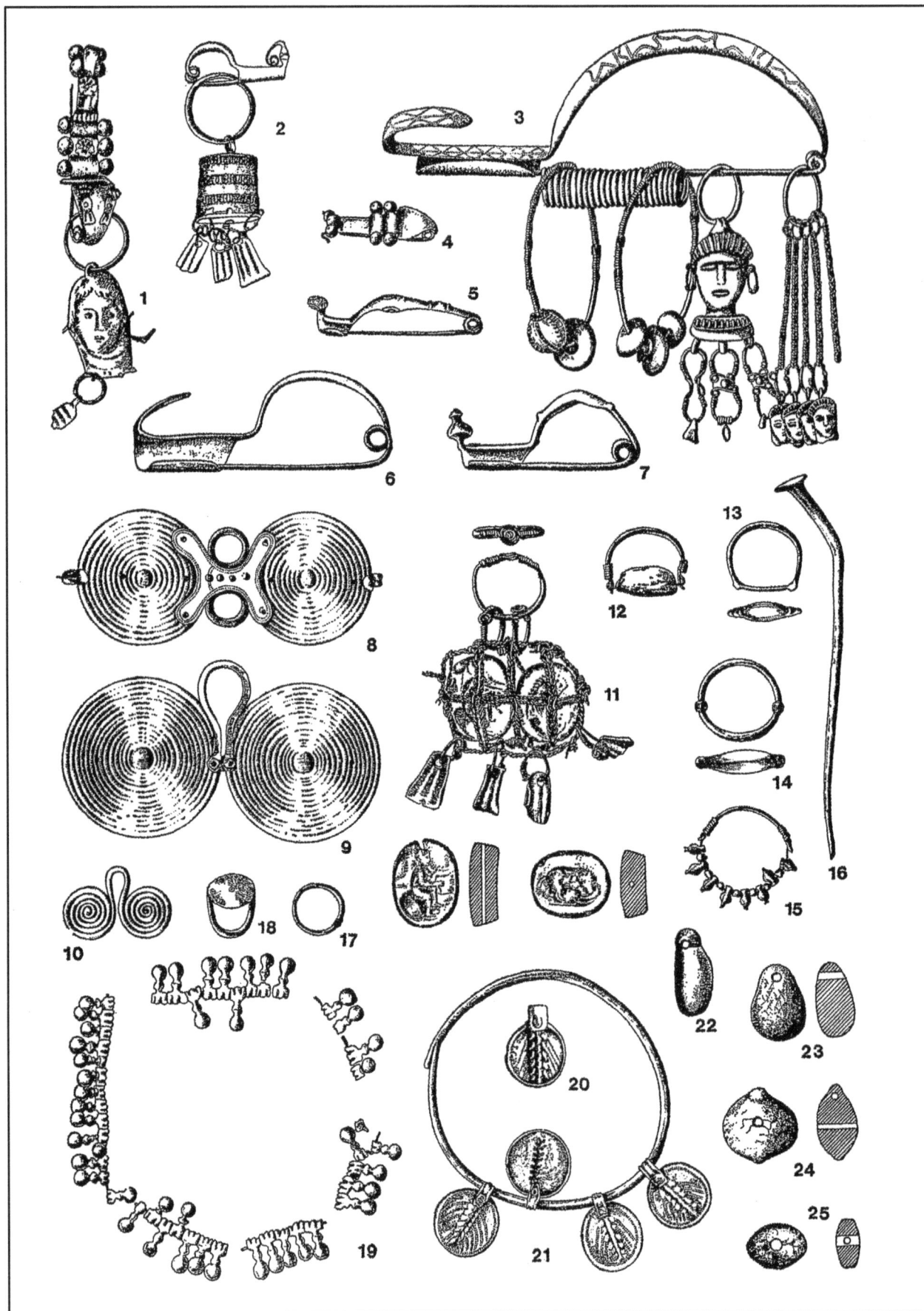

Fig. 2. Basic jewellery forms of phase V A of the Liburnian Culture of the Iron Age, 4th-3rd centuries BC
1: Nin, grave 76; 2: Asseria, grave 80; 3: Baška (island of Krk) hoard; 4-5, 7, 11-13, 16-18, 20-25: Jagodnja Gornja, hoard; 6, 9-10, 14: unknown provenience; 8: Nin; 15: Asseria; 19: Nin-Solana, grave 42. 1-4, 7, 11-15, 20, 21 silver; 5-6, 8-10, 16, 17-19 bronze; 22-25 amber. Not to scale.

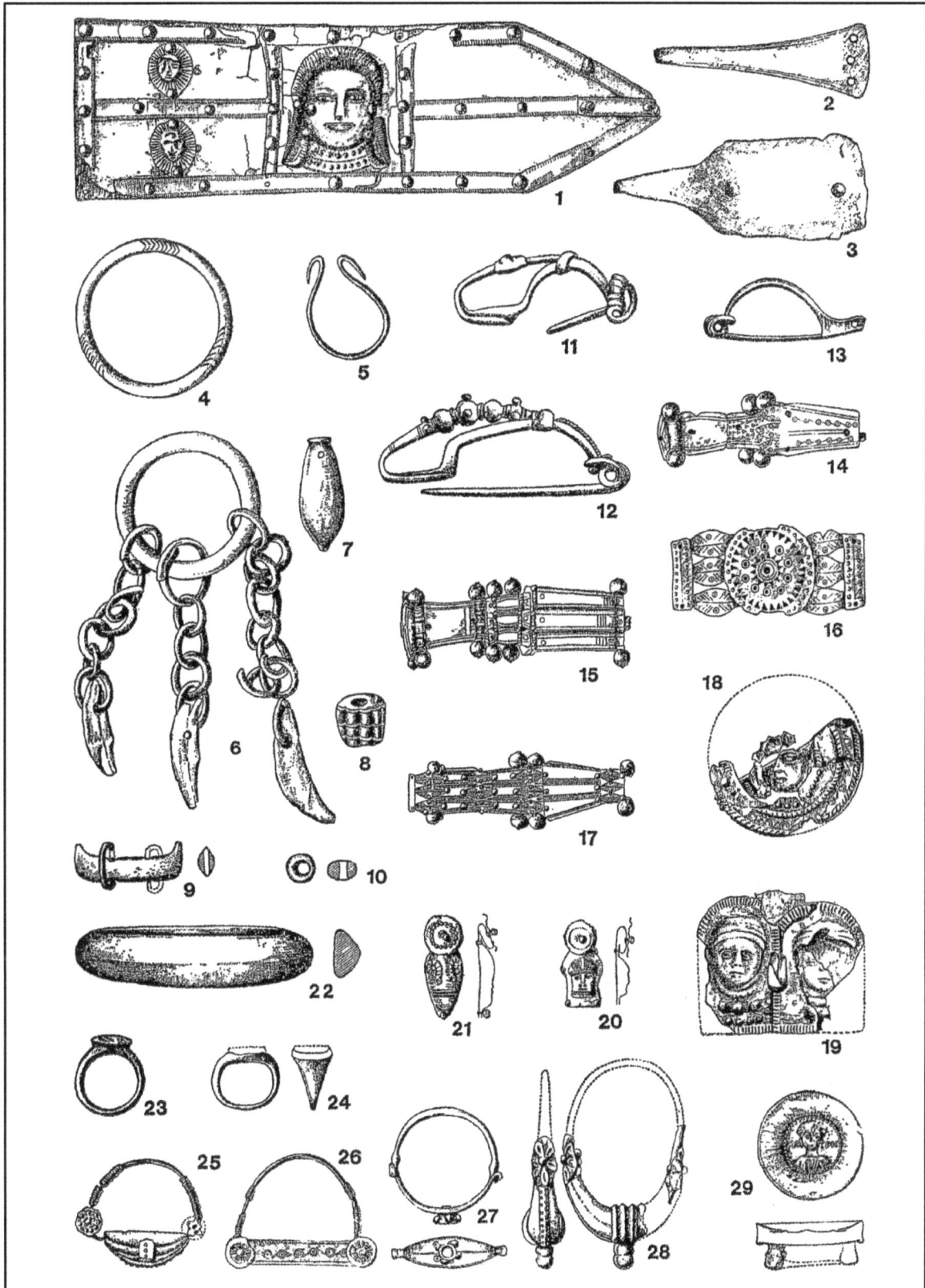

Fig. 3. Basic jewellery forms of phase V B of the Liburnian Culture of the Iron Age, 2nd-1st centuries BC
1, 15, 20, 21: Asseria; 2-5, 7-9, 13, 23-24: Nadin, grave 1; 6: Nin, grave 50; 11, 12, 14, 16, 18, 19, 28:
Nin, grave 82; 17: Nin; 10, 25, 26: unknown provenience; 27: Medviđa; 29: Nin-Ždrijac.
1, 12, 14-21, 25-29 silver; 2-6, 9, 11, 13, 22-24 bronze; 7 amber; 8 glass. Not to scale.

An important difference in relation to the previous phase is the appearance of fibulae of the Middle La Tène type in sub-phase B of the fifth phase (Fig. 3, 11.12). Š. Batović considered the La Tène fibulae to be the products of local workshops, while some fibulae of this type were imports from northern Italy. In terms of the development of

Liburnian plate fibulae in sub-phase B, there are later variants of Liburnian plate fibulae (Fig. 3, 14-17) and Gorica type fibulae (Fig. 3, 13).

At the very beginning of the Liburnian fifth phase objects appear that undoubtedly are modelled on Hellenistic or Roman jewellery, such as rings with a spiral crown, rings with an oval crown, gems, pendants depicting a face, and amber beads of bag or bottle shape. Metapontan coins were strung as pendants on the necklace from Jagodnja Gornja (Fig. 2, 21). Earrings or rings with a loop in the shape of the letter U with an amber bead (Fig. 2, 12) were manufactured according to examples of Hellenistic jewellery.

Fibulae of the Baška type, of the Certosa type *VII f*, and Certosa fibulae with a bottle-shaped foot are not limited merely to the Liburnian region, rather they show the circulation and exchange of goods within the broader Illyrian association in the 4th and 3rd centuries BC.

The situation is similar in the later, sub-phase B of the fifth phase in terms of the supra-regional types, i.e. forms that were not specifically Liburnian. Of all the types of sub-phase B of the fifth phase only the Middle La Tène type fibulae are still generally considered to be prehistoric. The Gorica type fibulae is located at the boundary, with a beginning in the Roman period, while the remainder were widely distributed types of Hellenistic and Roman jewellery, including glass beads. Spectacle fibulae, as a specifically Liburnian element, cease to be in use only in sub-phase B of the fifth phase.

Celtic coins are occasionally found at Liburnian sites from the period of the last, fifth phase. It is presumed that they were recognized as a means of payment at the end of the Liburnian Iron Age (Batović Š 1974, 225; Bonačić-Mandinić 2003, 438 ff.).

In the last phase of the Liburnian Iron Age culture, Hellenistic influences overlap in artefacts of local production, along with Hellenistic-Roman imports, and traditional Bronze Age forms, such as spectacle fibulae. Certain attire elements and jewellery of coarse local production, particularly utilitarian ones, from the fifth phase are insignificant chronologically, such as hooks, tweezers, and a pendant-amulet with animal teeth (Fig. 3, 2.3.6). On one typological table of sub-phase B of the fifth phase, an object from Nin was placed that definitely does not belong there, the lid of a box-shaped fibula (Fig. 3, 29) from the end of the 6th and beginning of the 7th centuries (Preložnik 2008, 203, Fig. 1).

THE HISTORICAL CONTEXT OF THE FIFTH PHASE OF THE LIBURNIAN IRON AGE

The Liburni, like other Illyrian peoples in Dalmatia, arrived on the historical scene at the time of their first contacts with the Greeks.

Greek navigation along the coast of the central Adriatic began in the 8th century BC. A pre-colonial interest in the sense of trade with the native populations in the northern and central Adriatic is proven archaeologically by the many finds of imported goods from the late Archaic and Classical periods at Liburnian sites. These include the well-known Attic skyphos from Nin, dated to the end of the 6th century BC (Brusić 2010 b, 103).

However, reports about voyages and attempts to found Greek settlements on the coast further north than the island of Corfu and Dyrrhachium on the Albanian coast are in the domain of myth and legend, so the credibility of the early written sources remains the subject of scientific discussion.

Hence a tradition exists of a Liburnian thalassocracy and the notorious Liburnian piracy throughout the entire Adriatic Sea. However, any real domination by the Liburnians along the entire eastern Adriatic coast is questionable, although the theory of a Liburnian thalassocracy does have its supporters among scholars of Croatian history. Information about the native population of northern Dalmatia is gradually increasing for the period of the founding of the Greek colonies in the Adriatic.

According to Slobodan Čače, the Greek presence in the central Adriatic can be confirmed with certainty in terms of historical and archaeological arguments through four essential elements (Čače / Kuntić-Makvić 2010, 68 ff).

The first is epigraphic proof, in the form of the inscription from Lumbarda that refers to intervention by the Issaeans in events on the eastern part of the island of Korčula at the beginning of the 3rd century BC, this being the date of the inscription, known as the Lumbarda Psephisma.

The foundation of Tragurium and Epetium on the coast is the second element, or the second secure proof of the presence of the Greeks on the Dalmatian coast. The date of the foundation of Tragurium and Epetium has not been reliably established, and Slobodan Čače supports an earlier date – in the 3rd century BC, in contrast to some researchers who place the foundation of these Greek settlements in the 2nd century BC.

The third argument is largely archaeological. The archaeological excavations at Cape Ploče near Rogoznica, somewhat south of Šibenik, have confirmed the existence of a Greek maritime shrine at this promontory point along the central Adriatic coast (Šešelj 2010, 110-113). It was established before the end of the 4th century BC, and the most obvious candidates for the founders would be the Greek Issaeans, i.e. the Greek settlers on the island of Vis.

It is well known that at the very beginning of the fourth century, the colony of Issa was founded by Syracusan Greeks at the site of the present town of Vis on the island of the same name. Soon after the founding, Issa began to mint its own coinage, develop crafts, and produce pottery. The settlers planted vineyards in the interior parts of the island and started wine production and trade. The settlement prospered and Issa remained economically and politically the most influential Greek colony in the central Adriatic.

We have finally arrived at the fourth element of Greek presence in the Adriatic Sea that refers to the complicated political and military circumstances of the Roman conquest of the Illyrian lands. In this the Greeks from *Issa* and *Pharos* (Starigrad on the island of Hvar) played an important, in fact vital role representing in general terms the mutual Greek and Roman interests in conflicts with the local inhabitants. At the end of the third century and in the second century BC, the ascendant Illyrian kingdom fought against the Romans, and lost the war in 167 BC. After the fall of the Illyrian kingdom, the Delmatae became strengthened and militarily opposed the Romans, which ended in the Roman subjugation of large territories of central Dalmatia. The triumph over the Delmatae was celebrated by P. Cornelius Scipio in 155 BC. The Liburnians, together with the Iapodes, were defeated in military operations commanded by C. Sempronius Tuditanus in 129 BC. The Liburnian territory was definitively included into the Roman province of Dalmatia around 35 BC, this marking the end of the prehistory of Liburnia.

The Greek colonizing activities in Dalmatia, followed by the Roman expansion into the Illyrian regions was in fact the historical background to the fifth and final phase of the Iron Age of the Liburnians (4th-1st centuries BC).

THE HILLFORT OF DRAGIŠIĆ IN THE FRAMEWORK OF THE FIFTH PHASE OF THE LIBURNIAN IRON AGE

The site of Dragišić hillfort is located in the close hinterland of the city of Šibenik (Fig. 4) in central Dalmatia in the southern Liburnian territory. The hillfort is positioned on a hill 166 m above sea level above the hamlet of the same name to the northeast of the elevation. The hillfort is surrounded by fields and fertile land, with the villages of Grabovci and Gačelezi to the southeast. The fertile land, ponds, and the nearby streams of Kriva Draga and Gudača, as well as rocky ground overgrown with macchia were all suitable for grazing stock, ensuring good living conditions even in prehistory. Good visual communication existed from the hillfort of Dragišić with other prehistoric hillforts in the vicinity, and it was possible to monitor the route that led further into the interior towards Bribirska Glavica. Traces of settlement in the form of buildings were found on the peak of the ellipsoid plateau of the hillfort with dimensions of ca. 250 x 150 m, while the remains of houses were also noted along the edges of the plateau. The hillfort settlement has no evident defensive wall. The entrance to the hillfort was considered by Brusić to be on the eastern side, as a path exits there leading to the foot of the hill. The cemetery and graves are located alongside that path leading to the top of the hillfort of Dragišić.

Fig. 4. Detailed map of Dragišić and Mrdakovica

ARCHAEOLOGICAL EXCAVATIONS AT THE HILLFORT OF DRAGIŠIĆ

The archaeological excavations of the cemetery carried out by Zdenko Brusić in 1973 and 1976 uncovered eighteen graves, fourteen of which were from the late Iron Age, three were Hellenistic grave vaults, and one was Roman period cremation burial.

Zdenko Brusić published the results of his excavations, and described the entire situation with the graves at the hillfort, so that it was possible to use Brusić's descriptions of the hillfort and cemetery (Brusić 2000 a, 1-15).

The remains of the graves at the cemetery were visible on the surface as oval indentations in the soil. The hollows were partially surrounded by stones, as documented by photographs in Brusić's publication (Brusić 2000 a, Pl. 25, 1.2.3). Brusić writes that during field survey of the hillfort position above Dragišić it was not clear whether there really were burial traces from the prehistoric period. However, the excavations proved that these truly were graves, i.e. the cemetery, of the settlement on the hilltop. All of the excavated graves, with a few exceptions, were multiple burials. These facts were confirmed by the later excavation of graves carried out by the curator of the Municipal Museum of Šibenik, Marko Menđušić, in 2001, 2002, and 2003. The archaeological material published here came from the twenty-four graves excavated by Menđušić at Dragišić.

As the graves were at the surface of the terrain and had been present throughout a long chronological period, they were subject to the natural erosion or deposition of soil. They were overgrown with natural vegetation, and were crossed by grazing stock, etc. All of these factors caused a gradual destruction of the graves and fragmentation of the grave goods throughout time. This could also have been, among other things, a factor in the mixing of the archaeological material, as well as the accumulation of large quantities of objects in one spot in the original grave pit.

The archaeological material from the graves excavated by Menđušić at Dragišić is stored in the Municipal Museum in Šibenik in bags with the grave number, and on the basis of this the grave units and catalogue with the grave inventories were created. Some of the graves are very rich and contain hundreds of objects, but there were also graves with a modest number of finds. It should be noted that the finds were generally in a poor state of preservation, so that they consist mostly of fragmentary, almost crushed material.

The pottery from the graves, mostly Liburnian Hellenistic relief pottery, was separated from the grave units. It is stored separately in the museum and is not a subject of this catalogue. The pottery finds will be analysed and discussed in the publication of the entire material from the hillfort of Dragišić, including the finds from all excavated graves at the site, currently being prepared.

The remains of bones, i.e. the skeletons from the graves excavated in 2001-2003 were sent to the Archaeological Institute of the Croatian Academy of Sciences and Arts. The osteological analyses were carried out by Mario Šlaus, PhD, and Mario Novak, PhD. In the list of finds from the graves in the catalogue only brief information was offered on the number of buried individuals, and their sex and age, inasmuch as it was possible.

Considering the multiple burials at the cemetery in Dragišić, grave units cannot be utilized as closed finds relevant for dating. For this reason, the analysis of the material is typological, i.e. based on the types of objects. An attempt was made, inasmuch as was possible, to arrange the material in chronological order from the earliest to the latest, while also not neglecting to arrange the finds according to importance.

It should once more be emphasized that the material is highly fragmentary and at first glance appears as a pile of debris, meaning that the challenge to determine it typologically and chronologically was even greater.

THE TYPOLOGY AND CHRONOLOGY OF FINDS
FROM THE GRAVES EXCAVATED IN 2001-2003

FIBULAE

Certosa fibulae

The fibula from grave **14** must first be discussed (Pl. 9b, 54). It has a biconical or poppy-shaped extension to the wide banded foot, the bow has a C-shaped section, and a double loop. It can be compared to the fibula from Otišić with an identical foot and a multiple loop (Marović 1984, 57, Fig. 23, 15). The fibula from Otišić has a massive bow with a shallow D-shaped section. A fibula of the same form as that from Otišić was published by Fulvia Lo Schiavo. It was found at an unknown site in northern Dalmatia (Archaeological Museum of Split, inv. no. 1714). The cross-section of the massive bow is roof-shaped (Lo Schiavo 1970, 448, Pl. 20, 1). A similar fibula from Picugi has a foot with a C-shaped section and a poppy – shaped head on the top. Kristina Mihovilić defined this fibula as variant *d* of type *I*, according to the classification of Certosa fibulae made by Biba Teržan. She also emphasized the fact that this form of foot was present on earlier fibulae of a proto-Certosa type (Mihovilić 1995 a, 86, 87, Pl. 1, 3).

Despite certain differences in details, the fibulae from Dragišić, Picugi, Otišić, and an unknown site in northern Dalmatia form a morphologically homogenous type of fibula. This type is close to fibulae of the Certosa type *I* varianta *c* and *d* (Teržan 1977 a, 319-320) and this group of fibulae could be somewhat earlier than the true Certosa fibulae.

The Certosa fibulae of the Dragišić – Picugi type (Pl. 9b, 54) have the following common typological characteristics: a tall semicircular bow, smooth and undecorated. The bow can be roof-shaped or have a C- or D-shaped section. The broad foot is sometimes decorated and ends in an obliquely placed biconical or poppy-shaped button with a cork-like or conical protrusion.

Šime Batović defined type *I* variants *b, c, d* according to Biba Teržan as *a variant of Certosa-like fibulae with an extended foot in the shape of a bottle*. According to Batović they were further divided into three variants of version *I* with a smooth undecorated bow. The sites of discovery of these variants were: Nin, Asseria, unknown site in Dalmatia, and Jezerine, Ribić, and Golubić (Batović Š 1974, 187).

Fragmentary fibulae of this type, i.e. with a biconical button and cork-like protrusion at the end of the foot, according to Batović *bottle-shaped*, were found at Dragišić in grave **14** (Pl. 9b, 61) and in grave **20** (Pl. 13a, 1). The fibula fragment from grave **14** has a flat banded foot without a catchplate for the pin, while the fragment

of the foot of a fibula from grave **20** has a J-shaped section and a sharp biconical outline of the button with a cork-shaped knob. Fibulae with this shape of button were further divided by both Teržan and Batović into sub-types on the basis of the articulation or moulding on the bow. As not a single bow was preserved of these Certosa fibulae from Dragišić, they cannot be classified in greater detail according to these criteria.

The Lika – Iapodian Certosa fibulae were analysed by Tihana Težak-Gregl. The so-called *Certosoid* fibulae with a foot extension in the shape of a bottle, or fibula tipa *I*, variant *b, c, d* according to Teržan, were classified by Težak-Gregl into type *8* (Težak-Gregl 1981, 32, 33).

Fibulae with an undecorated smooth bow were according to Š. Batović *the first, basic variant of Certosoid fibulae*, (see above), while the example of this variant from Prozor in Lika (Težak-Gregl 1981, 44, Pl. 6, 8) should be added to Š. Batović's list of sites (cf. Batović Š 1974 188, Map 2).

Certosa fibulae with a semicircular bow and a foot ending in a biconical button with a cork-like knob are one of the earlier forms of Certosa fibuae, which otherwise appear from the middle of the first millennium BC. In the Liburnian and Iapodian cultural groups and also in Istria, they develop certain specific variants and morphological features, such as a completely undecorated bow, an obliquely placed biconical or poppy-shaped extension to the foot, and so forth. In terms of the Liburnian culture, the date of the Certosa fibulae with a bottle-shaped foot extension is the 4th and 3rd centuries BC, i.e. the last phase (sub-phase A) of the Liburnian culture.

Several fibulae were found at Dragišić that according to Š. Batović belong to one of the *latest variants of the classic Certosa type fibulae* (Batović Š 1974, 185). Teržan defined these as type *VII* with nine variants (from *a* to *i*). Most of the Liburnian fibulae belong to variant *f* of type *VII*, and the list of sites of discovery in Š. Batović mostly corresponds to the list of finds published by Biba Teržan. These fibulae are characterized by a shallow peak of the bow shifted unsymmetrically forward. At the widened point of the banded bow are multiple arched incisions that appear like eyes. The button on the foot is also decorated with incisions, while the upper broadened surface of the foot bears various decorative motifs (cf. Osor-Kavanela: Glogović 1982, 40, Fig. 4, 1.2.4). An illustrative example of a fibula of this type is the fibula from Jagodnja Gornja (Batović Š 1974, 169, Pl. 14, 1). Težak-Gregl arranged the Certosa fibulae from Lika with the same morphological traits into several variants of type *3*, while the fibula from Jagodnja Gornja was specifically referred to under type *3c* (Težak-Gregl 1981, 29).

The broken Certosa fibula from grave **13** (Pl. 8a, 8) at Dragišić has a hemispherical protrusion between two ribs at the slope of the bow and double loop typical for this form. The front part of the fibula is incomplete, damaged, with a patina. The fibula from grave **20** (Pl. 13b, 38) at Dragišić has a much shallower moulding of the relief decoration on the slope of the bow. The remains of arched incisions can be seen on the widest part of the bow that are characteristic for this kind of Liburnian Certosa fibula. The fibula from grave **11** (Pl. 6a, 14; Fig. 5) no longer has a protrusive element on the bow, but rather an incised decoration of a hatched web. However, the triangle on the button is highly characteristic and can be found on the majority of Certosa fibulae of the late Liburnian type (cf. Glogović 1982, 40, Fig. 4, 1.4). A web pattern can also be found on the bow of a Certosa fibula from grave **10** (Pl. 5b, 29), and the same grave contained another four fragments of the foot endings of Certosa fibulae with a button on the end (Pl. 5b, 27.30a. 32.37).

Fig. 5. Dragišić. Fibula from grave 11

The fragmentary fibula no. 23 from the same grave (Pl. 5b, 23) was part of the bow of a Certosa fibula with lateral arched incisions at the widest point. In place of the decorative webbed motif, which had replaced the original hemispherical relief protrusion and rib, instead there was a sheaf of transverse incisions. Good analogies for a webbed band at the end of the bow, as well as transverse incisions, can be found on the fibulae from Hellenistic grave 1 at Nadin (Batović A 2001, 22, Pl. 9, 3, 5).

Considering the fibulae from Dragišić, on the one hand we can note a degradation of the basic decorative elements of the late Certosa fibulae, i.e. fibulae of type *VII f*, while on the other hand there was a distinct tendency to vary the basic pattern and replace it with the occasional decoration of local provenience. This category of a local variant includes a webbed motif on the surface of the button on several Certosa fibulae from Nadin (Batović Š 1987, 35, Pl. 41, 14; Batović A 2001, 22, Pl. 9, 2.5.7) and on the bow of the fibulae from Dragišić.

Certosa fibulae of type *VII f* (or the latest variants of the classic Certosa fibula) are dated in the western Balkans from approximately the middle of the 4th century BC (Teržan 1977 a, Add. 2), while they were noted by Batović as a type of sub-phase A of the last phase of the Liburnian culture (Batović Š 1974, Fig. 7, 7). The Jagodnja Gornja hoard with a Certosa fibula of type *VII f* is dated to the earlier sub-phase of the last phase of the Liburnian culture, to the 4th and 3rd centuries BC.

According to Š. Batović, the hoard was deposited at the end of the third century BC in relation to the first penetration of the Romans on the eastern Adriatic coast (Batović Š 2011, 28). Hence it is earlier than the hoard from Baška on the island of Krk, which is dated to the third or beginning of the second century BC.

In grave 126 at the site of Kapiteljske Njive in Novo Mesto (Dolenjska/Lower Carniola) in Slovenia, a Certosa fibula of type *VII* was discovered in the context of material from the LT B 2 to LT D phases of the Late Iron Age (Križ 2005, 33, 52 ff., Pl. 15, 3), meaning that this type of fibula had continued into the second century BC.

The Certosa fibulae from Dragišić and Nadin represent at least the second generation of the original form of Certosa fibula type *VII f*, and hence were created somewhat later as a local form of popular jewellery.

Fibulae of the Baška type

This type of fibula is named after the Baška hoard found on the island of Krk. The fibula from the hoard is silver, and has decoration on the bow and on the leaf-shaped extension of the foot (Vinski 1956, 20, Fig. 1a).

The Archaeological Museum in Zagreb possesses a large collection of Baška type fibulae from Kastav (Glogović 1989 b, 31 ff., Pl. 27, 3.4; 30, 1-5, 7-8), which was published in catalogue form by Martina Blečić (Blečić 2002, 88-91, Pl. 3-7). In terms of the central Liburnian region, the relatively recent find of a silver Baška type fibula from the hoard of Jagodnja Gornja near Benkovac is important. This hoard contained several bronze Baška type fibulae, with one decorated silver fibula of the same form (Batović Š 1974, 169, Pl. 18). Batović described the development and emergence of this type of fibula, which he considered derived from the *local pre-Certosoid fibulae* (Batović Š 1974, 190). According to Š. Batović, in the 4th and 3rd centuries BC it acquired its full form with the leaf-shaped extension to the foot and greater dimensions. The distribution map of Baška type fibulae or *the western Balkan local type of proto La Tène fibulae* exhibits a distinct density of finds in the central Liburnian region (Batović Š 1976, 53, Map 9), suggesting they are autochthonous in this area. Hence Zdenko Brusić considered (Brusić 2005, 10) that they should be called *Liburnian fibulae with a leaf-shaped foot*, which is certainly an appropriate name. However, in the interest of briefness and clarity, we shall remain with the term in the title of this chapter. Additionally, it should not be forgotten that the fibulae with a leaf-shaped foot, i.e. the Baška type, was an intercultural phenomenon involving the Delmataean, Liburnian, and Iapodian cultural groups (Marić 1968, 20, 21, Map 3).

The Baška type fibulae, or the Liburnian fibulae with a leaf-shaped foot, can be dated at the earliest to the end of the 5th century BC on the basis of imported pottery from graves at Viča Luka on the island of Brač (Brusić 2005, 11; Glogović 1989 b, 32; Barbarić 2006, 56). They are characteristic for Š. Batović's phase V a of the Liburnian Iron Age (Batović Š 1981, 21, Fig. 6, 3.6), as well as phase V a of the Delmataean Culture (Batović Š 1986, 58, Fig. 10, 1-3.5), which are both dated to the 4th and 3rd centuries BC.

The Baška type fibulae found in graves at Dragišić are all fragmentary. The leaf-shaped extension to the foot on the fibula from grave **11** has two bands of tiny transverse incisions as a decoration (Pl. 6a, 18), and the Baška type fibula from grave **17** (Pl. 11b, 25) is decorated by groups of transverse lines along the bow and on the leaf-shaped foot.

Viewed as a whole, a great variety can be noted in the decorative motifs of the Baška type fibulae, such as the zigzag band along the edge of the fibula from Kastav (Glogović 1989 b, 32, Pl. 30, 7.8). A double zigzag ornament composed of a dense row of incisions can be found on the fibula from Otišić (Glogović 1989 b, Pl. 31, 4) and on the fibula from Jagodnja Gornja (Batović Š 1974, 16, 11), while a leaf motif can be found in the fibula from Asseria (Brusić 2005, Fig. 8, 1). A wavy line is formed from dense incisions on the silver fibula from Baška on the island of Krk (Vinski 1956, 1956, 20, Fig. 1a), representing a stylized birds (Teržan 2013, 256 ff.). The variety of motifs and the total quantity of the discovered examples of the Baška type fibulae bear witness to the great popularity of this jewellery form throughout a lengthy chronological period.

Through systematic analysis, and first the catalogue presentation of all the Baška type fibulae, perhaps specific features would come to light or the frequency of individual decorative motifs in provinces and small cultural zones, which at present is only hinted at. An example would be two fibulae from the islands of central and southern Dalmatia. The Baška type fibula from Vis (Protić 1985, 41, Fig. 3 a) and the fibula from Viča Luka on the island of Brač (Marović / Nikolanci 1969, 27, Fig. 14, 3) are both decorated with a punched (dotted) row of triangles.

In grave 27 at Asseria there were six examples of the Baška type fibulae, versus one Certosa fibula (Brusić 2005, 15, Fig. 8, 1-3. 9, 4-7. 27). The same ratio of these two types of fibulae exists in grave 5 at Asseria – 6 to 1 in favour of the Baška type fibula (Klarin 2000, 33 ff.). The Baška type fibulae, as can be seen from the above, were a form of simple *local* jewellery, while the Certosa fibulae may have been imported elements in Liburnian attire, but were nonetheless widely accepted as an expensive piece of jewellery.

Liburnian plate fibulae

Fragments of Liburnian plate fibulae were found at the cemetery of the Dragišić hillfort in graves **6** (Pl. 1, 12), **9** (Pl. 4, 13, 14), **10** (Pl. 5b, 42, 43), and **13** (Pl. 8a, 15). On one fragment of a small ball from grave **26** (Pl. 21a, 24) there is a little green patina that was created through the mixture of bronze or copper that was added to the silver

to increase its hardness (Glogović 2006 b, 130, Fig. 3a, 3b).

Plate fibulae of the Liburnian type (Fig. 2, 1.4; Fig. 3, 14-17) were introduced to Croatian archaeological literature by Šime Batović. This interesting form of jewellery was described in detail and defined typologically in the late 1950s in two articles (Batović Š 1958, 361-372; Batović Š 1959, 425 ff.). He based his analysis of the plate fibulae primarily on the material held by the Archaeological Museum in Zadar, but he also took into account other finds of plate fibuae known until then.

Among earlier finds of this type of jewellery, plate-shaped fibulae of the Liburnian type were found in the hoard of Lički Ribnik in the 1930s (Klemenc 1935, 105-107). Publishing a hoard with two silver fibulae of this type, Klemenc added a photograph with the legend *Bronze plate fibulae from Prozor near Otočac* (Klemenc 1935, 115, Fig. 1).

Zdenko Vinski also referred to fibulae of this form in his publication of plate fibulae from Baška and Osor (Vinski 1956, 21, 23, Fig. 3, 5). For the silver fibula from Baška, which was shortly afterwards placed by Batović among the plate fibulae of the Liburnian type, he wrote that it was *Sonderform,* i.e. with a special, unusual shape. The term *plate fibula* (*Plattenfibel*), would according to Vinski truly correspond to the fibulae from the Lički Ribnik hoard, while the fibula from Baška would be better called a serpentine fibula because of the wavy bow (Vinski 1956, 26).

A collection of silver jewellery with several examples of Liburnian plate fibulae comes from graves at Asseria that were excavated in 1911-1914 by Mihovil Abramić.

So, at the time when Š. Batović was writing about plate fibulae, in the 1960s, the list of sites where this distinctive type of Liburnian jewellery had been discovered included: Nin, Asseria, Zadar, and Murter in the central Liburnian territory, an unknown site in the vicinity of Rijeka, Osor, and Baška on the island of Krk in the northern Liburnian region, and Lički Ribnik and Prozor from the territory of the Iapodes.

The silver fibula with serpentine characteristics that Š. Batović claimed in 1959 had been found in the *vicinity of Rijeka*, was placed by Fulvia Lo Schiavo in the city itself (Lo Schiavo 1970, 451 ff., Pl. 22, 5), so that ever since the distribution maps for plate fibulae have included Rijeka (Batović Š 1974, 204, Map 3; Batović Š 1976, 71, Map 12; Guštin 1984, 345, 360, Fig. 30), which is the northernmost point of discovery of plate fibulae of the Liburnian type on the Croatian side of the Adriatic. The densest concentration of this type of jewellery is understandably in the central Liburnian territory.

The distribution map of finds of silver plate fibulae (Glogović 2006 b, 132, Map 1) was moved towards the Caput Adriae at the beginning of the 1990s when Kristina Mihovilić published several fragments of plate fibulae among the silver jewellery discovered at her excavations in the area of the Roman temple as Nesactium. She also published a fragment of a plate fibula found in the storerooms of the Archaeological Museum of Istria (Mihovilić 1995 a, 81-100, Pl. 2, 1-3).

In 1974, two fibulae were published from grave 1 at Nadin (Batović Š 1974, 194, 197, Fig. 4, 3; 5, 8), so that the Nadin hillfort appeared for the first time in the literature in the middle of the 1970s as a site of discovery of Liburnian plate fibulae. Later Ante Batović (Batović A 2001, 19-45) created a complete catalogue of grave 1 from Nadin with several plate fibulae.

Seven examples of Liburnian plate fibulae with serpentine characteristics were discovered in the hoard from Jagodnja Gornja (Batović Š 1974, 172, 173, Pl. 19, 15-19).

The assortment of silver jewellery from Jagodnja Gornja has direct parallels with the selection of silver jewellery from grave 80 at Asseria (Batović Š 1965, Pl. 12, 13, 1-15). The ratio is interesting between the two variants of plate fibulae with serpentine characteristics in these two finds. At Jagodnja Gornja there were two examples with two folds and five fibulae with three folds on the bow, while the opposite was the case in grave 80 at Asseria – only one fibula was more luxurious with three folds and six small balls, while the remainder were of the more modest variant with two folds and four balls on the bow. One fibula with serpentine characteristics from the Jagodnja Gornja hoard has no decoration whatsoever on the bow, while the others have technically and stylistically uniform geometric decoration (Batović Š 1974, Pl. 19, 15-19), and are hence probably from the same goldsmith workshop (Glogović 2006 b, 134 ff.).

The third cumulative find of Liburnian plate fibulae, in addition to Asseria and Jagodnja Gornja, are examples from graves at Ljubač Kosa. In 2002 Zdenko Brusić published photographs of unfortunately inaccessible (privately owned) finds from the above cemetery at Ljubač. They include six to seven Liburnian plate fibulae (Brusić 2002, 213-242).

As the discovery of the hoard at Jagodnja Gornja resulted in much new knowledge, Š. Batović revised some of his earlier opinions on the development of plate fibulae of the Liburnian type, and also their position in the chronology of the last phase of the Liburnian Iron Age culture (Glogović 2006 b, 136). In his earlier articles on this form of jewellery, Batović created a basic division into simple plate fibulae and plate fibulae with serpentine characteristics. The fibulae with serpentine characteristics of the third and fourth variants of stage A of the fifth phase of the Liburnian Iron Age include those with a transverse shaft with a ball on each end placed at the end of the foot of the fibula. Thin sheet metal wraps the shaft and covers the banded foot (Batović Š 1974, 195, Fig. 4, 3.4). The balls in pairs on the sides of the bow, like those at the end of the foot, are fixed onto nail-like protrusions. These protrusions are extracted or constructed from the

same silver band or silver plate from which the bow of the fibula is made. The fibulae of the fourth variant have an emphasized banded shape and lose the stepped moulding between the bow and foot of the fibula, *"which all leads to a pure plate-like form that is prominent in the later phase"*, as Š. Batović wrote.

The later B stage, the last phase of the Liburnian Iron Age (2nd and 1st centuries BC), features plate fibulae in ten variants, with variants *1* to *5* constructed with a shaft with two balls (Batović Š 1974, 197, Fig 5, 1-10). The occasional fibula has two shafts, with one on the end of the foot, like the fibulae of the third and forth variants of stage A (see above). The second shaft with balls is located at the transition point towards the bow of the fibula. This can best be seen on the fragment of a plate fibula from Nesactium (Mihovilić 1995 a, Pl. 2, 1) as well as a fibula from Asseria (Marović 1970, 281, Fig. 4) that is one of the rare fully preserved Liburnian plate fibulae.

In the final phase of development of the Liburnian plate fibuae, the bow completely loses any serpentine characteristics. These are fibulae of Š. Batović's second group of Liburnian plate fibulae, i.e. variants *7, 8,* and *9* of the second stage (Batović Š 1974, 201). Also, in the last phase – phase B – gilding began to be used. The banded saddle at the very end of the foot is wound around the shaft with the balls facing downwards and is circularly edged, as can be seen on the fragment from Dragišić, grave **10** (Pl. 5b, 43). That fragment has a small hole for the rivet that connected the base of the end of the foot and the gilded coating band.

The gilded plate from Dragišić (Pl. 5b, 43) and the short silver rod-shaped shaft with balls on each end (Pl. 5b, 42) are parts of Š. Batović's variant 4 phase B (Glogović 2006 b, Fig. 5). A shaft of larger dimensions but the same form (Pl. 4, 14) would be part of a fibula of variant *3* phase B, and those are fibulae that have two shafts – one at the end of the foot and one in the centre of the fibula (Glogović 2006 b, 136, Fig. 6). For smaller fragments of Liburnian plate fibulae from graves at Dragišić (Pl. 1, 12; 4, 13; 8a, 15) neither the type nor the variant to which they would belong can be determined.

The dating of all fragments of plate fibulae from graves 6, 9, 10, 13, and 26 from the hillfort of Dragišić is clear according to Š. Batović's chronology of the Liburnian Iron Age. Fibulae of variants 3 and 4 are typical forms of phase B, the later stage of the fifth and last phase of the Liburnian Culture that extended throughout the 2nd and 1st centuries BC.

The list of finds of Liburnian plate fibulae (Glogović 2006 b, 132, Map 1; Note: the list has been supplemented by the discovery of no. 16. Trošenj – grad):

1. Nesactium (Vizače): Mihovilić 1995 a, 83, 84, Pl. 2, 1.3 (temple "C", western area).
2. Rijeka: Lo Schiavo 1970, 452; Batović Š 1959, Pl. 6, 20.

3. Krk: Lo Schiavo 1970, 451, Pl. 22, 5; Batović Š 1974, Pl. 39, below.
4. Baška (island of Krk): Vinski 1956, 21, 25, Fig. 3; Batović Š 1974, Pl. 39, above.
5. Osor: Vinski 1956, 26, Fig. 5; Batović Š 1959, Pl. 6, 10.
6. Prozor (Lika): Klemenc 1935, 114, 115, Fig. 1.
7. Lički Ribnik: Klemenc 1935, 105 ff., Pl. 2, 1.2.
8. Ljubač Kosa: Brusić 2002, 228 ff., 230-233, Fig. 25, 30, 31, 33, 1-5.
9. Nin: Batović Š 1959, 429, 438, Pl. 3, 2; 6, 9, 11-13.
   Grave 76: Batović Š 1968, Pl. 18.
   Grave 82: Batović Š 1962, Y 40, 1-4.
10. Zadar: Batović Š 1959, 432, Pl. 7, 21, 22.
11. Nadin, grave 1: Batović Š 1974, 194.197, Fig. 4, 3, Fig. 5, 8, Pl. 38; Batović Š 1987, 364, Pl. 41, 16.
12. Asseria (Podgrađe): Marović 1970, 276, 281, Fig. 4, Pl. 4, 2.
    Grave 80: Batović Š 1959, 443, Pl. 7, 15-19; Batović Š 1965, 66, Pl. 12, 4.5.11.12, Pl. 13, 14.
13. Jagodnja Gornja: Batović Š 1974, 172 ff., Pl. 19, 15-19; Pl. 28, 1-5.
14. Murter: Batović Š 1958, 366, Fig. 2, 4.5; Batović Š 1959, 437, Pl. 5, 7.8.
15. Dragišić: Grave 6 (Pl. 1, 12),
                      9 (Pl. 4, 13. 14),
                     10 (Pl. 5b, 42. 43),
                     13 (Pl. 8a, 15),
                     26 (Pl. 21a, 24).
16. Trošenj – grad: Balen-Letunić 2010, 136, Pl. 1, 2, 3.

Fibulae of the Middle La Tène type

The graves at Dragišić contained a large quantity of fragments of La Tène fibulae. Grave 8 (Pl. 3, 6) contained part of a bow with a large circular loop. Bow fragments of Middle La Tène fibulae were found in grave 14 (Pl. 9b, 43, 58, 59). A bow fragment of a Middle La Tène fibula was hung through the circular loop of a fibula on a pendant, in fact an omega fibula, from grave 21 (Pl. 14a, 12). This grave contained 65 catalogue units with immense amounts of La Tène fibulae. Fragments 27, 47, 49, 51, 52-56 from the catalogue (Pl. 14b, 27; 14c, 47, 49, 51; 14d, 52-56) are parts of Middle La Tène fibula types with an external circular loop. Almost all the fragments, and particularly the pins, are deformed. A fragment of a fibula from the same grave (Pl. 14c, 49) has a loop and the remains of the external tendon. A fragment from grave 26 belonged to a La Tène fibula with a large circular loop (Pl. 21a, 2). The fragment from grave 21 was part of a folded over foot with a moulded clamp that attached the foot to the bow, which is typical for Middle La Tène type fibulae (Pl. 14a, 16).

Fibulae with a smooth bow and a wire relatively large circular loop, which can have an outer as well as an inner spring cord, originated in the late Middle La Tène period (Dizdar 2001, 109 ff.), and are dated to the LT – D or the Mokronog III or Mokronog 5 and 6 phases (Guštin 1984, 333 ff.), with an absolute dating in the period from ca. 110 BC to the beginning of the new era (Božić 1987, 876-881). The Middle La Tène fibulae of this form in the

Iapodian cemeteries in the Una River valley are dated identically, to phase V (Marić 1968, 45-50).

The rod-shaped pieces of bronze with three ribs from grave 14 (Pl. 9b, 44, 48, 57; Pl. 9d, 92) are fragments of La Tène fibulae of the Vir variant, type Picugi (Guštin 1987 a, 51, 52, Fig. 12; Marić 1962, 67, Pl. 2, 10: Vir near Posušje), along with perhaps also a fragment of a small rod from both grave 15 (Pl. 10a, 6) and grave 26 (Pl. 21a, 17). Fibulae of the Vir variant have a sharp knee-shaped transition of the bow to the foot, a spiral loop with many coils and an external spring cord or crossbaw, so that the fragments of spiral fibula loops from grave 9 (Pl. 4, 16-18) might belong to fibulae of the Picugi type, Vir variant.

In terms of finds of Middle La Tène fibulae from the northern Liburnian region, two fibulae are known from the archaeological collection in Osor that were published by Jasminka Ćus-Rukonić. One of the fibulae from Osor belongs to Guštin's Picugi type (Ćus-Rukonić 1981, 8, Pl. 2, 3; Guštin 1987 a, 52), and possibly also two fragments of La Tène fibulae from Baška on the island of Krk (Glogović 1989a, 98, Fig. 1, 1,2).

According to Mitja Guštin, La Tène fibulae of the Kastav type have a wire wound around the bow, hence several fragmentary fibulae from grave 10 at Dragišić could be attributed to this type (Pl. 5b, 19, 30, 40, 44). The broken bow of a fibula from grave 11 (Pl. 6a, 11) probably belongs to the same form of La Tène fibula. Mitja Guštin composed a list of fibulae of the Kastav type, variant Kastav, and this included several Liburnian examples, such as the fibula from grave 19 at Nin (Guštin 1987 a, 51), later published by Gundula Hiller (Hiller 1991, 370, Pl. 26, 284). Other fibulae published include a fibula of Middle La Tène type from grave 82 at Nin (Batović Š 1962, Y 40, 2 (2), 9) with a double-sided loop with three coils and an external spring cord, and the fibula from grave 1 at Nadin (Batović Š 1990, 121, 122, Fig. 32, 5).

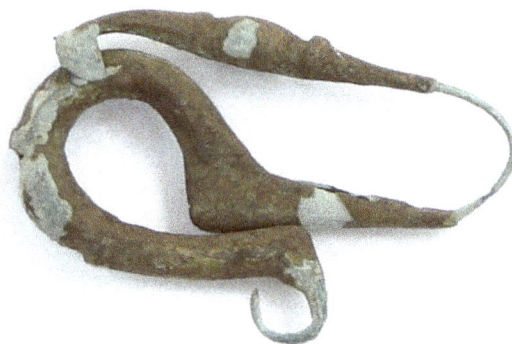

Fig. 6. Dragišić. Fibula from grave 10

The small banded pieces of bronze rods with transverse incisions and hemispherical protrusions are elements of the overlapping elements on the feet of La Tène fibulae.

These include two fragments (Pl. 6a, 9, 10) from the above mentioned grave **11**, as well as a fragment from grave **13** (Pl. 8a, 10). A fragment of bronze from grave **13** (Pl. 8a, 11) might be part of a La Tène fibula with a discoid overlapping cover onto which a decoration of other material was applied (amber, coral, etc.). A large quantity of fibulae of this type was found in graves of the penultimate phase of the Iapodian cemeteries in the Una River valley (Marić 1968, 45-50, Pl. 5, 169, Pl. VI, 209). An attractive example of a fibula of this form comes from Donji Lapac in the Lika region (Arte e cultura 1993, 114, no. 93).

Most of the fragmentary La Tène fibulae from Dragišić cannot be precisely determined according to type, and hence they were described on the basis of a minimum of characteristics in the catalogue of graves.

Šime Batović wrote that the Liburnian fibulae with a leaf-shaped extension to the foot (Baška type), perhaps under Celtic influence, developed in the 2nd and 1st centuries BC into Middle La Tène clasps where the plate at the end of the foot was elongated and joined to the top of the bow with a ring. The final form of the development of this type, the distinctive Late La Tène fibula, were not popular in this region to the end of the prehistoric period and appeared rarely, probably under Roman influence (Batović Š 1981, 21 ff., Fig. 8, 34). Nonetheless, two fibulae of the Middle La Tène type were designated as the basic type of jewellery of the V B phase of the Liburnian culture of the Iron Age, and both are from grave 82 at Nin (Fig. 3, 11.12). The pure La Tène material from the former Archaeological Collection of Obrovac, which was collected somewhere in the Liburnian region, should also be taken into consideration (Stipčević 1960, 87-93).

One Middle La Tène fibula of the Picugi type from grave 1 at Nadin was published in 1987 (Batović Š 1981, 116; Batović Š 1987, 35, Pl. 41, 15), and the full inventory of that grave showed that fragmentary fibulae of the Middle La Tène type were the most common among of all types of fibulae (Batović A 2001, 73).

The newly published material from the site of Ljubač Kosa contains a large number of Middle La Tène type fibulae (Brusić 2002, 229, 236, 238, Fig. 36, 3. 5; Fig. 37, 7; Fig. 38, 5-10). They were discovered among material considered typical for the last Liburnian phase. This fact also contradicts Š. Batović's thesis that La Tène fibulae were not widely accepted in the Liburnian culture.

The fibula from grave **10** is particularly interesting (Pl. 5b, 28, Fig. 6), as it was deliberately deformed. The bow was bent into a ring. It had a hemispherical thickening between two ribs on the upper bent segment of the foot, so the fibula would belong to the Kastav type, Ribić variant (Guštin 1987 a, 50). The thickening on the bow of the fibula is corroded, so it cannot be seen whether or not it was notched (serrated), like the notched or serrated thickening on the fibula from Picugi (cf. Picugi: Guštin 1987 a, Fig. 3, 5). Another example of a La Tène fibula

with an obliquely notched nodule on the bow comes from grave **17** (Pl. 11a, 2) at Dragišić. The fibula is too incomplete to be able to determine it typologically.

Slanted incisions on a hemispherical thickening on the foot, as well as slanted notches on a protrusion on the bow are characteristics of the *Nesactium type* fibula according to Maša Sakara Sučević. She listed the fibulae of this type from sites in Istria and the coastal Primorje region of Slovenia: Socerb (San Servolo), Kopar, Beram, Picugi (Guštin, 1987 a, Fig. 3, 5; Guštin 1987 b, 37, Fig. 3, a 2; Mihovilić 1991, 158, 162, Fig. 1, 16), and Nesactium (Sakara Sučević 2004, 24 ff., no. 65; Mihovilić 2001 b, 269, 272, Fig. 6, 4: Nesactium).

Publishing recent finds of La Tène fibulae from Istria, specifically from Nesactium, Kristina Mihovilić confirmed the validity of defining this kind of fibula as the Nesactium type with two examples (Mihovilić 2009, 290, Fig. 2, 5, 6). The characteristics of the Middle La Tène fibula of the *Nesactium type* consist of a nodule or thickening on the bow, which otherwise is not specific to the Kastav type fibulae, with the exception of the already cited fibula from Picugi, and perhaps the fibula from Koper (Guštin a 1987, Fig. 2, 3; 3, 5). The fibula from Dragišić (Pl. 5b, 28) has an untypical cross-section of the bow, also without transverse ribbing on the segment of the foot above the nodule (Cf. Guštin 1987, 45, Fig. 3, 5).

Maša Sakara Sučević wrote that the Nesactium type fibula was specific to Istria (Sakara Sučević 2004, 25), however, the presented examples of two fibulae from Dragišić (Pl. 5b, 28; 11a, 2) in the southern part of the Liburnian territory should indicate a widening of their domain into the central Adriatic, into Liburnian territory.

The form of the fibula from grave **10** is unusual (Pl. 5b, 45), where only the low bow and a section of the multipart spring with a cord wound around the bow was preserved. In terms of the form and decoration of the bow, this was similar to the low long-footed fibulae that are characteristic for the Santa Lucia / Most na Soči group in Slovenia (Teržan / Lo Schiavo / Trampuž-Orel 1985, 22, 1; Guštin / Knific 1973, 838, 835, Fig. 3). The same type of fibulae with a lowered bow and a long foot can be found in the Villanova and Este cultural circles in northern Italy (see v. Eles Masi 1986, 187-191). Fibulae with a low flat foot can also be found elsewhere in Slovenia, i.e. at Stična (Griže, tumulus 66: Gabrovec *et al.* 2006, 171, Pl. 145, 3.4).

A fibula from Magdalenska Gora has the same form of bow – the decoration of the bow is somewhat different, but part of a long grooved foot is preserved (Hencken 1978, 59, 239, Fig. 261, f). A fibula from Santa Lucia / Most na Soči has the same type of foot (Marchesetti 1993, 158, 226, Pl. 10, 9), and it can be conjectured that this fibula from Dragišić also had an elongated grooved foot.

Considering that the spring cord on the fibula from Dragišić (Pl. 5b, 45) was wound around the bow in the same manner as on the Middle La Tène fibulae, we would not connect it in terms of dating to the above analogies that refer to the shape of the bow. Additionally, the northern Italian and Slovenian late Hallstatt fibulae that we cited most often have an inner double loop, and hence the fibula with a low bow from Dragišić, just like the other La Tène fibulae, is placed among the Middle La Tène material from Dragišić.

The iron bow fibula from grave **10** at Dragišić (Pl. 5b, 34) with a fragment of a foot can be related to a find from Istria, specifically to the newly published iron La Tène fibula from Pula, which has a similarly shaped foot (Mihovilić 2009, 214, Fig. 3, 27).

Many fragmentary fibulae from graves at Dragišić cannot be more precisely classified, but on the basis of analogies with recently published fibulae from Istria (Mihovilić 2009, 211, 213, Fig. 1, 2, 3) the fibulae from grave **10** (Pl. 5a, 9; 5b, 35), from grave **13** (Pl. 8a, 14), fragments from grave **14** (Pl. 9b, 43, 51), and from grave **21** (Pl. 14d, 57) at Dragišić can in general be included among La Tène fibulae.

The Jezerine type fibulae

Jezerine type fibulae were found in grave **14** (Pl. 9d, 94) and in grave **32** (Pl. 23, 6). The basic characteristics of the Jezerine type fibulae are a broad banded segment on the bow – the so-called "cuff", as well as a four-coiled spring with an inner cord and a rectangular foot with a raised button on the end. Jezerine type fibulae in earlier literature had been placed in the group of early Roman fibulae of the Late La Tène type, which suggests both their origin and development. The ring on the narrowed banded part of the bow thus represents a rudimentary remnant of a La Tène fibula where the foot is bent upwards and attached to the bow (Koščević 1980, 12; Težak-Gregl 1982, 101). The form of the foot with a button on the top is reminiscent of the Certosa fibulae, although a significant chronological gap exists between the Jezerine type fibulae and the Certosa fibulae. The spiral coil with an interior cord for tightening a fibula was developed in the first century BC and can be found on fibulae of the Nauheim type, Cenisola type, and others (Adam / Feugère 1982, 146). According to Elisabeth Ettlinger, the influence of the Aucissa fibula was important in the formation of the Jezerine type fibula, particularly in terms of the button on top of the foot. She wrote that the fibulae with a "cuff" were a cross between the Aucissa and Late La Tène fibulae (Ettlinger 1973, 42).

It is generally concluded that northern Italy was the area of the origin and first production of the Jezerine type fibula, so that they are considered as an Italic element in the Celtic culture in our regions (Božić 1987, 896). Stefan Demetz added southern France as a possible source for the fibulae of this type (Demetz 1999, 103, 104). The distribution map of Jezerine type fibula in Europe (Adam / Feugère 1982, 154, Fig. 13) shows five groups of larger concentrations of finds: Languedoc (France), northern

Italy / Slovenia, central and southern Italy, the central Danube basin, and Dalmatia. According to Adam and Feugère this would permit a hypothesis about workshops of the Jezerine type fibula in the above areas. This could also include the coastal area of Croatia, Dalmatia. Firm proof for such a hypothesis does not exist, and hence the only certain place of production of Jezerine type fibula remains, as was established earlier, the northern Italian – Eastern Alpine region (Adam / Feugère 1982, 150-158).

Two fibuae of the Jezerine type from Sisak were published among the Late La Tène fibulae from the Archaeological Museum in Zagreb. Remza Koščević placed them in a European context and dated them to the end of the first century BC. She noted that they continued in use, judging from the grave units in the Una River valley, throughout the entire first century (Koščević 1980, 12, 45, Pl. 1, 1.3).

Jezerine type fibulae from Slavonia were published by Nives Majnarić-Pandžić (Majnarić-Pandžić 1970, 42, 114, Pl. 4, 9, Pl. 38, 3.4, Pl. 51, 9). The fibula from Orolik was published among the finds of the La Tène culture from Vinkovci (Dizdar 2001, 110, Pl. 7, 6). Somewhat earlier, in an exhibition catalogue about archaeology in the Vinkovci region, another two Jezerine type fibulae were published, so that the quantity of such fibulae found in eastern Slavonia have greatly increased in the recent period (Dizdar 1999, 116, 120, no. 163, 181).

The earliest publication of a Jezerine type fibula from Croatia was of an example from Prozor near Otočac (Ljubić 1889, 122, no. 8, Pl. 19, 72). This fibula of the Jezerine type can be tied to finds of the same kind from the Iapodian cemeteries of Jezerine, Golubić, and Ribić in the Una River valley. They represent forms of phase V b and phase VI, extending from 35 BC to 110 AD (Marić 1968, 32-38).

Joachim Werner published data about a Jezerine type fibula from Salona. The same information was also noted by Sabine Rieckoff (Rieckoff 1975, 97, no. 62; Werner, 1979, 141, 142, Fig. 2, 2).

Fibulae that have a roof-shaped bow section with notched longitudinal ribs, according to Demetz's classification, create the quantitatively greatest group among the Jezerine type fibulae, and this was the type to which the fibula from Salona belonged (Demetz 1999, 250, no. 40).

The list of sites composed by A.M. Adam and M. Feugère contains two Jezerine type fibulae from Narona, i.e. Vid near Metković (Adam / Feugère 1982, 182, no. 109). Demetz placed one of the fibulae from Vid on the list of fibulae of group *IIa1* (Demetz 1999, 248, no. 6).

In terms of the Liburnian territory, a fibula of the Jezerine type was published in 1981 in the catalogue *Jewellery in Northern Dalmatia from Prehistory to the Present* without any data about the site of discovery (Nedved 1981, 166, Fig. 5, 202). This is very probably the same fibula that was included in the list of Adam and Feugère from 1982 (Adam / Feugère 1982, 180, no. 97). This fibula is listed in Demetz as among the examples of Jezerine type fibulae whose drawings were not accessible (Demetz 1999, 252).

The fibula from grave **32** at Dragišić is missing the front side of the bow, the foot, and the pin (Pl. 23, 6). Two notched ribs run along the raised edges of the banded part of the bow, which has a roof-shaped section, so that it is classified to Demetz's group *IIc1* (Demetz 1999, 249 ff.; Glogović / Menđušić 2007 b, 148, Fig. 2).

The Jezerine type fibula from grave **14** (Pl. 9d, 94) according to Demetz would belong to group *IIa2* (Demetz 1999, 248; Glogović / Menđušić 2007 b, 148, 149, Fig. 3). Grave 14 was a typical mass grave with at least seven individuals of various sexes and ages. The grave contained many fragments of metal, and also fragments of fibulae that we consider to have been from the Late Iron Age along with two Aucissa fibulae (Pl. 9b, 56, 60). Accordingly, no elements are present at Dragišić for a more precise dating of Jezerine type fibulae.

A large quantity of Jezerine type fibulae was discovered in the northern part of the Liburnian territory, in the Croatian Primorje region. The finds from the islands include a fibula from Krk (Lo Schiavo 1970, 424, Pl. 22, 4). Five Jezerine type fibulae were found in Osor on the island of Cres and were published in 1982 (Težak-Gregl 1982, 99, 101, Fig. 1, 1), which S. Demetz did not take into consideration.

Two Jezerine type fibulae from Grobišće (Grobnik) were published by Martina Blečić (Blečić 2005, 69, 90, Fig. 16, Pl. 5, 1.5.1, 1.5.2). The smaller of the Jezerine type fibulae from Grobišće (Blečić 2005, Pl. 5, 1.5.2) with a completely smooth banded segment of the bow belonged, according to Demetz, in the smallest group of Jezerine type fibulae, group *Ic* with an undecorated bow, of which only five or six examples have been found (Demetz 1999, 99, 100, 248).

The sites of discovery of Jezerine type fibulae from the Croatian part of Istria, as listed by Mitja Guštin, are: Picugi, unknown site (Poreč Museum), and Kaštelir near Nova Vas / Brtonigla (Guštin 1987 a, 45, Fig. 3, 7.8.15.16). The latter is one of the largest castellieri sites in Istria. The finds from Kaštelir near Nova Vas / Brtonigla were analysed by Maša Sakara Sučević, so that the Jezerine type fibulae were classified according to the typology of S. Demetz. They are dated similarly as in the rest of Europe from around the middle of the first century BC to the end of the first decade AD (Sakara Sučević 2004, 25, no. 78, 80-87).

In terms of the silver jewellery from Nesactium (Mihovilić 1983, 127, Fig. 68; Mihovilić 1995 a, 82, Pl. 1, 4), the attribution of the fragmented and bent Jezerine type fibula is not uniform. M. Guštin characterized this piece of jewellery as a fragment of a Jezerine type fibula (Guštin 1987 a, 46). K. Mihovilić described the fragment

as a fibula *with a willow leaf-shaped bow* (Mihovilić 1995 a, 82). The lengthwise rib in the middle of the band is the only element that connects this bow fragment with the Jezerine type fibulae. The decoration, composed of tremolo lines on both sides of the band, as well as the material used to make the fibula (silver), are untypical for Jezerine type fibulae.

However, recently a fragment of a fibula from Nesactium was published that undoubtedly belongs to the Jezerine type (Mihovilić 2009, 212, 214, Fig. 2, 22), so that Nesactium can now be definitely placed on the list of places where Jezerine type fibulae were discovered (see below).

The various opinions on dating the first appearance and length of use of the Jezerine type fibulae are listed in Adam / Feugère. The creation of the Jezerine type fibulae in the summary of their chronology is dated to 40-30 BC, while they placed the massive use of these fibulae from 30-20 BC to 1-10 AD (Adam / Feugère 1982, 167). S. Demetz made a table of the theoretical development of the Jezerine type fibulae, with no significant chronological shifts. All dates earlier than around 40 BC are questionable, and the upper limit of the Jezerine type fibulae was moved to approximately 30 AD (Demetz 1999, 104, Fig. 7). This can thus be used to date the two fibulae from Dragišić.

The list of finds of Jezerine type fibulae from Croatia:

1. Dalj: Rieckhoff 1975, 97, no. 150; Majnarić-Pandžić 1970, Pl. 4, 9; type *IIc1* (Demetz 1999, 250).
2. Dragišić: grave 14 (Pl. 9d, 94); grave 32 (Pl. 23, 6); type *II a 2* and *II c 1* (Demetz 1999, 99-102).
3. Grobnik – Grobišće: Blečić 2005, 90 ff.; Fig. 16, Pl. 5, 1.5.1, 1.5.2; type *IIa2* and *Ic* (Demetz 1999, 99-102).
4. Kaštelir (Nova Vas – Brtonigla): Sakara Sučević 2004, 25; types *IIa2*, *IIc1*, *IIc2* (Demetz 1999, 99-102, 248, 249, 151).
5. Krk: Lo Schiavo 1970, 424, Pl. 22, 4; type *IIa2* (Demetz 1999, 249).
6. Nezakcij (Istra), western area of temple B: Mihovilić 2009, 212, Fig. 2: 22; type *IIa* (Demetz 100 ff.).
7. Orolik – Gradina: Majnarić-Pandžić 1970, 114; Dizdar 2001, 110, Pl. 7, 6; type *IIc1* (Demetz 1999, 99-102).
8. Osijek – Mursa: Rieckoff 1975, 150, no. 157; type *IIc1* (Demetz 1999, 250).
9. Osor: Težak-Gregl 1982, 99, Fig. 1, 1.2; type *IIb* (Demetz 1999, 99-102).
10. Picugi: Guštin 1987 a, 45, Fig. 3, 7.8; type *IIb1*, *IIc1* (Demetz 1999, 249, 250).
11. Poreč – museum (unknown site): Adam-Feugère 1982, 180, no. 88.
12. Prozor near Otočac (Lika): Ljubić 1889, 122, Pl. 19, 72; Adam-Feugère 1982, 180, no. 91; type *IIc* (?).
13. Salona – Solin: Rieckhoff 1975, 97, no. 162; Werner 1979, 141, 142, Fig. 2,2; type *IIc1* (Demetz 1999, 250).

14. Sisak: Koščević 12, 45, Pl. 1, 1, 3; type *IIc1, IIc2* (Demetz 1999, 250, 251).
15. Sotin: Majnarić-Pandžić 1970, 42, Pl. 38, 3,3a. type *IIa1* (Demetz 1999, 248).
16. Vid – Metković (Narona): Adam-Feugère 1982, 182, no. 109; type *IIa1* (Demetz 1999, 248).
17. Vinkovci: Dizdar 1999, 116, 120, no. 163, no. 181; type *IIb, IIc* (Demetz 1999, 99-102).
18. Vukovar: Majnarić-Pandžić 1970, 100, Pl. 51, 9. (Demetz 1999, 251).
19. Zadar-museum (unknown site): Nedved 1981, 166, no. 202, Fig. 5, 202; type *IIc1* (Demetz 1999, 99-102).

The Gorica type fibula

In grave **21** (Pl. 14c, 45), which contained many fragmentary fibulae, was part of a bow with a section of the loop of a fibula classified to the Gorica type, although it lacks an important element for this type of fibula, a rectangular foot with a button on the top.

The Gorica type fibulae differ from the Jezerine type in terms of the lack of a cuff-shaped or banded part of the bow, rather the bow was solid cast with an oval or triangular section (Rieckhoff 1975, 24, with earlier literature). The spiral construction on the fragment from Dragišić with four coils on the spring – two on each side, is a common element of the Jezerine and Gorica type fibulae (Demetz 1999, 106).

Stefan Demetz described the Gorica type as the "Late La Tène Gorica wire fibula" and divided them into two forms, where the Gorica *IIa* type has a triangular section to the bow. This form has an often barely emphasized reinforcement or decorative band on the upper side of the bow, which can be seen on the bow of the fibula from Dragišić (Pl. 14c, 45). According to Demetz the form *IIa* is further subdivided into *IIa1* with a decoration of tiny incisions on the bow and *IIa2* without decoration. Fibulae of the Gorica *IIb* type have a square or rhomboid bow section, while fibulae of the Gorica *IIc* type have a circular or oval section. The fibula from Nadin was classified to this latter type (Demetz 1999, 253, no. 15), and was published by Š. Batović in the article about the hoard from Jagodnja Gornja (Batović Š 1974, 229, Fig. 9, 6), and also in the catalogue to the exhibition on Liburnian jewellery in 1981 in Zadar (Batović Š 1981, 106, Fig. 7, 13). The cross section of the fibula from Nadin was not drawn in either of these publications, but in the list of objects from grave 1 at Nadin, the fibula can be recognized from the description: *A clasp with a triangular section, a lengthwise notched rib, a circular plate at the end of the foot, and a circular opening on the foot, 5.6 cm long.* Accordingly, it can be placed in Demetz's group *IIa*.

The BA thesis of Ante Batović from 2001 discussed the graves from Nadin. The material from grave 1 at Nadina had long been sporadically used, for example in the chapter about the Liburnian Group in volume V of the series on the prehistory of the Southern Slavic Lands

(*Praistoriji jugoslavenskih zemalja*), from 1987 (Batović 1987, 351, Pl. 41, 12-21). The complete catalogue of grave 1 at Nadin *de facto* describes three fibulae of the Gorica type with a triangular section of the bow. All three have a decorative band with notches on the bow (Batović A 2001, 25, Pl. 11, 17, 18, 20), and hence belong to Demetz's Gorica *IIa1* type. They are termed *fibulae of a late Certosoid type* in the BA thesis of A. Batović (Batović A 2001, 25, 72).

The fibula from grave **21** at Dragišić (Pl. 14c, 45) belongs to Demetz's type *IIa2*, these being fibulae without a decorative band.

Gorica type fibulae are in general chronologically parallel to Jezerine type fibulae. The earlier type, form Gorica *I* according to Demetz, can be dated at the earliest from the middle of the first century BC, while the others are dated from 40 / 30 BC to around 10 AD (see above). The list of form *I* fibulae includes one from Vid near Metković (Narona), located in the *Natural History Museum* in Vienna (Demetz 1999, 252).

Ćiro Truhelka published the finds from Gorica in 1902, the eponymous Herzegovinian-Bosnian site located in Sovići Plain by the Trebižat River. He described the form of the fibula, which was later called the Gorica type, as an Early Roman fibula (*frührömische Fibel*). Demetz placed this fibula from Gorica, together with a fibula from Debelo Brdo near Sarajevo (an equally old find), on the list of form *IIa1* (Demetz 1999, 252: triangular section of the bow with a tiny incised decoration).

Fibulae from Istria do not need to be discussed, since they were analysed by Guštin (Guštin 1987 a 43-57) and Sakara Sučević (Sakara Sučević 2004, 26), and these are the remaining sites where Gorica type fibulae were discovered: Sisak, Jezerine, Putovići near Zenica, Mušići near Višegrad, and further towards the east, in the eastern Balkans: Sočanica (Kosovska Mitrovica), Ohrid, Trebeniško Kale (Ohrid), Rečica (Požarevac), and also Irinaj (Gramsh) in Albania (Demetz 1999, 252).

Demetz's distribution map for the Gorica type fibulae has two dots that represent two sites on the Dalmatian coast approximately at the latitude of the island of Brač (Demetz 1999, map 32), buit which are not on the list, so that it is impossible to know to which Dalmatian sites or fibulae they refer.

Demetz shows that Gorica type fibulae were worn by members of both sexes on the basis of several female graves from Italy. He cites, for example, the female grave III Groppelo Cairoli (Pavia province). Grave 237 from Jezerine is cited as an example of a male grave with weaponry and a Gorica fibula (Demetz 1999, 108, 235).

The analysis of the distribution of Gorica type fibulae displays a greater concentration of finds in the Caput Adriae region and in the Po River valley, but also in contrast to the Jezerine type fibulae, Gorica fibulae were also present in Dalmatia, Bosnia and Herzegovina, and in the central Balkan territory (Demetz 1999, 108).

It should be noted that the majority of authors who write about the Gorica type fibulae and their distribution refer to Dalmatia in the sense of the Roman province of Dalmatia, as only two, in fact three sites of discovery of Gorica type fibulae exist in the region of present-day Dalmatia. These are Nadin and Dragišić in northern Dalmatia, Vid (Narona) in southern Dalmatia, along with nearby Gorica in Herzegovina in the immediate Adriatic hinterland. Sisak is in Pannonia, four sites are in Bosnia and further to the east towards the central Balkans, so the use of the geographical term *Dalmatia* for the home region of the Gorica type fibulae is really quite confusing from the modern point of view.

Grave **17** (Pl. 11b, 26) at Dragišić contained one part of the bow of an **Alesia *I*** type fibula (Demetz 1999, 157-160) with an incised pattern of slanted webbing. This decorative motif can be compared to the decoration on the bow of a fibula of the same type from Split (Buora 1999, 134, Pl. 3, 6). According to M. Buora, the decoration on the fibula from Dragišić as well as on the cited fibula from Split, was decoration no. V, while for Demetz fibulae with a similar decoration belonged to group Alesia *Ia1* (Demetz 1999, 157-164, 273, with an incomplete list of sites). In his article, M. Buoara published an Alesia type fibula from Asseria with a distinctive decoration, or it could be a sub-variant of decoration V (Buora 1999, 110, Pl. 4, 1).

The characteristics of Alesia I type fibulae are: a bow composed of triangularly cut sheet metal, a head with a jointed socket, and a foot with a grooved catch-plate with a protrusion on the top. This is considered to be the earliest fibula with a hinge system for moving the pin, and that the Alesia type is a stage in development leading up to the Aucissa type fibula. The fibula from Sisak with a smooth bow would hence represent a prototype (Koščević 1980, Pl. 2, 11). This is also proven by a fibula from Solin that has a triangular bow with a spear-shaped perforation. The Alesia type fibulae from Demetz's *Id* group have an identical perforation. However, the Solin fibula has a triangular foot with a button on the end, like an Aucissa fibula. The fibula from Solin was classified by Sanja Ivčević among the *early hinged fibulae* (Ivčević 2002, 247, no. 6).

The Alesia type fibulae are dated at the earliest to the middle of the 1st century BC, but continue longer, parallel with the Aucissa fibulae. In the analysis of the Roman fibulae from Sisak, Remza Koščević defined a small group of fibulae with a triangular bow as a group of early hinged fibulae (Koščević 1980, 12 ff.). The amount of discussion about this type of fibula, called the *Alesia I type*, has increased considerably, and many sub-types, variants, and derived forms have been created. The Sisak fibula with a triangular perforation on the bow (Koščević 1980, Pl. 2, 9) is now included in Demetz's *Id* group (Demetz 1999, 274), just like the fibula from Nin (Nedved 1981, 168, no. 215, Fig. 5, 215). The fibula from

Osor (Težak-Gregl 1982, 100, Fig. 2, 3) and the fibula from Nin have a perforation in the shape of an arrow or spear on the bow, or as Demetz puts it, the fibulae have a small triangle at the base of the bow. Fibulae with this shape of perforation are also classified to group *Id* (Demetz 1999, 159, Pl. 40, 5).

The above mentioned fibula from Nin was cited recently by Dragan Božič while discussing the dating of fibulae of this group. Božič opposes Demetz's opinion that the Alesia type fibulae with a triangular or spear-shaped perforation represent the youngest variant of this type (Božič 2009, 106-108, Fig. 55, 1-5). In fact, according to Božič, this variant of the Alesia fibula can be dated to around the middle of the 1st century BC.

Many authors composed comprehensive lists of sites where Alesia type fibulae were found. In the mid-1970s a map and list were composed by Sabine Rieckhoff (Rieckhoff 1975, 96, Pl. 11), while Stefan Demetz published his list fifteen years ago (Demetz 1999, 163, n. 1019, 273 ff.). Maurizio Buora was particularly involved in the finds of this type of fibula in Friuli, and he offered several distribution maps of various variants, types, and groups of Alesia fibulae (Buora 1999, 116, 118, 120, Fig. 1-3), while Mitja Guštin made a list of sites in the Caput Adriae region, Slovenia, and the ex-Yugoslavia (Guštin 1991, 43). The lists are often contradictory, and are constantly being supplemented with new findings and elaborations in terms of form and type. I have composed a list of Alesia type fibulae from the Liburnian-Dalmatian region according to current knowledge. From north to south, the finds are:

1. Osor: Težak-Gregl 1982, 100, Fig. 2, 1.3.
2. Nin: Nedved 1981, 168, no. 215, Fig. 5, 215.
3. Asseria: Buora 1999, 138, Pl. 4, 1.
4. Ivoševci (Burnum): Šeparović / Uroda 2009, 51, no. 88.
5. Dragišić, grave 17 (Pl. 11b, 26).
6. Vrelo Cetine / Source of the Cetina River: Marović 1959, 46, Fig. 30, 1; 60, Fig. 40, 3.
7. Salona: Ivčević 2002, 247, no. 5, Pl. 1, 5.
8. Vid – Narona: Buora 1999, 120, no. 16.

An Alesia type fibula, of unknown provenience from the Archaeological Museum in Zadar, has a triangular bow decorated with small circles and a row of lengthwise notches in the middle. The foot of the fibula is missing. The same decoration is present on a fully preserved fibula of the same type from Burnum (Ivoševci) that has a coiled end to the foot (Šeparović / Uroda 2009, 11, 51). The fibula from Zadar has a peculiar feature – a double pin. Only one is preserved, while only a slit on the hinged remained from the second (Nedved 1981, 214, Fig. 5, 214). The two pins are the element that makes this fibula from the Archaeological Museum in Zadar close to the Aucissa fibula from Vrelo Cetine. Ivan Marović listed many Roman fibulae with double pins from Dalmatia and Herzegovina, and suggested that they be called the Adriatic-Dalmatian variant of the Aucissa fibula (Marović 1959, 39 ff., 77, Fig. 24, 3).

Aucissa fibulae and other Roman fibulae

Aucissa fibulae were found in several graves at Dragišić: in grave **14** (Pl. 9b, 56, 60), and grave **21** (Pl. 14d, 59), while the best preserved example was found in grave **26** (Pl. 21b, 42). The same grave contained a fragment of a bronze fibula or rather a fragment of the hinge of a fibula with small, flattened lateral buttons. This is a fragment of another Aucissa fibula (Pl. 21b, 32).

A silver Aucissa fibula from Dragišić or Zaton or Velika Mrdakovica was on display at the exhibition of jewellery at the Archaeological Museum in Zadar in 1981 (Nedved 1981, 169, no. 226, Fig. 5, 226).

Fibulae with a semicircular bow and a button on the end of the foot, or Aucissa fibulae, were originally from Italy, although the greatest quantity of these fibulae come from the northern provinces of the Roman Empire. The Aucissa fibulae received their name from the stamp impressed on the head plate of such fibulae. The name belongs to the Celtic onomastikon. The basic characteristics of an Aucissa fibula consist of a hinged construction of the device for fastening, a head plate with a legend or some other decoration, and a triangular foot with a button on the end. The bow is symmetrically arched, in some cases almost semicircular (Koščević 1980, 15). The bow of the fibula can be variously decorated or moulded. It is commonly considered that Aucissa fibulae with a banded bow are earlier than those with a bow with a semicircular section. The local grouping has been noted of individual names on the workshop stamps of Aucissa fibulae.

The finds and frequency of Aucissa fibulae are in general tied to the Roman army. R. Koščević published around sixty examples of this type of Early Roman fibula from Sisak in her monograph on Roman fibulae from the Sisak region (Koščević 1980, 15-17). Ivan Marović wrote a study on Aucissa fibulae with legends from Croatia, from the archaeological museums in Split, Zadar, and Zagreb (Marović 1961, 106-120). At the end of the 1990s Tomislav Šeparović supplemented Marović's article with another twenty Aucissa fibulae from the collection of the Museum of Croatian Archaeological Monuments in Split (Šeparović 1998, 177-187). Most of the Aucissa fibulae come from well-known Roman sites in Dalmatia such as Zadar, Nin, Asseria, and Bribir, while the finds of Roman fibulae from Solin / Salona were recently analysed by Sanja Ivčević (Ivčević 2002, 231-273).

The military character of the Aucissa fibulae is also confirmed by the recently published finds of this type of fibula from Tilurium at Gardun (Šeparović 2003, 219, 228, Pl. 1-9).

T. Težak-Gregl composed a catalogue of a small but interesting collection of Roman fibulae in Osor. They include almost twenty Aucissa fibulae (Težak-Gregl 1982, 100 ff., Fig. 3, 1-8; 4, 1-7). They come from the graves of the Roman cemetery at Kavanela, which was on the Lošinj side of the Osor channel.

The chronological characteristics of the Aucissa fibulae are very reliable. They appeared at the beginning of the AD era, and were use in the first century, particularly during the rule of the Flavian dynasty.

The multiple moulded fibula from grave **13** has a slightly later date (Pl. 8b, 17). Only the bow is preserved. This type of fibula has many variants with varied forms of decoration on the bow. Their mutual characteristic is the two-part structure with a hinge mechanism for the pin, making it close to the Aucissa fibulae. The bow is low and completely decorated so that they had a primarily decorative function. The vast majority of fibulae of this type from Sisak range in size from 3 to 6 cm (Koščević 1980, 19).

Analogies for the fibula from Dragišić can be found among several examples from Sisak (Koščević 1980, Pl. 26, 222, 225; 27, 228). This type of jewellery was analysed by Rieckoff-Pauli in the group of hinged fibulae with a lengthwise moulded bow (*Scharnierfibeln mit längsprofiliertem Bügel*) divided into several sub-groups. The fibula from Dragišić can be placed in group *B1*. This group has a very direct relation to the Aucissa fibulae, and it is dated to the Claudian and Vespasian periods both in Germany and England (Rieckoff-Pauli 1977, 14, Fig. 2, 25-32; 3, 33-47). Six fibulae from Salona belong to the same group – *B1* (Ivčević 2002, 238).

Several multiple profiled fibulae from the Liburnian territory (Asseria, Burnum, "Obrovac Collection") were published in 1981 by Branka Nedved (Nedved 1981, 174, fig. 7, 264-271).

The pendant from grave **21** (Pl. 14a, 12) was originally an annular brooch. The brooch can be compared to the find from Nin that was described as a *belt attachment in the form of a circlet with a pin,* and dated to the 2nd-1st centuries (Batović Š 1981, 126, Fig. 11, 15). The same brooch was also placed among the jewellery types of the Iron Age with a date from the 9th to 1st centuries BC (Batović Š 1981, Add. 1). It seems to me that there are no firm arguments for such an early date, i.e. in the beginning phase of the Iron Age in the Liburnian region, for annular brooches.

One circlet with an attached short wire with a coil (hence it could be an annular brooch) was found in grave 7 of the excavations by Z. Brusić at Dragišić. The grave belongs to the earliest group of graves at the cemetery of the hillfort of Dragišić (Brusić 2000 a, 6, Pl. 9, 2).

Sanja Ivčević, while publishing several examples of this from of clasps from Salona, illustrated the manner in which they were used to fasten clothing, similar to that of the Roman omega-shaped fibulae (Ivčević 2002, 244-246, no. 217, 2217-221).

Nine examples of omega fibulae from Roman sites in central Dalmatia were published in the 1980s in the catalogue of the exhibition of jewellery from northern Dalmatia (Nedved 1981, 170, 238-244). They came from the

Obrovac Collection, from Nin and Starigrad (*Argyruntum*). The omega fibula from an unknown site (Nedved 1981, 172, no. 242) has a circular section identical to the *fibula* from Dragišić, which is not typical for this type of fibula. Omega fibulae more often have rhomboid or flat – rectangular sections of the circlet (Koščević 1991, 64-66).

Roman omega fibulae appeared in the 1st century, but they were primarily utilized in the 2nd and 3rd centuries (Ivčević 2002, 244), however, they also continued further into the 4th century throughout the entire Empire (Koščević 1991, 65), including in Dalmatia (Busuladžić 2008, 26, 34-37) and Liburnia.

The fibula from Dragišić published here apparently was not used for its original purpose. The question remains open as to whether this was an early Liburnian annular brooch or a true Roman omega fibula, so that the dating remains very uncertain.

The fragmentary bronze pieces from the graves at Dragišić include small and large fragments that belong to fibulae, such as the "safety pin" from grave 6 (Pl. 1, 9). On the straight bar of the bow some decorative or similar elements were attached, but since its complete appearance is unknown, we did not enter into typological speculation. If this fragment of a clasp were part of a spectacle fibula, it would represent the earliest fibula among those analysed, and would have been inherited from the previous phase of the Liburnian Iron Age.

PINS

Roll – headed pins

Almost all the graves at the hillfort of Dragišić contained many pin fragments. Most often they cannot be determined typologically or in terms of function because of poor preservation and fragmentation, however, several types of pins can nonetheless be identified.

Graves 7 (Pl. 2, 1), 14 (Pl. 9a, 5, 6), and 26 (Pl. 21a, 20) contained roll – headed pins (with spirally wound heads). Roll-headed pin from grave 7 morphologically and in terms of dimensions can be compared to Bronze Age pins of the same type from Klaćenica and Garica in the northern Libiunian region (Glogović 1989 b, 9, Pl. 5, 1.2). Roll-headed pins were also found in the central Liburnian territory, such as in grave 26 from Nin, which is dated to phase II of the Liburnian Iron Age, i.e. in the 8th-7th centuries BC (Batović Š 1976, 65, Fig. 13, 3). One pin of this type was found as a scattered find at Beretinova hillfort (Batović Š 1968, 61, Pl. 20). An roll-headed pin was found in similar circumstances during excavations at Bribirska Glavica (Batović Š 1980, 74, Pl. 4, 4). A pin with a roll-top head and spirally twisted neck comes from Nin (Batović Š 1981, 122, Fig. 10, 46). Two pins of the same type were found some fifty years ago, also in Nin, when several graves were discovered by

chance while landscaping the garden outside the town administration building (Brusić 2002, 214, 223, 224, Fig. 3, Fig. 16, 3.4.).

Good analogies for roll-headed pins, and particularly those from grave 14 (Pl. 9a, 5.6) and grave 26 (Pl. 21a, 20), can be found in the recently published find from Nadin. Grave 4 (tumulus 13) contained two pottery urns filled with soil and bones. It could not be established whether or not these represented the bones of two different deceased individuals. The globular urn with two horizontal handles, where neither the upper section nor the mouth were preserved, contained a roll-headed pin. This grave from Nadin is dated on the basis of the shape of the pottery urn to the 9th-8th centuries BC (Kukoč 2010, 97-107, Fig. 14).

Roll-headed pins are an old form of jewellery and extend from the early Bronze Age to the end of the Iron Age (Vasić 2003, 20). They remained in use for a long time in the Liburnian region (Glogović 1989b, 9), as was proven once again by graves 14 and 26 at Dragišić. One of the pins from grave 14 (Pl. 9a, 6) has a curved neck, while the other has a knee-shaped bend in the middle (Pl. 9a, 5), just like the pin from grave 20 at Nin (Batović Š 1962, 39, 3). It should be mentioned that roll-headed pins are not noted as typical forms of the late Bronze Age or the earlier phase of the Liburnian Iron Age. One pin of this shape of unknown exact provenience from Dalmatia was published (Marović 1981, 49, 56, Fig. 16, 5).

According to Boško Marjan, roll-headed pins are typical for the Iron Age in the southern Adriatic region and in eastern Herzegovina. They are placed there in the forms of phase II = the 7th century BC (Marijan 2001, 59, 65, Fig. 12, 8). Many finds of roll-headed pins in the Caput Adriae region and in Slovenia show their supra-regional character. They are often found in the Inner Carniola / Notranjska Iron Age group, and in Istria, where they were found at Beram, Kaštel near Buje, Kaštelir near Nova Vas / Brtonigla, Limska hillfort, and Nesactium (Sakara Sučić 2004, 17 ff.).

The dating of roll-headed pins from graves 26 and 14 cannot be based in the contents of the grave unit, as both graves contained several burials and a chronologically broad range of material from prehistoric to Roman finds, such as Aucissa fibulae, a Roman coin, belt buckle plates, etc.

Not even grave 7, with a pin that in terms of workmanship and dimensions could be an earlier Bronze Age pin and hence the earliest pin with a coiled head from Dragišić, could not be significantly earlier, as the grave also contained fragments of iron nails and bars (Pl. 2, 11.12).

Nonetheless, roll-headed pins in this context represent an old and conservative form that survived many changes in terms of forms of jewellery and clothing among the Liburnians.

Pin with a globular head

The pin with a globular head and a hole in the thickened part of the neck below the head from grave **20** (Pl. 13a, 14) most probably belongs to a two-part serpentine fibula with analogies to the fibulae from Grižane and Klaćenica (Glogović 1988, 5-18, Pl. 2, 5.6; Glogović 2003, 47-49). Two-part serpentine fibulae from Liburnian territory are placed among forms of the first phase (approximately 9th century BC) of the Iron Age Liburnian Culture (Batović Š 1987, 363-366, Fig. 20, 6). Some variants of two-part serpentine fibulae can also be dated somewhat earlier, i.e. to the 10th century BC (Glogović b 1989, 40, 41; Blečić 2007, 112).

The pin with a globular head from Dragišić, which was once part of a serpentine two-part fibula, was reused in some manner, losing its original purpose. Like the roll – headed pins, it is reminiscent of earlier Bronze Age attire and jewellery.

Multiheaded pins and Liburnian imitations of astragal belts

In grave 5 from Brusić's excavation at Dragišić (Brusić 2000 a, 9) a parallel row had been arranged of eight of the upper sections of the heads of multiheaded pins (Glogović 2008, 325, Fig. 1, 4a-h). The heads of the pins were, as Brusić suggested, sewn onto a leather belt, while the circlet found in the vicinity was perhaps a buckle for this imitation of an astragal belt.

The Iapodian-Liburnian multiheaded pins that have two or four globular heads alternating with moulded discs and a spirally twisted neck are a typical form of the Liburnian Iron Age Culture (Batović 1982, 17-21; Škoberne 2003, 204). The pins with four globes and discs were called type *A* by Fulvia Lo Schiavo, while the type *B* pins have two globes (Lo Schiavo 1970, 461). The list of Liburnian sites of multiheaded pins are: Nin, Obrovac, Zaton near Nin, Radovin, and Ljubač (Hiller 1991, 218, 414, Fig. 68). Multiheaded pins have also been found at Osor and Rijeka (Marchesetti 1924, 145, Fig. 22; Glogović 1989 b, 12, Pl. 8, 1-4) in the northern Liburnian region, and information about a multiheaded pin from Vrbnik on the island of Krk was recently published (Blečić 2007, 113, Fig. 5).

A multiheaded pin of type *A* that was remodelled into an pendant was found at Dragišić in grave **9** (Pl. 4, 10).

A multiheaded pin in its original function was found in grave 5 of Brusić's excavations at Dragišić, while fragments were found in graves 11 and 14. The five pieces of heads from multiheaded pins in grave 7 similarly suggest an attempt to modify them into a astragal-like type of jewellery (Brusić 2000 a, Pl. 7, 13; 8, 11; 10, 3; 14; Glogović 2008, 328, Fig. 2, 16-20).

Throughout the entire Liburnian territory altogether around a dozen multiheaded pins of the Iapodian-Liburnian type were found. Dragišić, where some twenty pieces

were documented, by far surpasses the total number of multiheaded pins in the Liburnuan region, as was pointed out by Želimir Škoberne in his publication of the multiheaded pins from Budinjak in the Žumberak region.

Since the finds from Dragišiću consist of a modification or change or function – as the heads of the pins were deliberately gathered to be placed on a belt – these pins and fragmentary pins will not be counted among the modest amount of finds of multiheaded pins from Iron Age Liburnia.

A considerably larger quantity of pins of the Iapodian-Liburnian type has been found at Iapodian sites. Around fifty examples were found at Prozor (Škoberne 2003, 203, 204), while the other sites are: Duga Gora / Kordun (Balen-Letunić 1986, 46, 47, Fig. 1, 7), Kompolje, Smiljan, and Vrebac (Hiller 1991, 414). The multiheaded pins from the Liburnian and Iapodian Iron Age groups have an even number of globes (2 or 4) alternating with discs, while the Istrian multiheaded pins have three or five globes with discs, such as the pins from Beram (Kučar 1979, 96, 97, 100, 104, Pl. 6, 3.7; Pl. 8, 3; Pl. 11, 5). The list of site of multiheaded pins in Istria, in addition to Beram, consists of Limska hillfort, Nesactium, Picuga, Štramar near Milje / Muggia, Sv. Martin near Tar, and Kaštelir near Nova Vas / Brtonigla (Sakara Sučević 2004, 22). Multiheaded pins are thus a mutual component of Iapiodian, Liburnian, and Istrian cultural groups, with an earliest date from the late 8th century BC (Gabrovec / Mihovilić 1987, 310).

The western boundary for finds of multiheaded pins is in Lombardy (northwestern Italy), while on the east it extends to the central Danubian basin with Croatian sites in eastern Slavonia. The southernmost finds were in Dalmatia with several unpublished multiheaded pins from Otišić in the Sinj area (Škoberne 2003, 205, 207, Fig. 3). Multiheaded pins are usually attributed to male attire. Iapodian-Liburnian pins with an astragal-like head and a spirally twisted neck are synchronized to the third phase of the Iapodian Culture (Drechsler-Bižić 1987, 404, 405, Fig. 23, 10; Pl. 43, 16) and phase II of the Liburnian Culture of the Iron Age (Batović 1982, 18 ff.).

The astragal form was popular in the Iapodian cultural milieu, with rod-shaped pendants utilizing this form (Dreschler-Bižić 1966, 82, 2: Kompolje). This was also the case in the Liburnian Iron Age group, as shown by the pendants from Dragišić (Pl. 4, 10; Brusić 2000 a, Pl. 15, 3) and Ljubač – Kosa (Brusić 2002, 235, Fig. 35, 4). Another astragal-shaped pendant was found at an unknown site in northern Dalmatia (Batović Š 1981, 136, Fig. 14, 12).

Astragal belts originated in the 6th century BC, and possibly earlier, in the western Balkan – Illyrian territory. Grave I – Ararev tumulus at Glasinac contained a Corinthian helmet and several typical Glasinac fibulae, much amber, and other types of Glasinac jewellery, along with a luxuriously decorated astragal belt (length 100 mm), and was dated to the third quarter of the 6th century

BC. Staša Babić considered that this had been the burial of a female with princely rank, just as in grave 2 from Pilatovići, which contained several astragal-like elements (Babić 2004, 122; Jovanović 1998, 44, Pl. 4, 1). Women, according to the theory of S. Babić, performed the function of hereditary tribal chieftains in the central Balkan region and as such were buried with princely grave goods (Babić 2004, 117-133). In terms of the question of astragal belts, this would be an important, although indirect proof that they belonged to female attire in the late 6th century BC. However, Rastko Vasić questioned several of the arguments for such a sexual attribution of the princely graves, particularly at Glasinac (Vasić 2007, 558 ff.). In fact, one astragal element from a belt comes from the male princely grave at Kličevo (Jovanović 1998, 44, Pl. 3, 3; Babić 2004, Add. B, Pl. 2), so that the astragal belts in the central Balkan princely graves cannot be reliably defined in terms of the sex of the deceased.

Astragal belts from the central Balkan – Illyrian region spread into the southern Pannonian plain, which shows the cultural and trade connections of the Balkan peninsula and the Illyrian world with the Carpathian basin in the late Hallstatt period (Jerem 1974, 229-242). The astragal belts were adopted here from the newly arriving Celtic populations and the Celtic-influences indigenous inhabitants and became a characteristic of the Celtic – La Tène Culture.

The grave from Vučedol contained an astragal belt, two Certosa fibulae, several spearheads, and a single-edged sword (Brunšmid 1902, 68-71: found *supposedly in one grave with a skeleton*) and was analysed in the context of the horizon of warrior graves of the 5th and 4th centuries BC in the Danubian basin (Teržan 1977 b, 14 ff., Fig. 4, 1-12). The belt from Vučedol is a typical form of the Iron Age Srijem / Syrmia group, specifically its earlier phase, i.e. the 5th century BC, and was classified as the Syrmian type of astragal belt (Vasić 1989, 106).

Among the La Tène astragal belts a bell-shaped loop appears with a raised button for attachment. Dragan Božić classified the belts into three types. The Osijek type, just like the Syrmian type of Late Hallstatt belts, has horizontal incisions along the square areas between the elements of the astragal. The Osijek type is somewhat earlier, classified to the Beograd 2 phase, i.e. LT C, while the other types of astragal belts are dated to the Late La Tène and worn by the Scordisci (Božič 1981, 47-54; List of finds, in: Todorović 1964, 64).

It is widely considered that astragal belts continued in use from the middle of the last millennium BC to the beginning of the AD era, while certain indications exist from recent excavations in Syrmia that astragal belts also remained in use in the Roman (Jovanović 1998, 39).

Astragal belts were attributed in earlier texts to a warrior caste, and were hence considered to have been worn by men, and this was indirectly reaffirmed in the 1970s by Biba Teržan (Teržan 1977 b, 14). Today it is predominantly thought that they were part of female attire or were not gender differentiated. D. Božić based his arguments for a female attire element on the problematic credibility of the closed finds of astragal belts in combination with weapons, particularly in terms of the grave from Vučedol (Božič 1981, 53; Todorović 1964, 47). Astragal belts in the central Balkan region in earlier periods were part of ceremonial attire, and perhaps a sign of a higher, princely status.

Donja Dolina is the western boundary for finds of astragal belts. A belt buckle of the Syrmian type and a bell-shaped La Tène buckle were found as scattered finds at the cemetery of Donja Dolina (Marić 1964, 40, Pl. 14, 24.28.29; Arsenijević 1998, 29). A small astragal-like fragment was found at Pod near Bugojno (Jovanović 1988, 42, Pl. 2, 8), hence at a site that in geographic terms is the closest to central Dalmatia and the Liburnian territory.

The astragal-like finds from Dragišić that are interpreted as local imitations of astragal belts were found in graves 5 and 7 of Brusić's exavations, in a group of graves that preceded the Hellenistic phase of the cemetery. They are dated to the 5th and 4th centuries BC. At that time, evidently from somewhere in the interior, from the central Balkan region or from the Danubian basin, the idea arrived about wearing astragal-like elements on a belt. The form itself had been affirmed among previous generations through the multiheaded pins and astragal pendants. As there are no astragal belts in the Iapodian cultural group, the communication and transfer of the fashion trends probably took place via Bosnia (Glogović 2008, 331).

Double pins

Double pins were found in grave **10** (Pl. 5a, 1.2), and grave **11** (Pl. 6a, 1). The second pin is deformed and evidently was not in its original function, The double pins in the Balkan region were classified and listed by Rastko Vasić at the beginning of the 1980s (Vasić 1982, 220-257). The pins from Dragišić belong to the very widespread and quantitatively well represented Vasić's type *IVa* (Vasić 1982, 242-250). Many pins of this type were found in Dalmatia and its immediate hinterland (Vasić 2003, Pl. 69). Vasić's distribution map of this type of pin can be supplemented by a double pin from the island of Hvar, from Starigrad – the ancient Pharos (Petrić, 1998, 28, Pl. 4, 5). One example of a double pin was found at Nin, in grave 17, with a fragment found in grave 85 – Ždrijac (Batović Š 1981, 118, Fig. 10, 48). A double pin of type IV from the island of Korčula has an additional detail – a transverse fastener on the neck with snake heads on the ends (Glogović 2006a, 9, 14, Fig. 3). As double pins are found only sporadically on Liburnian territory, while they are typical for Dalmatia and the Balkans, at the earliest from the second half of the 6th century BC (Čović 1987, 456; Marijan 2001, 80: 4th phase; Vasić 1982, 247), the finds of double pins at Dragišić are held to represent influences from southern Dalmatia and Bosnia and Herzegovina.

RINGS AND OTHER CIRCLET-SHAPED JEWELLERY

Rings

Rings with a semicircular or horseshoe-shaped contour with a decorated crown in the shape of a disc are typical forms of phase V A of the last stage of the Liburnian Iron Age culture, and the ring from the hoard of Jagodnja Gornja served as an illustration on the table of types (Batović Š 1981, 19, 150, Fig. 6, 18).

In the group of rings from Dragišić that belong to the last phases of the Liburnian Iron Age culture, and that correspond in form to the above described type of ring, the ring from grave 6 should first be noted (Pl. 1, 14). The hoop of the ring is missing, while the crown of the ring was preserved in the form of a circular bezel where concentric circles were stamped.

A fragment of the same type of ring with a semicircular-horseshoe section was found in grave 12 (Pl. 7, 4), but the surface of the crown of the ring has a considerable patina, so the decoration could not be seen.

A ring with a semicircular or horseshoe shaped section was found in grave 17 (Pl. 11a, 17; Fig. 11). The crown of the ring was damaged and missing the edges. Remains of decoration in the form of four groups of impressed concentric circles were visible on the preserved part of the upper surface. This ring is analogous to the ring from Jagodnja Gornja (Batović Š 1974, 177, 206, Pl. 24, 31).

A very similar, almost identical ring is known from Otišić with four small circles on the surface of the bezel (Marović 1984, 56, 57, Fig. 23, 2). The ring from Otišić is considered one of the main forms of the fifth phase of the Dalmatian Iron Age culture (Batović 1986, 51-59, 52, Fig. 10, 9). A fragment of the identically decorated bezel of the ring, i.e. with impressed concentric circles, can be found in the inventory of cremation grave 1 at Velika Njiva in Vrebac near Gospić (Drechsler-Bižić 1958, 43, Pl. 10, 71). Rings with an elliptical or circular bezel decorated with concentric circles are thus not exclusively Liburnian jewellery.

A second fragment of a horseshoe-shaped ring from the same grave 17 at Dragišić (Pl. 11b, 27) with an oval bezel has an ornament or figure in negative that cannot be identified.

A decoration composed of a group of concentric circles on the bezel of a ring is present on two rings from grave 10 (Pl. 5d, 63). This was a clump of several rings that were joined together by corrosion. The rings might have been packed together into a purse or had been tied together with some material that later decayed (Pl. 5d, 61, 63). These clusters of rings also contained examples of other types of rings classified to the last Liburnian phase or the V B phase, i.e. the 2nd and 1st centuries BC (Batović Š 1981, 150, Fig. 7, 23).

Fig. 7. Dragišić. Ring from grave 17

The rings from stage B of phase V have a crown with a lenticular section built onto the round circlet of the ring. The protrusive surface of the crown has an oval or circular shape and a geometrical pattern or figural depiction on the upper surface. Two corroded rings of this shape were found in grave 10 (Pl. 5d, 62, 64) and grave 11 (Pl. 6b, 20). The ring from grave 11 with an ellipsoid head has a hatched motif on the upper surface.

Four rings from grave 20 (Pl. 13a, 19; Pl. 13b, 20-22) are examples of the mentioned second type of ring from the last phase of the Liburnian Iron Age group. The same shape of ring can be found in grave 21 (Pl. 14a, 1), while four examples were found in grave 14 (Pl. 9c, 62-65), and one ring in grave 13 (Pl. 8b, 18). Rings with a lenticular crown can have, as was noted on these examples, circular or rhomboid sections of the rings.

Four rings with a lenticular-oval head were found in the Hellenistic grave 1 from Nadin (Batović A 2001, 34, nos. 98-100, 102), in addition to one small oval ring with an inlaid crown (Batović A 2001, 34, no. 101).

At Dragišić the wealthy grave 14, which contained many rings, had only one fragment of a ring with a crown (Pl. 9c, 66). Grave 20 from Dragišić was second in terms of the quantity of discovered rings. All the rings from this grave have decorative motifs impressed on the bezel, such as a rosette, a bird – or duck, a bucranium, a female figure (?), which were all motifs taken over from the rich decorative repertory of Hellenistic or Roman rings. Z. Brusić recently published eight rings of the same form from Ljubača Kosa which again confirms the frequency of finds of such jewellery in the central Liburnian territory (Brusić 2002, 239, Fig. 39).

The group of rings from grave 10 at Dragišić (Pl. 5d, 61, 63), composed of physically connected rings from two different stages of the fifth phase, A and B, show that these two stages of the last phase of the Liburnian Iron Age, at least in terms of rings, cannot be strictly distinguished chronologically, as had been thought.

Graves 10 (Pl. 5c, 48) and 23 (Pl. 18, 6) contain star-shaped circlets. This form of jewellery is not typical for the Liburnian Iron Age culture, nor is it a common find in the Iapodian region, so it has been connected to find of rings of this type from Istria (Mihovilić 2001 a, 213, Pl. 57, 56: Nesactium) and the Trieste Karst region (Carso). Several examples of star-shaped circlets, as well as circlets with hemispherical protrusions, can be found in the inventory of the prehistoric graves at Socerb / San Servolo (Crismani / Righi 2002, 81, Fig. 136-142: List of sites in the Caput Adriae region and in Slovenia). The finds of star-shaped hoops from Kastav indicate connections with the Histrian and Karst regions (Blečić 2002, 97, Pl. 10, 1.3.3, Pl. 11, 9.2.1, 9.2.3). They are dated from the 5th century BC onwards.

Almost all the graves at Dragišić that are being published contained ring-shaped objects, mostly fragmentary, and large and small circlets of various sections. There were two large rings in grave **10** (Pl. 5c, 46, 47), where no. 46 has a lenticular section, and the two fragments of a large circlet (no. 47) have a flat rhomboid section. There are also quite a few small ringlets, such as in grave **12** (Pl. 7, 2, 3). Their purpose cannot be determined with certainty, so they have not been analysed in detail.

BRACELETS

The bracelet, or rather a fragment of a deformed bracelet of circular section with ends in the shape of highly stylized snake head (?), from grave **20** (Pl. 13a, 16) can be classified as Roman jewellery. This form of bracelet is dated to the transition from the 1st to the 2nd century, and into the 3rd century (Cf. Koščević 1991, 32-34, Pl. VIII, 96. 99; Pl. IX, 105. 106; Budja 1979, 244 ff., Pl. 2, 15-17). The bracelet would thus belong to a Roman period burial at the cemetery of Dragišić.

The banded piece of bronze sheet metal from grave **13** (Pl. 8b, 16) with a simple decoration of slanted incisions was probably a bracelet. The workmanship is quite rustic, so it is possible it represents a relict from prehistoric times. The grave contained material from the last Liburnian phase and Roman material, such as a multiple profiled fibula.

PENDANTS

Basket-shaped pendants

Grave **20** (Pl. 13b, 37) contained a fragment of a basket-shaped pendant missing the loop for suspension, identical to the pendant of the same form from grave **24** at Dragišić (Pl. 19, 6).

Two examples of basket-shaped pendants were found in grave **4B** from Brusić's excavations at the cemetery of Dragišić (Brusić 2000 a, Pl. 4, 13), and the jewellery set from grave **10** of Brusić's excavations was composed of eight basket-shaped pendants strung on a squeezed bow fibula, which in turn was hung through the loop of a proto-Certosa fibula (Brusić 2000 a, Pl. 11, 6). One basket-shaped pendant was found in grave 18 of Brusić's excavations at Dragišić (Brusić 2000 a, Pl. 16, 3). Basket-

shaped pendants were used as rattles in a ring-shaped pendant on a fibula from Polače near Benkovac (Batović Š 1981, Fig. 5), similarly as the jewellery set from grave 10 at Brusić's excavations at Dragišić.

Basket-shaped pendants were found in several graves at Nin (Hiller 1991, 192, 194, 41 3, Fig. 61: Distribution map) and Zatona (Batović 1965, Pl. 15, 7), and several basket-shaped pendants from unknown sites in central Dalmatia were published among the Liburnian jewellery from an exhibition catalogue from 1981 (Batović Š 1981, 137, Fig. 14, 17, 18).

Three basket-shaped pendants were strung onto a ring excavated in the graves at Nin published by Brusić in 2002 (Brusić 2002, 223, Fig. 16, 1).

Of Liburnian sites, Osor can also be listed with two examples of basket-shaped pendants (Marchesetti 1924, 147, Fig. 24; Glogović, 1989 b, Pl. 39, 4; Lo Schiavo 1970, 469, 470).

The basket-shaped pendants decorated with a zigzag pattern from grave 10 at Dragišić have analogies to the basket-shaped pendants from Kompolje (Bakarić 1989, 9, Pl. 3, 2). According to Barbara Tessmann, they are type *1*, variant *1* of basket-shaped pendants (Tessmann 2007, 680 ff.). The cited article by Barbara Tessmann about basket-shaped pendants lists all the previous literature on this subject, and introduces a classification into eight types with variants and a list of finds of basket-shaped pendants arranged by type.

The list made by Barbara Tessman should be supplemented for the Liburnian region with the basket-shaped pendants from Dragišić, eleven of which Brusić published in 2000, while here are added another two from the later excavated graves at Dragišić, as well as a basket-shaped pendant from grave 4 at Asseria (Klarin 2000, 32). With the recently published basket-shaped pendants from Nin (Brusić 2002, 223, Fig. 16, 1), the total quantity of basket-shaped pendants from Liburnia has been considerably increased.

Our pendants, those from Liburnian finds, belong among the usual forms that had spread from their original region, that of the Golasecca and Este Cultures, through Slovenia and Istria to Iapodian sites, all the way to Dalmatia. B. Tessmann cited Dalmatian finds of basket-shaped pendants from Viča Luka and Solin as type *4*, variant *1* (Tessmann 2007, 686 ff.).

Basket-shaped pendants with impressed concentric circle are somewhat more rare. One pendant of this type was found in grave 18 of the earlier excavations at Dragišić (Brusić 2000 a, Pl. 16, 3). Sakara Sučević placed this pendant in type *3*. Not many of them have been found, and only three or four sites of discovery in northern Italy were listed (Sakara Sučević 2004, 33, n. 36). According to the classification of B. Tessmann, they would be pendants of type *1*, variant *1* or variant *2* (Tessmann, 2007, 681 ff.).

Pendants decorated with concentric circles, such as the one from grave 18 at Dragišić (see above) belong to the earlier type of basket-shaped pendants from the Golasecca II B phase, dated to the second half of the 6th century BC (de Marinis 1974, 70, Pl. 3).

A basket-shaped pendant – Tessmann type *2*, variant *1* – from northern Dalmatia (Archaeological Museum, Zadar) with a small receptacle and a large loop for suspension (Batović Š 1981, Fig. 14, 18) belongs to a scarce type of basket-shaped pendants. They are only two sites of this type, Most na Soči / Santa Lucia in Slovenia and Dosso del Pol – Gozzo Veronese in the province of Como in northern Italy (Tessmann 2007, 683; Warneke 1999, 129, Fig. 62, 643: basket-shaped pendants with a pointed base).

Hence two small basket-shaped pendants of the same type from Nesactium which were catalogued among *Oggetti dispersi* (Mihovilić 2001 a, 205, Pl. 53, 13) are important. This form of pendant with a small body and large loop would be classified according to R. de Marinis in the later forms of basket-shaped pendants that are placed in the Golasecca IIIA phase = in the first half of the 5th century BC (de Marinis 1974, 70, Pl. 3).

Both basket-shaped pendants from the more recent excavations at Dragišić (Pl. 13b, 37; Pl. 19, 6) are broken and unusable, but nonetheless have increased the amount of this type of European jewellery in the southern Liburnian territory.

Rod-shaped astragal pendants

Grave 9 at Dragišić contained a rod-shaped or astragal pendant (Pl. 4, 10), in fact the remnant of a multiheaded pin reworked into a pendant, while another fragment of the same type of jewellery was found in grave 21 (Pl. 14b, 29). One complete, well-preserved example of a rod-shaped pendant with several globular protrusions was found in inhumation grave 16 of Brusić's excavations at Dragišić (Brusić 2000 a, Pl. 15, 3). This subject has already been discussed under the heading *Multiheaded pins and Liburnian imitations of astragal belts*, so that the pendants need not be once again considered here.

An annular pendant of the Jagodnja Gornja type

A fragment of an annular pendant classified as the *Jagodnja Gornja type* was found in grave 10 (Pl. 5c, 59) at Dragišić. The eponymous find, the hoard of Jagodnja Gornja, contains a fully preserved silver example of a circlet that in terms of function was described as a bracelet or necklace (Batović Š 1974, 169, 173, Pl. 20, 20). The silver circlet is decorated with filigree in the form of a spirally wound wire interrupted by segments of wavy wire. An identical example of an annular pendant was found in the Baška hoard. It was strung onto a Baška type fibula along with beads (Vinski 1956, 20, Fig. 1), just like in the large find of silver jewellery in grave 80 at Asseria (Batović Š 1965, Fig. 19b, 14). The ensemble of silver jewellery from Asseria strikingly resembles the hoard from Jagodnja Gornja in terms of content

(Glogović 2006 b, 134 ff.), so that in the case of the jewellery from Asseria, perhaps this was in fact a hoard, i.e. the storing valuables – silver jewellery, just as the hoard from Jagodnja Gornja had been interpreted.

A fragment of a circlet with identical filigree decoration was found in Osor at Kavanela (Glogović 1982, 37, 38, Fig. 3, 3). So, the sites of discovery of annular pendants of the Jagodnja Gornja type are: Baška (island of Krk), Osor (island of Cres), Asseria, Jagodnja Gornja, and Dragišić (Pl. 5c, 59). Annular pendants of the Jagodnja Gornja type are dated on the basis of the example from Baška to the VA phase of the Liburnian Culture of the Iron Age, to the 4th and 3rd centuries BC.

A hollow lenticular pendant

Circular hollow pendants are generally made from one piece of sheet metal with two circular convex hammered parts. These parts are placed on top of one another and joined into a lenticular circular pendant, while the banded part of the sheet metal is formed into a short tubular loop for suspension. In the literature about the Liburnian Iron Age they are called *biconical* pendants (Batović Š 1981, 124, 136), and quite a few have been found in the Liburnian region. At Nin, for example, several lenticular hollow pendants were hung from a belt plate (Batović Š 1981, 122, Fig. 11, 1), and are dated to the 5th century BC or just in general to the Iron Age.

One half of a pendant of this type was found in grave 34 (Pl. 24, 18) at Dragišić. This half of a lenticular pendant has a hole in the centre through which a nail for attachment was inserted, just like on the above pendants from Nin. Hollow lenticular pendants were found in the graves of Brusić's excavations of the cemetery of Dragišić: grave 4B, grave 5, and in grave 16 (Brusić 2000 a, Pl. 4, 1.2; Pl. 7, 1; Pl. 15, 6).

In Istria, hollow lenticular pendants, called *bullae*, appear early on at Nesactium, in the graves of the first Histrian phase (= 11th and 10th centuries BC). However, Kristina Mihovilić doubts the authenticity of the grave units that would confirm such an early dating for ths type of pendant, considering that in northern Italy bullae are dated to the 9th and 8th centuries BC (Mihovilić 2001 a, 55 ff.).

The archaeological context of the finds of a hollow lenticular pendant at Dragišić is grave 34, with Roman glass, iron nails, etc, which would certainly indicate a later dating in the framework of the last phase of the Liburnian Iron Age.

ELEMENTS OF ATTIRE AND TOILETRY ACCESORIES

Hooks

Grave 14, which contained a large amount of finds, also included a pair of fasteners or loops for fastening (Pl. 9a, 7, 8). A fragment of a similar object was found in grave

30 (Pl. 22a, 2). A hook of identical form was found in the rich Hellenistic grave 1 at Nadin (Batović A 2001, 37, no. 124), so that such hooks for attachment belong to the accessories of the Hellenistic period.

Ordinary hooks with a triangular or trapezoidal platelet with rivets, probably for a leather belt, were found in grave graves from Brusić's excavations at Dragišić: grave 3, grave 4A, and grave 6 (Brusić 2000 a, Pl. 2, 9.12; Pl. 3, 7; Pl. 8, 14). The triangular hook from grave **17** is interesting (Pl. 11b, 32) with three holes for rivets, which was decorated with irregularly scattered hammered circles. A similar decoration can be found on a fragment of a hook platelet from grave **30** (Pl. 22a, 8).

Ordinary simple undecorated hooks with remains of sheet metal backing sometimes have traces of rust, meaning that they were repaired and generally in use for a long time. They were totally intended for everyday use, and were found in the wealthy graves **10** (Pl. 5c, 60) and **14** (Pl. 9c, 73, 74). Grave **21** (Pl. 14b, 30) contained a fragment of a hook with an oval platelet and a square hole for a rivet or nail.

Tweezers

Undecorated tweezers were found in grave **10** (Pl. 5d, 65), and also in grave **21** (Pl. 14b, 28). Tweezers are typical for the Liburnian and Iapodian Iron Age cultures. They were cosmetic instruments and as personal property were placed in the grave. A list of Iapodian and Liburnian graves with tweezers and their typology was composed by F. Lo Schiavo. Tweezers have been found at all important Iapodian sites (Lo Schiavo 1970, 481). They were also found at the cemetery of Nin-Ždrijac in grave 37 and grave 85, and are dated from the 8th century BC onwards (Hiller 1991, 233 ff.). Grave 3 of Brusić's excavations of the cemetery at Dragišić that contained tweezers belonged to a group of earlier pre-Hellenistic graves (Brusić 2000 a, 6-10, Pl. 2, 13). The tweezer finds from Dragišić published here belong to the last, Hellenistic-Roman phase of the Liburnian Culture.

Belt buckle

Grave **14** contained a fragmentarily preserved trapezoidal belt buckle (Pl. 9c, 75). An almost identical buckle was found at Velika Mrdakovica (Brusić 2000 b, 8 ff., 38, below). Interestingly enough, this specimen from Velika Mrdakovica was also broken and later repaired with the help of rivets and a backing plate. The decoration on the flat belt buckle from from Velika Mrdakovica is approximately identical to the geometric decoration on the fragment of the belt buckle from Dragišić. The belt buckle from Velika Mrdakovica was in one of he graves of the later phase of the cemetery, which are dated from the third to the first centuries BC, i.e. they belong to the Hellenistic phase of Velika Mrdakovica. According to Brusić, the graves contained buckles, beads, and imported relief pottery (Brusić 2000 b, 9-11), just as at the cemetery of Dragišić judging on the basis of the inventory of grave **14** (Pl. 9a-9d).

BUTTONS AND APPLIQUÉS

The only find that could be considered a button in the true sense of the word came from grave **14** (Pl. 9c, 70). It is shaped like a miniature hat, and analogies to this shape can be found in the Lika region, for example, the inventory of a grave from Prozor with several examples of a similar *appliqué*. Balen-Letunić considers that these buttons or appliqués were on a leather belt, and also that they were part of the attire of members of both sexes (Balen-Letunić 1996, 27, 37, Pl. 1, 4). These finds from Prozor are dated to the 2nd century BC, and this small button from Dragišić could also be dated to this period.

Grave **34** contained a fragment of a button with a spike in the middle (Pl. 24, 16), which in this context is a very old form of button or appliqué. A convex button with a long spike was found in grave 4B of Brusić's excavations at Dragišić (Brusić 2000 a, Pl. 4, 3). This form is characteristic for the Delmataean Iron Age culture in the 8th and 7th centuries BC (Batović Š 1986, 40, Fig. 13, 4). An convex button with a long spike is noted as the leading type of the third phase (= 5th century BC) of the Iron Age in the southern Adriatic region (Marijan 2001, 71-73, Fig. 13, 8).

Appliqués are metal platelets of various forms that are permanently attached to clothing, shoes or belts and do not unbutton. Two fragmentary appliqués were found in grave **10** (Pl. 5c, 57a, 57b).

TEMPLE-RINGS, HAIR-PINS, AND EARRINGS

Two doubly bent thin wires from grave **20** (Pl. 13a, 7, 8) at Dragišić are probably hooks or clips. They are thin and elastic, so that it is difficult to suggest that they could have served as equipment for fastening clothes. It is assumed that they served as hair-pins or as a decoration or accessory for hair.

Such a form of earring is known among Roman jewellery, but they are made from precious metal. The hooks or clips from Dragišić are made of bronze, so it is unlikely that they would have been worn directly on the body, as earrings, for instance.

Ivan Marović and Mladen Nikolanci described hooks of the same shape, discovered in Viča Luka as *a variant of a decorative pendant that could have been worn around the temples (temple-rings),* and they wrote that the ends had stylized snake heads (Marović / Nikolanci 1969, 31). The hooks or clips from Dragišić have an astragal-shaped moulding below the conical-pyramidal ends. A similar ending can be seen on the more detailed photographs of the same object – a *pendant* from Viča Luka published by Vedran Barbarić (Barbarić 2006, 55, Fig. 9), along with the information that the permanent collection of the Archaeological Museum in Split displays another two such silver *pendants* from the site of Klobuk – Omiška Rogoznica. These finds come from two graves that are dated to the 3rd and 2nd centuries BC.

Zdravko Marić placed the site of Klobuk on the list of sites of discovery of long fibulae of the Middle La Tène type while publishing the finds from Vir near Posušje. The report by Frane Bulić from the 1909 *Bulletin* was cited, which lacks illustrations of the material discovered at Klobuk, which is on display in the Archaeological Museum in Split (Marić 1962, 66, 68, Fig. 2, n. 11).

A detailed analysis of the grave goods in grave IV from Viča Luka and a certain correction of the inventory published in the 1970s date the burial in the grave containing the *temple-rings* or *pendants* to the 4th and 3rd centuries BC (Barbarić 2006, 51-56). Hence, these jewellery items from Dragišić are dated identically, while their purpose as clothing accessories, jewellery, or hair accessories cannot be determined with certainty.

Earrings

A thin silver wire with a loop and a coil on one end from grave **30** (Pl. 22a, 14) could be part of a horseshoe-shaped earring. It corresponds to forms of earrings or temple-rings of stage A of the last phase of the Liburnian Iron Age culture, as classified by Šime Batović. This fragment of an earring from Dragišić is missing the loop with the coil from the other end of the wire. These earrings or temple-rings had a wire with a row of various forms of pendants inserted through the loop (Batović Š 1974, 208-211, Fig. 6, 1, 2, 3).

GLASS BEADS

Introduction

Glass is transparent, glittering, and brilliant, and ideal substance for making jewellery. It first began to be used for decoration, and only much later for the manufacture of luxurious objects of everyday use. In chemical terms, glass is defined as an inorganic product of fusion solidified by rapid cooling without crystallisation. The composition of glass has remained unchanged from its first beginnings to the present, consisting of around two-thirds of quartz sand (silica), along with calcium oxide and sodium carbonate. The addition of various metals or metallic oxides result in various colours of glass, used widely for decorative purposes. The ancient Egyptian civilization is considered to be the source for the manufacture of glass beads for necklaces, dating from the middle of the third millennium BC (Šoufek 2006, 24-36).

In central Europe, the earliest glass artefacts, beads, appear in the Middle Bronze Age. Glass beads for necklaces remain the most common form of personal jewellery throughout the entire prehistoric period in Europe, and the peak in terms of quantity and variety began in the Late Hallstatt and Early La Tène period.

Single coloured beads, granules, and ring-shaped grains

Single-coloured beads as the simplest and most modest form of glass jewellery were found in many graves at

Dragišić: graves 9 (Pl. 4, 23), 15 (Pl. 10b, 16), 21 (Pl. 14e, 63), 18 (Pl. 17, 16.19), 22 (Fig. 12), 25 (Pl. 20, 1a-1d), 26 (Pl. 21b, 44), 30 (Pl. 22a, 27), and 34 (Pl. 24, 31-33).

Multicoloured beads and granules

Several graves of Brusić's excavations at the cemetery of Dragišić, specifically graves 4C, 6, and 7 (Brusić 2000 a, Pl. 5, 9; 8, 8; 9, 3), contained glass paste beads with multi-layered "eyes", one in each grave.

The richest graves among those from the new excavations by Menđušić, in terms of multi-coloured and varied glass beads and granules, were grave **14** (Pl. 9d, 88-90, Fig. 9. 10), and **21** (Pl. 14e, 63), although various types of coloured beads were also found in other graves.

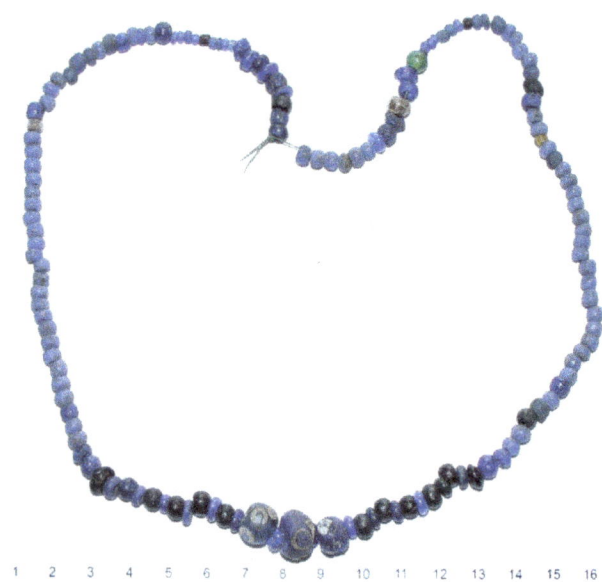

Fig. 8. Dragišić. Necklace from grave 14

Fig. 9. Dragišić. Detail of the necklace from grave 14

One fragment of a blue bead with white circular eyes was found in grave **32** (Pl. 23, 10) at Dragišić. Blue beads with white glass single eyes are the most common and widely distributed type of Hallstatt glass beads. The distribution map of this type shows the main concentration in central and northern Italy, Slovenia and northwestern Croatia, and in the Lika (Iapodian) region (Matthäus 1987, 10, Map 2). Natalia Venclova classified blue beads with four white-blue eyes as type 503, with many having been found. They are dated from the Ha C to the LT A phases (Venclova 1999, 68, Pl. 8). One dot on Matthäus' map of sites marks a blue-white bead from grave 6 at Zaton (Matthäus 1987, 70). This grave from phase III A of the Liburnian Iron Age is well-known and has been published several times (Batović Š 1965, 63, 64, Fig. 15).

Two glass beads with stratified or layered eyes were found in grave **9** (Pl. 4, 25.26). The blue bead has an opaque glass matrix with particles of white sand. It is damaged and has irregularly scattered multi-layered eyes, where yellow and blue alternate, with a dot in the centre of the eye (Pl. 4, 25). The other polychrome bead has a greenish matrix of transparent glass (Pl. 4, 26, Fig. 10) with seven layered eyes. One bead from grave **24** (Pl. 19, 11) belongs to the same category of stratified multi-coloured eyes.

Fig. 10. Dragišić. Bead from grave 9

All three examples of beads with eyes belong to a large group of polychrome beads – types 512 to 517 according to Natalija Venclova, and they are characterized by a very careful workmanship of the eye in several layers with a dot in the centre. All known examples from the Czech Republic are from the *oppidum* of Stradonice, while one glass bead was from the *oppidum* of Staré Hradisko, which limits the dating of this group to the second and first centuries BC. N. Venclova connected the beads from the Czech Republic with the classification of Black Sea polychrome beads, which differ technically from the described examples from central Europe, and are dated at the earliest to the third century BC (Venclova 1990, 70, Pl. 8).

Grave **34** at Dragišić contained several fragments of blue beads densely covered with white concentric circular eyes (Pl. 24, 28-30). They can be compared to geographically near finds, including the beads from Prozor in the Lika region (Kunter 1995, 362, Pl. 5, 20, 21) and from Viča Luka on the island of Brač (Marović / Nikolanci 1969, Pl. 8). The beads from Dragišić with white eyes are chronologically connected to the dating of graves II and III from Viča Luka on the island of Brač.

The cobalt blue bead in the middle of the necklace from grave **14** (Pl. 9d, 88, Fig. 8.9) was, according to the classification of N. Venclova, a three-pointed (with three

horns) bead with three white spirals, or type 412. Blue beads with white spirals are very widespread – from the Mediterranean Sea to northern Germany – and they appear quite early, such as in Ha A – Ha B in Switzerland. This earlier group, according to Venclova, is limited to northeastern Europe and Greece, while the later group of beads with white spirals are classified to the Middle La Tène period, and are a product of Celtic glassmaking that spread throughout all of Europe in the 3rd century BC (Venzlova 1990, 67, 68, Pl. 8).

Grave **21** (Pl. 14e, 63) contained a necklace of fifty-some dark blue round beads, and in the centre a larger bead with a matrix of dark blue transparent glass. The decoration was made in the mosaic technique, with white canes in yellow glass in the *reticello* technique. *Reticello*, a webbed or lace-like decoration, was used in the Hellenistic period in the manufacture of glass vessels, but also in the decoration of various types of beads. The production of objects with *reticello* decoration continued in the 3rd and 2nd centuries BC in workshops throughout the classical world, and perhaps also in Italy, and continued further throughout several centuries (Lazar 2003, 31).

The Liburnian Late Bronze Age or the early phases of the Iron Age culture were not characterized by finds of glass jewellery (Batović Š 1981, 28). For glass beads in the pre-Roman Iron Age, one necklace of varied glass beads is known and one large globular bead with protrusions and multi-coloured eyes from "Zadar-Aenone", as is written in the catalogue of Kari Kunter. The necklace and the described bead supposedly are located in Ancona, Italy (Kunter 1995, 372, Pl. 6, 10). Grave 38 from Nin contained a large circular bead of blue glass paste with yellow incrustation (Batović Š 1981, 140, Fig. 15, 16). This type of blue and yellow beads, which Thea E. Haevernick called *Kompolje – beads* (Dobiat 1987, 15 ff.) most probably arrived in Nin from the Iapodian region. Identical beads are strung on the luxurious necklaces from Prozor in Lika (Bakarić 2006, 62, 63, 156, no. 91; Balen-Letunić 2006, 42, Fig. 21). The local manufacture of glass with a very specific decorative style began to develop very early in the framework of the Iapodian culture, as early as the 9th century BC. It is not surprising that Iapodian bi-colour beads of dark glass paste with circles, dots, and zigzag lines of yellow glass, known as Kompolje – beads, can be found among the Liburnians. A bead of this type was recently also found at the site of Budinjak not far from Zagreb (Škoberne 1999, 31, Fig. 23).

Jewellery with glass beads was somewhat more popular in the Delmataean Iron Age culture. Glass beads in fact arrived in Dalmatia in the Late Bronze Age, hence earlier than among the Liburnians. Tiny ring-shaped and biconical beads are known from the site of Babino polje on the island of Mljet (Marović 1962, 18, 19; Fig. 8, 7-8; Batović Š 1983, 334, Pl. 51, 6,7).

Small glass beads for necklaces are mentioned for phase IV of the Iron Age Delmataean culture (5th century BC), while for the fifth phase (4th-1st centuries BC) they were specifically referred to as a *basic form* of this phase. Several specimens of small glass beads from the well-known find of Gorica near Ljubuški were cited (Batović Š 1986, 51, 55, Fig. 12, 4-8).

A wide repertory of glass beads can be found in the often previously cited jewellery from Viča Luka (Marović 1969, 48, Pl. 8, 9). The graves contained necklaces of beads with colourful eyes and rows composed of transparent biconical granules in combination with amphora-shaped beads. Glass beads were found in three graves dated to the end of the 5th and in the 4th centuries BC. The graves contained Greco-Illyrian helmets, and as Ivan Marović wrote: *The numerous beads permit the hypothesis, if it is taken that they primarily adorned women, that individuals of both sexes were buried in the graves (II, III, IV).*

However, considered in general, decorative glass objects – beads arrive in the Liburnian and Delmataean cultures only in the later phases, as a consequence of Hellenistic influences in central and southern Dalmatia.

Melon beads

Grave **21** contained two melon-shaped beads, one blue (Pl. 14e, 64), and the other green (Pl. 14e, 65). The melon bead from grave **26** (Pl. 21b, 44) was made of an opaque glass with a thick mixture of ingredients that resembles pottery.

Melon-shaped beads – *Melonenperlen* – were widely distributed throughout the eastern Mediterranean, Egypt, the Aegean, and also in Italy. They spread across all of Europe from the Mediterranean. They can also be found in Asia, along the Black Sea coast, in the Caucasus Mountains, etc. They were produced with numerous variants, in faience as well as glass. Melon-shaped beads are extremely old and are known from ancient Egypt and the Mycenaean culture. Individual examples of melon beads were found in central Europe and Italy as early as in the 12th century BC, but their frequency greatly increased in the 6th and 5th centuries BC. Melon-shaped beads were most often made from blue and green glass. They continued in use into the Roman period. From the Liburnian Iron Age culture, a pottery pendant in the shape of a melon bead from Radovin was published (Batović Š 1981, 138, Fig. 15, 7; Batović Š 1987, 372, Pl. 35, 16).

Mira Bertoncelj-Kučar analysed the amber and glass jewellery from Slovenia, including the melon-shaped ribbed beads, and offered parallels to the central Illyrian region and the region of the Iapodes. Bertoncelj-Kučar wrote that according to evidence from the Iapodian cemeteries in the Una River valley the use of glass beads continued into the 1st and 2nd centuries AD (Bertoncelj-Kučar 1977, 258).

The finds of this form of glass beads in graves at Dragišić are dated to the Roman period.

Iapodian melon bead

Grave **22** (Catalogue no. 17; Fig. 11) contained a small melon-shaped bead made of two layers of white glass. The inner nucleus is cylindrical with longitudinal lobes, while the exterior layer was made from thin, very fragile transparent wavy glass. The bead is fragmentary and one half of the exterior thin glass had fallen off.

A necklace composed of the same form of small beads was found in grave 76 from Prozor (Drechsler-Bižić 1973, 41, 42, Pl. 29). According to the description of the workmanship of the small biconical beads from the necklace found in grave 52 at Prozor, a thin gold foil was placed between two layers of glass (Dreshsler-Bižić 1973, 37). The necklace from Prozor that has beads with inserted gold foil was also described in the catalogue of the exhibition of Prehistoric Amber and Glass from Prozor in Lika and Novo Mesto in Doljenska. The necklace is dated to the Late Iron Age, in the 1st century BC (Bakarić 2006, 159, no. 106). Grave 52 and grave 76, with a necklace of small melon-shaped beads, belong to horizon III of graves at the cemetery in Prozor dated to the Middle and Late La Tène period (Drechsler-Bižić 1973, 10, 18-20).

There are no traces of gold on the bead from Dragišić, although it is composed of two layers of glass. Nonetheless, this broken melon-shaped bead from Dragišić can be connected to Iapodian jewellery made with a specific technique, and it is very likely that it arrived in Liburnian territory from the Lika region. Grave **22** from Dragišić contained a glass bead of the Adria type, a form that is dated to the Late La Tène period (Glogović / Menđušić 2007 a, 791, 793, Fig. 1, 2).

Fig. 11. Dragišić. Beads from grave 22

Glass beads in the shape of an amphora

Two incompletely preserved glass colourless and transparent beads in the shape of an amphora were found in grave **34** at Dragišić (Pl. 24, 34.35).

Two terms are used for this form of small bead. They are either called *vessel*-shaped or *amphora*-shaped, of which the first would be better, as an amphora, as its very name indicated, should have two handles. However, the term "amphora-shaped beads" is predominant in the literature.

The origin of this shape of bead should be sought in the northern periphery of the Greek world. At the beginning of the 4th century BC, this form of jewellery spread relatively quickly towards the Adriatic coast, into the eastern Balkan territory, all the way to the central Danube valley and the Carpathian basin, as Petar Popović argued when displaying the distribution of finds of glass amphora-shaped beads (Popović 2000, 269-272, Fig. 2).

Pendants and beads shaped like amphorae for use on necklaces, pectorals, earrings, and other items, were manufactured in various materials, for example from amber, pottery, and naturally, from precious metals – gold and silver. In addition to the examples gathered by P. Popović from the Adriatic-Western Balkan area, a hollow vessel-shaped pendant can be noted on jewellery from Kastav (Glogović 1989 b, Pl. 42, 2; Blečić 2002, Pl. 9, 4.1).

The form of pendants or jewellery beads in the form of an amphora or vessel is not unknown in Liburnian territory. Beads in the shape of amphorae can be found on the earrings or temple-rings that Š. Batović defined as *two-part horseshoe-shaped temple-rings*. One of the variants of this type of horseshoe-shaped earrings has alternating silver vessel-shaped pendants and tiny beads or ringlets. Š. Batović created a list of the finds of this type of jewellery from the Liburnian region: Nin, grave 76, Asseria, grave 80, and Nadin, grave 1 (Batović Š 1974, 211, Fig. 6: 2a, 2b, 3). This was silver jewellery in all three cases. Only one find of glass amphora-shaped beads is noted in the archaeological literature. These are the unpublished *pendants in the form of an amphora discovered in graves below the hillfort of Dračevac in Jesenice below the Velebit Mountains* (Popović 2000, 269, 272, Fig. 2: Distribution map; Batović Š 1974, 211).

Dragišić is the closest find of amphora-shaped beads, other than the hillfort of Dračevac below the Velebit Mountains, to the find from Viča Luka in Dalmatia. Grave III contained an amphora-shaped bead, while grave IV had a necklace with twenty-some glass beads of the same shape (Marović / Nikolanci 1971, 13, 29, Pl. 8, 1; 9, 1). It can be concluded that this form of glass jewellery arrived in the southern Liburnian region from the neighbouring Dalmatia or the interior of the Balkan region, considering the finds from Glasinac in Visoko (Vratnica) and from Sanski Most (Popović 2000, 270).

Glass beads of the Adria type

Green bead of the Adria type made of glass paste was found in grave **15** (Pl. 10b, 15). The same kind of beads can be found in graves **18** (Pl. 17, 20) and **22** (Fig. 11) at Dragišić. The surface of the pale green bead is smooth and shiny, and the granular structure of the glass mass was not as noticeable as for the blue beads from graves **18** and **22** (Glogović / Menđušić 2007 a, 791, Fig. 1, 3).

Similar cylindrical beads with protrusions of blue glass can be found in the Lower Carniola / Dolenjska group in Slovenia, for example on the necklace from grave V/35 at Kapiteljska njiva in Novo Mesto, while a pale blue bead with protrusions was found in grave 10/17 (Križ 2006, 179, no. 232; 190, no. 293). Beads with protrusions (or studded beads) are dated in Novo Mesto to the Lower Carniola / Dolenjska group of the 6th-4th centuries BC, in a period when glass jewellery in general experienced its height of popularity. Beads with protrusions in fact first appeared earlier in the late Urnfield Culture in female graves (Križ 2006, 108).

Cylindrical beads with three rows of protrusions were also documented at Donja Dolina. Studded beads and granules were found in graves VIII and X located on the raised land of S. Jakarić (Truhelka 1904, 106, 107, Pl. 54, 10, 22; Marić 1964, Pl. 23, 47). Several variants of studded beads from Sanski Most were published by F. Fiala (Fiala 1889, 166, Pl. IV), so it can be stated that small glass beads with studded protrusions represented an important element of the glass jewellery of the Donja Dolina – Sanski Most group. Zdravko Marić placed the graves in question in phase III a of Donja Dolina, dated from the middle of the 4th to the middle of the 3rd centuries BC (Marić 1964, 44-46). The glass from grave VIII (Jakarić) was dated by Marić to 360-300 BC. Biba Teržan prepared a chronological combination table of the graves from Donja Dolina that does not correspond completely to Marić's periodization, and grave 10 (Jakarić) was placed in the second section of the penultimate chronological horizon of Donja Dolina (Teržan 1974, 44, Fig. 7). Borivoj Čović created a thoroughly elaborated chronology of the Donja Dolina – Sanski Most group and listed all the relevant literature. Glass beads appeared in the 2 b phase, while the above grave 10 (Jakarić) was placed in phase 3 b, whose begin corresponds chronologically to the beginning of Marić's phase IIIa of Donja Dolina (Čović 1987 b, 246, 261, 266).

Nonetheless, the morphological differences between the beads from Dragišić and the similar items that were cited from Novo Mesto (Lower Carniola) are evident. The Slovenian beads have a smooth and shiny surface, the studs are randomly scattered and non-uniform in size, while the protrusions are sometimes made from glass of a different colour. The three studded beads from Dragišić, on the other hand, were made from opaque glass or glass paste according to a single model, strictly of the same shape and size.

Thea E. Haevernick, who devoted her entire life to the study and systemization of pre-Roman glass, composed a table of examples of small studded beads (= *Noppenperlen*), which was reproduced in the book by Kari Kunter. It should be noted that earlier literature about pre-Roman glass is not cited here, as it can be found *in extenso* in the works of K. Kunter and N. Venclova. Several variants exist of small green-blue cylindrical beads with three rows of protrusions (Kunter 1995, 82-85, Pl. 4, 47-49, 52). Natalija Venclova divided the studded beads into three types: 315, 316, and 317. The transparent, colourless, and round bead with one row of protrusions in the middle that was found at Stradonice in the Czech Republic belongs to type 315. Natalia Venclova related this bead to the Slovenian studded beads from the Late Hallstatt – Early La Tène period in light of the considerable concentration and variety of studded beads in Slovenia. She supported the otherwise widely accepted idea that the glass beads were produced somewhere locally in Slovenia, but considering the dispersal of the finds and their long continuity, she conjectured that there had been several workshop centres (Venclova 1999, 63 ff.; Križ 2006, 90).

Cylindrical beads with three rows of protrusions, opaque and pale blue, were classified as type 316, and opaque pale green beads of the same form are type 317. They were produced by coiling and pressing into a mould. Stradonice (Czech Republic) and Pteni (Moravia) are sites where types 316 and 317 were found. They are dated on the basis of the hoard of Pteni to LT D 1, in the last century BC. They arrived in central Europe from more southeastern regions (Venclova 1999, 63). Many authors, according to J. Meduna, support the hypothesis of a Slovenian or northern Italian origin for the studded beads (Meduna, 1996, 106).

Dragan Božič solved the question of the location of the workshops producing the Late La Tène beads with three rows of protrusions or Venclova's types 315-317. First, Božić defined them as *glass beads of the Adria type*. Seventeen examples were found in Adria (Towle *et al.* 2001, 33-35, Fig. 9, 60-76). D. Božič broadened the total list of sites of discovery with Italian finds of studded beads from Adria, Montereale Valcellina, and Giubiasco. At the *oppidum* of Manching, beads of this kind are dated to the LT C 2 phase. According to Božič, beads of the Adria type (Venclova's types 315-317) of blue, green, and white made from opaque glass or glass paste were not produced in Slovenia, but rather in Adria, and were further distributed from there across northern Italy (Božič 1998, 149, 156). Another two cylindrical beads with four rows of protrusions were recently found in the Caput Adriae region, discovered among the material from the cemetery of San Pietro al Natisone / Špietar (Pettarin 2006, 154, 235, Pl. 37, 633, 634). From northern Italy the studded beads of the Adria type arrived in Bavaria, Moravia, Bohemia, and Slovakia along the amber road (Božič 1998, 150).

The beads of the Adria type from Dragišić published here presumably arrived in the southern Liburnian region from northern Italy via Caput Adriae, as there are no finds on the Italian coast south of the Po River (hence *vis-a-vis* central Dalmatia). They came into use at the end of the last phase of the Liburnian Iron Age, during the period of Romanization of this area (Glogović / Međušić 2007 a, 794, Map 1).

COWRY SHELL

A cowry shell was found in grave **10** (Pl. 5d, 66). The smooth and otherwise shiny surface was completely worn. The shell has a hole resulting from wear.

Cowry shells belong to the Cypraeidae family, which has many species, the most famous being the "money cowry" or *Cypraea moneta*. These sea snails live in warm waters in the Indian Ocean, the southwestern part of the Pacific Ocean, and in the Red Sea. They are small, growing to 3 cm in size, with a white and shiny shell. Cypraea moneta was very widespread as a means of payment, and were also used in jewellery. They are also part of Croatian folk costumes, particularly in the Dinaric zone (Oštrić 1981, 203; www. hrvatskifolklor.net).

Ivan Marović found a snail shell, 29 mm long, when excavating a stone tumulus at Bogomolje on the island of Hvar, which he described as the species *Luria lurida* (Marović 1985, 17, 18, Fig. 9, b). This sea snail is called by various names locally, such *kravica, žabica, babica, gudanić,* or *zupka*, and it lives in the sea where the water is warmer. Marović noted that local fishermen claim that it can be found, although rarely along the coastline of the island of Hvar. Accordingly, one species of the Cypraeidae family also lives in the Adriatic Sea.

Ruža Drechsler-Bižić wrote a discussion about prehistoric jewellery from the region with cowry shells, particularly in reference to the cowry shells found in the Iapodian territory. A piece of Iapodian jewellery from Prozor stood out in particular – a torc with a "trefoil" pendant from which three cowries were hung (Lo Schiavo 416, Pl. 12, 1: Spöttel Collection, NMW; Drechsler-Bižić Pl. 45, 10). Drechsler-Bižić cited many more finds of cowry shells and based their dating on the accompanying finds, such as from two graves at Sanski Most, and grave 250 from Ribić, placed in phase V a by Z. Marić. Finds were also noted from Gorica in Herzegovina, at Glasinac in Bosnia, from Slovenia, etc. In conclusion, Drechsler-Bižić dated jewellery with cowry shells in the Iapodian region in Lika and in Bosnia from the Ha D phase of the Early Iron Age to the end of the LT C phase of the Late Iron Age (Drechsler-Bižić 1991, 79-86).

Pendants and jewellery with cowry shells, as well as their imiltations, were particulary popular in Picenum in Italy (Die Picener 1999, 128, 260, 261, Fig. 103, 104, no. 489, no. 501), where pendants with cowry shells were noted as a form of phase VI a (Lollini 1976, 135, Pl. 10: 11, 12).

Attached to cowry shells, as well as many other types of goods that come from distant and exotic lands, are various superstitious beliefs about their apotropaic and prophylactic effect, with good effects on fertility, etc. Hence, in graves they are always interpreted as amulets.

This digression about cowry shells from distant regions, however, does not apply to the shell from Dragišić. Advice was asked from an expert of shells, Drago

Marguš of Šibenik, who considers that this shell, like the shell from Hvar published by Ivan Marović, is from a species that lives in the waters around the island of Hvar. Nonetheless, it was placed in the grave with similar beliefs about protection from evil forces, both in life and in the afterlife.

ROMAN GLASS VESSELS

Several graves at Dragišić contained fragments of glass vessels, while in some graves there were only two or three pieces of glass. Some fragments have a recognizable form, and an attempt will be made to determine them in line with the typology and chronology of Roman glass.

Grave **9** (Pl. 4, 20-22) contained three fragments of the edges of glass vessels made from blue-green transparent glass. The form of the vessels to which the fragments belonged cannot be determined. The fragment with a reinforced tubular edge (Pl. 4, 22) could be a fragment of a base or foot (Cf. Buljević 1998, 172, 54, 55, 56; Lazar 2003, 112, 113, Fig. 34, 3.8.3).

The fragment of a glass dish or cup of green glass was found in grave **22**. Part of the flat base with an annular tubular foot was preserved (Pl. 15, 1). The fragment can be compared, for example, to the feet of glass vessels from Tilurium (Buljević 2003, 298, 329, Pl. 6, 7; 13, 6-7). The same grave at Dragišić also contained another two fragments of bluish and white curved glass, which represent fragments of small glass vessels (Pl. 15, 2.3).

Grave **27** at Dragišić hillfort contained a broken glass vessel (Fig. 12). It was composed of thin green transparent glass. Thickened circularly bent fragments (Pl. 16, 19) belonged to the mouth or rim of the vessel, perhaps a glass urn. The pieces of glass slag found in the same grave inspire interest (Pl. 16, 18). Similar finds can be found from the remains of glassworking, such as workshops or furnaces (Lazar 2003, 209-232, Pl. 3, 13-15: Ptuj). However, this was a cremation grave, so these were determined to be the remains of melted glass grave goods from the ceremonial incineration.

The neck of a small flask – a balsamarium of white transparent glass (Pl. 21b, 46) was found in grave **26**, which also contained several other fragments of glass.

Balsamaria, according to Ivo Fadić, are quantitatively the most represented form of Roman glass at the Roman sites in Liburnia, and they represent one half (50%) of the total amount of Roman glass vessels in Liburnia (Fadić 2004, 98 ff.). They are one of the forms of Romna glass vessel used to store oils and scents (Lazar 2003, 175-197). This fragment from Dragišić is too small to determine chronologically. The next fragment of glass from the same grave is the rim of a large glass dish, bowl, or lid, made of transparent blue glass (Pl. 21b, 47), in addition to a fragment of a handle (Pl. 21b, 45) made of white glass (Cf. Lazar 2003, 8, 11; Buljević 1998, 155, 173).

Fig. 12. Dragišić. Glass fragments from grave 27

Grave **32** (Pl. 23, 8) contained part of the body of a balsamarium of white glass with a narrowing at the base of the neck. This is a tubular balsamarium, but the fragment is too small to classify it to any of the sub-types in the typology composed by Zrinka Buljević for the balsamaria from Salona (Buljević 2004, 81-95). According to the typology of Irena Lazar for Roman glass in Slovenia, this fragment could be type 8.6.3 of tubular balsamaria (Lazar 2003, 177 ff.).

The forty-some objects from grave **34** at Dragišić included broken Roman glass. The fragment of the edge of a thick angled profile of blue glass (Pl. 24, 36) was perhaps part of a thin bowl or dish, and it could also be the horizontal rim of a larger glass vessel. The same grave contains a fragment of the lower part of a small flask with a wide body and a concave base (Pl. 24, 37). This form of base can be seen on the small vessels for oils and perfumes of Lazar's group 8.6.8, 10-12 (Lazar 2003, Fig. 50) or some forms of balsamaria with conical or bell-shaped bodies (Buljević 2004, 87-89: type 3 *l* and 3 *m*).

Small bottles for scents and oils (balsamaria) appeared towards the end of the first century and are the oldest form of Roman blown glass. There are insufficient elements among the several fragments of balsamaria from Dragišić for either specific typological or chronological determination, so they are approximately dated to the late first century and the second century, with the note that balsamaria with a wide body and an indented concave standing surface are slightly later than the tubular balsamaria (Lazar 2003, 196; Buljević 2004, 87-89).

From production and trade centres in the larger towns of the Roman province of Dalmatia, glass vessels were sent to customers in the smaller settlements in the hinterland. Remains from glass production, i.e. furnaces and semi-finished objects, were discovered at Salona. One clay oil lamp from Asseria depicts a glass furnace and glass blower, which is otherwise a rare find. This image on the lamp from Asseria is used as an argument for the local production of glass vessels in southern Liburnia (Buljević 2005, 100, Fig. 8). Only recently was a lamp with the same scene discovered on the Slovenian coast (Školarice / Križišče, near Koper). Both lamps that depict glassworkers by a gass furnace are dated to the end of the first and the beginning of the second centuries (Lazar 2006, 230, 232, Fig. 2.3).

In the second half of the third century, a glass workshop was active *perhaps in Zadar itself, or somewhere in the vicinity (Aenona, Asseria...?),* as Ivo Fadić wrote. This hypothesis is primarily based on the large quanitity of Roman glass vessels that were found in Liburnia, as well as certain distinctive forms of glass products (Fadić 2004, 100).

According to Irena Lazar, the manufacture of glass was located in Zadar (Lazar 2003, 169). This referred, among other thing, to the specialized production of balsamaria with a bell-shaped body, a form that is particularly specific to the Liburnian glass finds. Bell-shaped balsamaria are dated to the 2nd and 3rd centuries.

POTTERY FINDS

Three fragments of fine pottery were foun in grave **30** (Pl. 22b, 29-31). They include one fragment of the step-like moulded foot of a krater (Pl. 22b, 31), a form that was particularly characteristic for Liburnian Hellenistic relief pottery. Examples would be the krater from grave C at Velika Mrdakovica or the foot of the krater from grave 24 of Brusić's excavations at the hillfort of Dragišić (Brusić 1988, Pl. 9, 1; Pl. 22, 3). Several fragments of Roman pottery were found in grave **22** (Pl. 15, 9-12).

A tiny fragment of pottery with a relief decoration from grave **14** (Pl. 9d, 86) at the hillfort of Dragišić bears the usual decorative motifs from the Liburnian relief craters, just like the fragments of pottery nos. 39, 54, and 57 from Brusić's book on Hellenistic relief pottery (Brusić 1999, 66, 68).

The majority of the fine decorated pottery from Dragišić consists of Hellenistic relief pottery, which was the subject of detailed analysis by Zdenko Brusić, primarily on the basis of finds from the graves of two important southern Liburnian hillforts: Velika Mrdakovica and Dragišić. Studying the Hellenistic relief pottery, Brusić proved the existence of a special Liburnian group of relief pottery that was the product of eastern Adriatic pottery workshops. This pottery is distinguished by a greater stylization of the decorative motifs, and also the fabrix and colour of the pottery, which stands out from the other Hellenistic relief pottery from the other Mediterranean production centres. Finds of this group of Hellenistic relief pottery have been documented at fifteen sites in Liburnia itself, at several sites on the Adriatic coast beyond Liburnia, and on the Apennine peninsula. Workshops of Adriatic Hellenistic relief pottery were located in ancient *Issa* (Vis) and Resnik near Trogir (ancient *Siculi*). On the basis of a mould for making relief decorations on the vessels that was discovered in Zadar (ancient *Iader*), Brusić presumed that one branch of the pottery workshops was active in Zadar (Brusić 1999, 14). The krater is the most typical form of the eastern Adriatic relief pottery.

Several fragments of relief kraters were found in graves excavated by Brusić at Dragišić, such as grave 20 (Brusić 1999, 69). Krater fragments were also discovered in grave 22 (Brusić 1999, 62), while grave 24 at Gradina near Dragišić contained fragments of a krater (Brusić 1999, 71) and relief bowls (Brusić, 1999, 72, 73).

Z. Brusić also discovered other types of imported fine ware in the graves at the cemetery of Dragišić, including a relief-decorated skyphos of northern Italian production. It was discovered in a cremation grave with several other fragments of thin-walled pottery (Brusić 2000 a, 12, Pl. 29, 8), so that Brusić in his study on relief northern Italian *terra sigillata* specially analysed this category of Liburnian imports (Brusić 1989, 102).

Kraters and other high quality vessels were placed in the graves through the ritual of breaking vessels at the funerary feast, as Brusić hypothesized. The finds that are published here confirm this hypothesis.

In terms of the chronology of the eastern Adriatic Hellenistic relief pottery, which is dated approximately to the second and first centuries BC (Brusić 1988, 34), the more recent finds of pottery from the graves at Dragišić have not provided any new information. The graves published here had been utilized for burial several times, so that the pottery is fragmentary and mixed with material that cannot be precisely dated.

The eastern Adriatic Hellenistic relief pottery and the burial ritual, in which the former appears to have had an important role among the Liburnians, underscores the uniqueness of the Liburnian Iron Age culture.

CONCLUSION – SUMMARY

According to the records of the Šibenik Municipal Museum, around thirty graves were investigated during the second excavation campaign at the necropolis of the Dragišić hilllfort, carried out between 2001 and 2003. We have compiled a catalogue of the assemblages from twenty-four graves based on the notes on the deposited finds. Several graves have a large number of catalogue items, e.g. grave 14 with around a hundred objects, or grave 21 with seventy catalogue items. Nevertheless, there are around 27 catalogue items on average. Grave no. 28 contained only three glass beads.

The analysis of human bone remains from seventeen graves, all very fragmented and poorly preserved, showed that all graves contained the remains of more than one person. There were at least two persons in each grave, while grave 26 yielded the remains of as many as eleven persons.

Only one grave, no. 7, can be dated to phase V A of the Liburnian Iron Age. It contained an ancient, Bronze Age roll-headed pin.

In our opinion, seven graves—no. 8, 10, 12, 17, 18, 23 and 24—should be dated to phase V B, due to the lack of indisputably Roman finds – primarily glass, Roman fibulae, Roman coins etc. Typical Liburnian forms from those graves include Certosa fibulae with a bottle-shaped foot, Certosa fibulae of type *VII f*, Baška-type fibulae, Liburnian plate fibulae, tweezers and a ring-shaped pendant of the Jagodnja Gornja type. In the opinion of Š. Batović, the fibulae of the Middle La Tène scheme from three graves are atypical for the Late Iron Age of the Liburnian area. The star-shaped ring from grave 23 can also be considered atypical for the core area of the Iron Age Liburnian culture. We associated them with the contemporary cultures in the Caput Adriae.

All of the other supposed *grave assemblages* contain mixed Roman and—in a manner of speaking—prehistoric objects. Among the latter, the predominant forms belong to the Liburnian phase V – the last phase of the Liburnian Iron Age.

The ornamentation of some of the later Certosa fibulae from Dragišić, for instance the reticulate pattern on the bow, is executed in the local tradition. We singled out from the assemblage of the Certosa fibulae the type Dragišić-Picugi, connecting the Istrian, Liburnian and Dalmatian Iron Age cultures. Liburnian plate fibulae are a specific feature of the Late Iron Age culture and the Hellenistic period in the Liburnian territory. Judging by the quantity and concentration of finds, they originated in the central Liburnian area, from where they spread to the Iron Age cultural groups of the Iapodes and the Histri.

The Dragišić graves yielded a large number of fibulae of the Middle La Tène scheme. The Dragišić hillfort had already earlier yielded a Celtic silver coin, while the nearby site of Balina Glavica near Drniš yielded a hoard of Celtic coins (Kos 2002, 147-158). Moreover, the imitation of astragaloid belts documented at the Dragišić hillfort is connected—albeit indirectly—with the influence of the Celtic Scordisci.

Oval grave pits (Božić 1987, 885; Dizdar 2007, 123, Fig. 2: Zvonimirovo-Veliko polje) documented in Brusić's excavations at the Dragišić hillfort also point to the influence of the Celtic La Tène culture on the burial rite, which is a strong factor in the ethnic interpretation of any culture. However, we cannot overlook the fact that round grave structures were found at the Liburnian necropolis of Ždrijac-Nin, e.g. graves no. 9 and 11. However, based on the find of an incomplete fibula of the Baška type (?) from grave no. 9, here, too, we are dealing with a burial from the fifth phase of the Liburnian Iron Age (Brusić 2002, 218 seq, Figs. 7, 9, 11; Fig. 8, Fig. 14, 2).

As we know from linguistic and onomastic studies, Celtic traces in the onomastics of the Liburnian area are scarce (Matasović 2003, 15-17), particularly when compared with the territory of the ethnic Iapodes, which was a widely discussed topic in the 1970s and 1980s (Matasović 2003, 8). Accordingly, the possible Celtic ethnic presence in central Dalmatia is unlikely, while the manifestations of the Celtic La Tène culture in the Liburnian area are generally interpreted as a consequence of the Roman presence, more precisely their military campaigns in Dalmatia. As regards the hints of Celticism within the last phases of the Liburnian Iron Age, it is nevertheless interesting that the toponym *Arausa* was categorized as a *Celtic-looking name*, same as *Blandona*. This would have to be considered as only a coincidence, because it had already been known that the territory where they were documented had not been a classical Celtic region (Sims-Williams 2006, 5-15, 222, 256, 259, Map 7.1).

In the recently published assemblage from Ljubač Kosa there are around a dozen fibulae of the Middle La Tène scheme. Together with the La Tène material from the former Obrovac Collection, as well as, naturally, the La Tène finds that are published here, we deem it necessary to highlight the Celtic-La Tène element in the Late Iron Age of the Liburnian group.

The fibulae of the Jezerine and Gorica types and the glass beads of the Adria type belong to the Late Liburnian or Early Roman phase of the necropolis, while the Aucissa type fibulae, a multiply-profiled fibula and an omega-shaped fibula all belong to Roman burials at the Dragišić necropolis. The same is true of the few fragments of Roman glass balsamaria, as well as a fragment of a bottle with a concave base and fragments of glass vessels in general. The Roman coin from grave 26 belongs to the

Late Augustan period, and comes from the imperial mint in *Lugdunum*. The graves contained a number of glass beads, and, considering that glass jewellery is not typical for the Late Iron Age Liburnian cultural group, we are more inclined to attribute the glass objects to the Roman burials at the Dragišić necropolis.

Grave 27 is a Roman burial. It yielded the remains of cremated bones belonging to a single person. The grave contained a large broken glass vessel, possibly an urn, that is, a receptacle for the ashes, while the glass slag found in the grave comes from glass grave goods that melted on the pyre (Pl. 16, 18; Fig. 12).

The published burials from Dragišić yielded several fragments of fine imported and Hellenistic relief ware. Considering that imports of Hellenistic relief ware and Italic ware in the Liburnian area have been extensively discussed, we refer the reader to the papers and book published on the subject by Zdenko Brusić (Brusić 1989; Brusić 1988; Brusić 1999).

Fine ornamented ware played an important role in the funerary rituals of the Liburnians. The vessels were in all likelihood broken at the grave during or after the burial rite, which further underlines the specific character of the Liburnian Iron Age group.

Finally, we can say that the published assemblage covers the chronological period from the late fifth century BC until the middle or the end of the second century AD.

We shall briefly review the ethnographic and topographic picture of the studied area in antiquity. The Krka river (*Titius f.*) is considered to have been the southern border of the ethnic Liburnians in prehistory and history, dividing them from the Delmatae. The Dragišić hillfort would then belong to southern Liburnia. The first contacts with Rome, followed by wars and conquests, as well as the activity of the state territorial administration, are reflected in the written sources for the Liburnians and the territory they inhabited.

It was precisely due to the several-year-long excavations at the hillfort near Dragišić and at Velika Mrdakovica, as well as their results, that certain places mentioned by ancient historians and geographers for the eastern coast of the Adriatic could be placed on the map with more accuracy. The correlation of those sources with the situation in the field and with the data obtained from archaeological finds has been a lasting interest of many students of early history.

To keep things concise, we shall highlight only points of direct relevance for the hillfort at Dragišić. Focusing his research on the territory of south Liburnia in the works of geographers, Slobodan Čače has advocated the idea that ancient *Arauzona* was located either at the Gradina near Dragišić or at Velika Mrdakovica, an idea championed also by Brusić (Čače 1990, 204; Brusić 2000 a, 7 seq). The same dilemma between Dragišić and Velika Mrdakovica appears in the discussion about the number of Liburnian municipalities, that is, in Pliny's text on the subject (Čače 1993 a, 25, 35, Appendix 3), as well as in a chapter dedicated to *Arausiona* in the Ravenna Cosmography (Čače, 1993 b, 374).

The Liburnian territory was definitely incorporated into the Roman province of Dalmatia around 35 BC. In the new economic and social circumstances brought about by the Roman provincial administration a gradual process started in which larger and more important Liburnian settlements—including Dragišić—eventually became municipal centres (Čače 1990, 204, 208). However, even these would eventually be abandoned after a couple of generations, which matches the dates for the Roman burials at the Dragišić necropolis, if we take that three generations account for a period of around a hundred years.

In the classification of the size and economic significance, in the hierarchy of settlements under Roman administration, a hillfort the size of Dragišić would be classified as a *vicus* or *pagus*, unlike *Scardona* (Skradin), which acquired the status of a *civitas* during the Flavian period, or e.g. *Varvaria* (Bribir) which in time acquired the status of a *municipium* (Suić 2003, 125). The major Roman towns with continuity from prehistory in central Liburnia were Nin – *Aenona*, Nadin – *Nedinum*, Asseria, Bribir – *Varvaria*. The capital, the Roman colony of Iader – Zadar, situated ot the coast, is not so rich in prehistoric remains precisely due to intense construction in the Roman period and later.

Despite economic growth, population migration to cities etc., the ancient prehistoric hillforts, situated at excellent strategic positions, remained important points in the network of Roman roads in the territory of southern Liburnia (Miletić 1992, 63-66), albeit somewhat removed from the main routes.

CATALOGUE

Frag. = Fragment; L = Length; W = Width; D = Diameter;
H = height; dim. = dimensions; G = Grave; Pl. = Plate

Grave 6, Pl. 1, 1-20.
1. Frag. of a pin, L 59 mm;
2. Frag. of a pin, L 48 mm;
3. Frag. of a pin, L 31 mm;
4. Frag. of a bent pin, L 31 mm;
5. Frag. of a fibula bow with an oval cross section, L 36 mm, W 5 mm;
6. Frag. of a fibula bow with a cruciform incision and a group of transverse incisions, L 29 mm, W 7 mm;
7. Frag. of a bronze band with transverse incisions, L 40 mm, W 3 mm;
8. Frag. of bronze sheet metal, dim. 11 x 4 mm;
9. Fibula with a double loop. The foot is missing. There are two rivet holes on the bow, one above the loop, the other on the terminal, L 51 mm;
10. A foot of a Baška type fibula, L 55 mm;
11. Frag. of a fibula foot, L 53 mm;
12. Silver perforated small sphere. It is a part of a Liburnian plate fibula, D 9 mm;
13. Frag. of bronze sheet metal, dim. 13 x 10 mm;
14. A rounded, flat bezel (the upper part of a ring setting) decorated with concentric circles, D 25 mm;
15. Frag. of a pear-shaped piece of iron covered with rust, L 29 mm;
16. Frag. of a flat piece of iron covered with rust, L 24 mm;
17. Frag. of an iron nail with a circular section, L 20 mm;
18. Frag. of an iron nail, L 24 mm;
19. Frag. of an iron nail with an oval section, L 21 mm;
20. Frag. of a flat oval bluish glass bead with longitudinal perforation, L 21 mm.

Grave 7, Pl. 2, 1-12.
1. A roll-headed pin, L 130 mm, W of the head 3 mm;
2. Frag. of a fibula loop with a fragmentary pin, L 19 mm;
3. Frag. of a pin, L 45 mm;
4. Frag. of a pin, L 29 mm;
5. Frag. of a pin with oval section, L 16 mm;
6. Frag. of a pin, L 14 mm;
7. Frag. of a pin, L 12 mm;
8. Frag. of a thin pin, L 34 mm;
9. Frag. of a pin, L 14 mm;
10. Frag. of a bronze rod, L 12 mm;
11. Frag. of a rusted iron nail, L 42 mm;
12. Frag. of iron nail covered with rust, L 35 mm.

Grave 8, Pl. 3, 1-8.
1. Frag. of a pin, L 44 mm;
2. Frag. of a pin, L 36 mm;
3. Frag. of a pin, L 20 mm;
4. Frag. of a spiral coil made from a bronze band, L 39 mm; W of band 4 mm;
5. Frag. of a spiral coil, probably a spring from a fibula with a fragment of the pin, L 40 mm;
6. Frag. of a Middle La Téne fibula bow with large external coil. On the fragmentary bow with a D-shaped section, the pincer element of the foot is preserved, L 53 mm; D of a coil 11 mm;
7. Frag. of an iron nail with rectangular section, dim. 40 x 10 mm;
8. Frag. of translucent glass, dim. 33 x 11 mm.

Grave 9, Pl. 4, 1-22.
1. Frag. of a pin, L 35 mm;
2. Frag. of a pin, L 14 mm;
3. Frag. of a pin, L 18 mm;
4. Frag. of a rod with a D-shaped section, partly ribbed, L 31 mm;
5. Frag. of a small pin, L 13 mm;
6. A bronze ring, D 7 mm;
7. Frag. of a tube made of thin bronze sheet metal, L 30 mm;
8. Frag. of a bronze band, L 29 mm;
9. a – d. Four fragments of rounded wire, L 16 mm, 24 mm, 17 mm, 11 mm;
10. An astragal pendant made from a reused multi-globular pin of the Liburnian – Iapodian type. The short remnant of a pin is bent into a loop, L 50 mm;
11. A shapeless piece of bronze with a corroded surface, L 20 mm;
12. A silver fragment of jewellery with incisions, L 34 mm;
13. A silver sphere, part of a Liburnian plate fibula, D 7 mm;
14. A silver rod with polygonal section and small spheres at each terminal. Part of Liburnian plate fibula, L 14 mm;
15. Frag. of a fibula foot terminal, L 20 mm;
16. Frag. of a spiral coil with a part of a crossbow from a fibula, L 46 mm;
17. Frag. of a fibula spring with the pin and part of the crossbow, L 34 mm;
18. Frag. of a spiral spring with a part of the crossbow from a fibula, L 44 mm;
19. a – c. Three iron nails, fragmented and rusty, one bent, L 65 mm, 26 mm, 50 mm;
20. Frag. of the rim of a blue-green glass vessel, L 15 mm;
21. Frag. of glass, L 15 mm;
22. Frag. of green glass, L 23 mm;
23. Four dark blue annular glass beads, D 2 mm – 3 mm;
24. Twenty-four blue and dark blue glass beads, approximately of the same size, D of the largest one 12 mm, D of the other beads 5 mm – 6 mm;
25. A blue glass bead with stratified yellow-and-blue eyes, D 11 mm;
26. A green glass bead with stratified yellow-blue-dark brown eyes with a blue spot in the middle of the eye, D 10 mm.

Grave 10, Pl. 5a, 1-16; Pl. 5b, 19-45; Pl. 5c, 46-60; Pl. 5d, 61-66.
1. Frag. of a double pin, L 70 mm;
2. Frag. of a double pin, L 34 mm;
3. A pin of a fibula with a frag. of spiral coil, L 73 mm;
4. A pin of a fibula with remains of a loop, L 53 mm;
5. A pin of a fibula with a spirally coiled band, part of a loop, L 41 mm;
6. A pin with a spiral end, L 46 mm;
7. A pin with the remains of a spiral loop, L 55 mm;
8. A pin with a spirally-coiled band terminal, L 45 mm;
9. Frag. of a fibula with a thin banded bow, L 55 mm;
10. Frag. of a fibula with engraved lines on the bow, L 28 mm;
11. Frag. of a fibula pin ending in an oval-section spiral coil, L 21 mm;
12. Frag. of a fibula pin with a spiral coil with a banded section, L 29 mm;
13. Frag. of a banded bow from a fibula with part of a spiral loop, L 16 mm;
14. A pin of a fibula with a fragmentary preserved loop, L 55 mm;
15. A pin of a fibula with a frag. of a loop with rectangular section, L 64 mm;
16. Frag. of the spiral loop of a fibula, L 21 mm;
17. Frag. of a spiral loop, L 14 mm;
18. Frag. of the pin and loop of a fibula, L 34 mm;
19. A bow of a Middle La Tène fibula with a frag. of spring wound about the bow, L 54 mm;
20. Frag. of a fibula bow with diagonal cross incisions and a segment of transverse lines, L 21 mm;
21. Frag. of a bronze band, L 51 mm;
22. Frag. of a bronze band, L 87 mm;
23. Frag. of a Certosa fibula bow with a loop and part of pin, L 47 mm;
24. A loop of a fibula with part of the bow, L 22 mm;
25. Frag. of a fibula with part of the bow and pin, L 35 mm;
26. Frag. of a banded fibula bow and loop, L 37 mm;
27. Frag. of a Certosa fibula foot terminal, L 15 mm;
28. A deformed La Tène fibula with brown corrosion. The external spiral is missing. The knob on the foot has diagonal ribbing, L 37 mm;
29. A Certosa fibula, flattened, with an ovally enlarged bow. The diagonal net-pattern is incised at the ending of the bow, L 68 mm;
30. a. A foot of a Certosa fibula, L 25 mm;
30. Frag. of a La Tène fibula, the banded spring wound about the bow, L 26 mm;
31. Frag. of a banded bow with a part of a loop, L 23 mm;
32. A foot of a Certosa fibula, L 23 mm;
33. Frag. of the foot of a fibula with a fragmented leaf-shaped terminal, L 35 mm;
34. Frag. of an iron fibula bow, L 23 mm;
35. A flattened fibula bow, L 43 mm;
36. Frag. of a bronze band with knotted and transverse lines, L 16 mm;
37. Frag. of a Certosa fibula foot, L 22 mm;
38. A bow of a Certosa fibula with a broken end, L 48 mm;
39. Frag. of a fibula foot with a J-shaped section, L 28 mm;
40. A bow and spiral loop of fibula wound about the bow, L 45 mm;
41. Frag. of the bow of a fibula, L 30 mm;
42. A small silver rod with square section and hollow spheres on the terminals, part of a Liburnian plate fibula, L 18 mm;
43. Thin silver sheet metal, gold-plated, broken in two. It is bordered by a band filled with two rows of dots. Piercing is present on the wider part of the sheet. Part of a Liburnian plate fibula, dim. 17 x 19 mm;
44. Frag. of a fibula with a part of a loop, L 21 mm;
45. A fibula with a lowered bow with twig-pattern decoration, L 39 mm;
46. A ring with a lenticular section, W 4 mm; D 38 mm;
47. Frag. of a large ring with a flattened rhomboid section, W 4 mm; D 38 mm;
48. A knobbed ring, D 16 mm;
49. A spiral ring with spirally coiled endings, D 14 mm;
50. An open ring, D 9 mm;
51. A small ring, D 8 mm;
52. Frag. of a ring, L 11 mm;
53. Frag. of spirally coiled wire, partly stretched, L 35 mm;
54. A U-shaped loop with hook terminals, L 25 mm;
55. Frag. of rounded wire with one spiral end, W 24 mm;
56. A thin wire bent into a ring, D 12 mm;
57. a, 57 b. Two disc-attachments with hemispherical bosses, D 19 mm and 17 mm;
58. Frag. of bronze sheet with a hole, S 9 mm;
59. Frag. of a pendant of the Jagodnja Gornja type. It is a part of a hollow silver ring with filigree decoration, L 51 mm;
60. A hook with a riveted piece of sheet attached, L 28 mm;
61. An accumulation of many rings joined together by rust and corrosion, dim. 33 mm x 37 mm;
62. A ring with a lenticular bezel, corroded, D 18 mm;
63. A large accumulation of rings with different shapes of bezels, dim. 33 x 33 mm;
64. A ring with a lenticular bezel, D 18 mm;
65. Bronze tweezers, broken in two, L 113 mm; W of one arm 20 mm;
66. A cowrie-shell pendant, L 36 mm.

Grave 11, Pl. 6a, 1-18; Pl. 6b, 19-35.
1. A double pin, the head part of the pin is flattened, one shank is deformed, L 96 mm;
2. A fibula pin with a banded cross section of spiral loop, L 78 mm;
3. A fibula pin broken in the middle with a spirally coiled terminal, L 60 mm;
4. A fibula pin with two banded coils in a loop, L 61 mm;
5. Frag. of a spiral coil, L 22 mm;
6. Frag. of a spiral coil, L 9 mm;
7. Frag. of a bronze band, L 16 mm;
8. A fibula bow bent into a ring. Part of the foot has a J-shaped section, L 30 mm;
9. Frag. of a bronze rod with a D-shaped section and a convex knob, possibly part of a La Tène fibula foot, L 13 mm;

10. Frag. of a bronze rod with a trapezoid section and a convex knob, perhaps part of a La Tène fibula foot, L 16 mm;
11. A broken bow of a La Tène fibula with a frag. of the spring wound around the bow, L 74 mm;
12. Frag. of a bronze band with transverse incisions, L 36 mm;
13. Frag. of the bow and spring of a La Tène fibula, L 30 mm;
14. A Certosa fibula with a rhomboid bow with two incised lines on each side of the bow. A diagonal net-pattern is incised on the back of the bow, L 64 mm;
15. Frag. of a fibula foot with a J-shaped section and raised terminal, L 24 mm;
16. Frag. of a fibula foot with a raised tongue-shaped terminal, L 24 mm;
17. Frag. of a fibula foot with a fragmentary raised terminal, L 24 mm;
18. A foot of a Baška type fibula with a leaf-shaped terminal. The "leaf" is decorated with two *a tremmolo* bands, L 34 mm;
19. A trapezoid plaque with holes in each corner. It is bordered with a zigzag band, dim. 43 mm x 35 mm;
20. A ring with an oval bezel with an incised net pattern, D 19 mm;
21. Frag. of a ring, L 14 mm;
22. Frag. of a curved pin, L 56 mm;
23. Frag. of thick wire, L 46 mm;
24. Frag. of wire bent into a ring, D 20 mm;
25. Frag. of wire, L 34 mm;
26. Frag. of a rusty iron rod, L 41 mm;
27. Frag. of a rusted iron pin, L 24 mm;
28. Frag. of a bronze band, L 49 mm;
29. Frag. of the spiral coil and pin of a fibula, L 14 mm;
30. Frag. of a ring with a lenticular section, L 24 mm;
31. Frag. of a fibula bow with incision, L 24 mm;
32. A spring and frag. of a crossbow from a fibula, L 39 mm;
33. Frag. of a pin, L 60 mm;
34. Frag. of rounded green glass, dim. 12 mm x 20 mm;
35. Frag. of rounded green glass, dim. 14 mm x 20 mm.

Grave 12, Pl. 7, 1-5.
1. Frag. of a corroded fibula with a double-spiral loop, L 28 mm; W of banded bow 6 mm;
2. A bronze ring, D 11 mm;
3. A rusted iron ring, D 9 mm;
4. Frag. of a ring, D of bezel 18 mm;
5. An iron nail of square section with a pyramidal head, L 65 mm;

Grave 13, Pl. 8a, 1-15; Pl. 8b, 16-23.
1. Frag. of a pin, L 61 mm;
2. Frag. of the pin with a loop from a fibula, L 38 mm;
3. A bronze pin, L 106 mm;
4. Frag. of spiral coil, L 8 mm;
5. A bent pin with a flat spiral terminal, L 16 mm;
6. Frag. of a pin with a loop, L 19 mm;
7. A terminal of a Certosa fibula foot with a T-shaped section, L 20 mm;
8. A Certosa fibula with a rhomboid enlarged bow. There are two parallel curved lines on each side of

the rhomb and a hemispherical knob on the descending outer part of the bow, L 80 mm;
9. A foot of a fibula with a J-shaped section. The terminal is folded over to the bow, L 35 mm;
10. Frag. of a La Tène fibula foot, L 14 mm;
11. A disc with a perforated hole and ribbed protrusion. Possibly a fragment of a La Tène fibula foot, L 23 mm; D of disc 14 mm;
12. Frag. of a banded fibula (?), L 45 mm;
13. Frag. of the channel-shaped foot of a fibula (?), L 24 mm;
14. A bow of a fibula, L 36 mm;
15. A hollow silver sphere with transverse rivets, D 6 mm;
16. A bronze band with two rows of short diagonal incisions. It was rounded to form a bracelet or an earring, W 16 mm; L 47 mm;
17. A Roman muliple moulded fibula, L 36 mm;
18. A corroded ring with lenticular bezel, D 17 mm;
19. A bronze bead, D 11 mm;
20. A bronze ring, D 22 mm;
21. A bronze spindle-whorl, D 25 mm, D of perforation 12 mm;
22. Frag. of colourless glass, dim. 20 mm x 20 mm;
23. Frag. of a rusted iron rod, L 19 mm.

Grave 14, Pl. 9a, 1-42; Pl. 9b, 43-61, Pl. 9c, 62-82, Pl. 9d, 83-94.
The human bones of pale brown colour from grave no. 14 were fragmented and poorly preserved. There were at least seven individuals, based on the seven mandibles. Three mandibles were from adults – two males and a female, and four were from children.
1. Frag. of a pin, L 30 mm;
2. Frag. of a pin, L 45 mm;
3. A pin, L 48 mm;
4. Frag. of a pin, L 30 mm;
5. A roll-headed pin, broken in the middle, L 92 mm;
6. A roll-headed pin, L 79 mm;
7. A U-shaped loop with a hook at each terminal, L 28 mm;
8. A U-shaped loop with a hook at each terminal, L 26 mm;
9. Frag. of a spiral coil with triangular section, L 5 mm;
10. Frag. of a spiral coil, L 6 mm;
11. Frag. of a coiled bronze band, D 7 mm;
12. Frag. of the spring and crossbow from a fibula, L 24 mm;
13. A bronze band with a D-shaped section coiled into a ring, D 18 mm;
14. A small fragment of spiral coil, L 8 mm;
15. A fragment of a bronze band with a hammered spirally coiled terminal, L 20 mm;
16. A fragment of a ring, D 10 mm;
17. A spiral disc made of wire, D 16 mm;
18. A pin of an Aucissa fibula (?), L 33 mm;
19. Frag. of a ring, D 20 mm;
20. Frag. of a ring, D 21 mm;
21. Frag. of a ring, D 22 mm;
22. Frag. of rounded wire, L 23 mm;
23. Frag. of a spiral coil, L 23 mm;
24. Frag. of a spiral bronze band, L. 9 mm;

25. Frag. of a spiral bronze band, L 15 mm;
26. Frag. of a spiral coil, L 25 mm;
27. Frag. of a spring with a part of the crossbow from a fibula, L 18 mm;
28. Frag. of a spiral spring from a fibula, L 14 mm;
29. Frag. of spiral coil, L 13 mm;
30. Frag. of a spiral bronze band, L 17 mm;
31. A spiral spring of a fibula wound around a rod, L 13 mm;
32. Frag. of a spring, L 13 mm;
33. A ring made of thin wire, D 10 mm;
34. Frag. of deformed wire, L 33 mm;
35. Frag. of a loop and part of pin from a fibula, L 40 mm;
36. Frag. of a loop and the pin from a fibula, L 30 mm;
37. Frag. of a channel-shaped foot of a fibula (?), L 15 mm;
38. Frag. of a large ring with a lenticular section, L 38 mm;
39. Frag. of a bent rod, L 20 mm;
40. Frag. of a rounded flat bronze band, L 31 mm;
41. Frag. of a bronze band with a lenticular section, L 31 mm;
42. Frag. of a flat rod, L 27 mm;
43. A fibula bow with an external loop, L 38 mm;
44. Frag. of the upper part of a foot of a La Tène fibula with three ribs, L 35 mm;
45. A fibula bow with a loop, L 45 mm;
46. A deformed fibula bow with a double loop, L 44 mm;
47. Frag. of a fibula foot with an upward-turning terminal, L 44 mm;
48. A small fragment of a fibula of the same type as no. 44, L 12 mm;
49. A foot of a Baška type fibula with a part of the bow, L 42 mm;
50. Frag. of a fibula bow with a banded section and spiral loop, L 41 mm;
51. Frag. of a fibula bow, L 34 mm;
52. Frag. of a fibula foot, L 13 mm;
53. Frag. of a large Baška type fibula foot with a J-shaped section, L 80 mm;
54. A Certosa fibula made from a thin band with a C-shaped section. A biconical or poppy-shaped knob is on the terminal of the foot, L 40 mm;
55. Frag. of the channel-shaped foot of a fibula (?), L 15 mm;
56. An Aucissa fibula with a broken bow, L 25 mm;
57. Frag. of a La Tène fibula, the same type as no. 44 and no. 48; L 16 mm;
58. Frag. of a fibula bow with a pincer element in the middle of the bow; L 48 mm;
59. Frag. of a fibula with part of the spring riveted to the bow, L 50 mm;
60. An Aucissa fibula with the bow broken in two, L 40;
61. Frag. of a foot from a Certosa fibula, with a conical knob with a cylinder-shaped protrusion on the foot terminal, L 33 mm;
62. A ring with an oval bezel. The impressed motif cannot be identified, D 19 mm;
63. A ring with an oval bezel, D 17 mm;
64. A ring with a circular bezel with impressed dots, D 17 mm;

65. A ring with a lenticular bezel with an impressed bird, D 18 mm;
66. Frag. of a ring with an oval-shaped bezel, the impressed motif is unclear; L 15 mm;
67. A large bone bead with a circular incision around the perforation, D 38 mm, D of perforation 7 mm;
68. A large clay bead of red-brown colour. The surface is rough, D 39 mm, D of perforation 8 mm;
69. A twisted bronze rod, L 48 mm;
70. A convex button with the loop inside, D 39 mm;
71. Frag. of thick bronze sheet metal with a bronze rivet attached, dim. 38 mm x 19 mm;
72. Frag. of the spiral spring and crossbow from a fibula, L 21 mm;
73. A hook with a trapezoidal catch-plate and rivet, L 32 mm;
74. Frag. of a flat bronze hook with a rivet, filled with iron rust, L 15 mm;
75. A trapezoidal belt plate, slightly curved, part broken off. A button is riveted to the broken edge on the back; L 81 mm; W 30 to 38 mm;
76. Frag. of a ring with a diamond-shaped section, D 21 mm;
77. Frag. of a ring with an oval section, L 25 mm;
78. Frag. of a ring with an oval section, L 21 mm;
79. Frag. of a ring with an oval section, L 22 mm;
80. Frag. of a rounded rod, L 28 mm;
81. Frag. of an iron nail, L 71 mm;
82. Frag. of an iron nail, L 26 mm;
83. A pin and loop of a fibula, L 56 mm;
84. A pin and loop of a fibula, L 58 mm;
85. Frag. of a pottery vessel rim of greyish colour, L 26 mm;
86. Frag. of relief pottery, dim. 30 x 25 mm;
87. A glass oval gem with an impressed image of a bee (?); D 7 mm;
88. A cobalt blue glass bead with three corners ornamented with white spirals, D 13 mm;
89. A blue glass bead with six randomly inlaid eyes consisting of blue-white layers, D 10 mm;
90. A blue glass bead with four stratified blue-white eyes, D 9 mm;
91. Frag. of a ring with a band wound around the middle, L 25 mm;
92. Frag. of a D-section rod with three knobs, L 21 mm;
93. Frag. of a fibula foot terminal, L 25 mm;
94. Frag. of a Jezerine type fibula, L 25 mm; W 9 mm.

Grave 15, Pl. 10a, 1-12, Pl. 10b, 13-17.
The pale brown bones from the grave were fragmented and badly preserved. There were two frontal bones, one of an adult and one of a child. Hence, at least two individuals were buried in this grave.

1. A fibula bow with a fragment of a spring with a rod pulled through it, L 55 mm;
2. Frag. of bronze sheet metal with an impressed line and a hole, dim. 34 mm x 28 mm;
3. Frag. of a thick bronze disc with three parallel impressed lines and three impressed circlets, dim. 27 mm x 20 mm;

4. a – d. Four fragments of bronze sheet metal with different thicknesses, dim. 20 x 20 mm; 14 x 14 mm; 15 x 8 mm; 17 x 4 mm;
5. Frag. of a bronze band with a flat D-shaped section, L 17 mm;
6. Frag. of a rod with ribbing, L 15 mm;
7. A small fragment of a rod with an oval section, L 8 mm;
8. Frag. of a rod, L 9 mm;
9. Frag. of bent bronze sheet metal, L 19 mm;
10. Frag. of a bronze band, L 14 mm;
11. Frag. of a curved bronze band, L 25 mm;
12. a – d. Four fragments of spiral coils, D 3 mm;
13. A blue cylinder-shaped glass bead. All of the inlaid eyes have fallen out, D 13 mm; L 11 mm;
14. a – f. Six fragments of blue-green coloured glass of different thickness, parts of vessels, dim. 16 x 16 mm; 20 x 21 mm; 18 x 13 mm; 24 x 20 mm; 24 x 14 mm; 21 x 10 mm;
15. A green bead of the Adria type, D 5 mm; L 5 mm;
16. A bluish glass bead, D 5 mm;
17. A black glass bead, D 5 mm.

Grave 17, Pl. 11a, 1-22; Pl. 11b, 23-32.
1. Frag. of a fibula bow with an enlarged area and a segment of incised lines, L 43 mm;
2. A fragment of a fibula bow with a hemispherical knob and part of a spring. The knob is ornamented with diagonally incised lines, L 34 mm;
3. Frag. of a bow and a foot from a fibula. The foot ends in an upward tongue, L 43 mm;
4. Frag. of a banded fibula bow with incisions, L 54 mm;
5. Frag. of a spring from a fibula, L 12 mm;
6. Frag. of a spiral spring from a fibula, L 22 mm;
7. Frag. of a pin, L 35 mm;
8. Frag. of a banded bronze sheet with mouldings, dim. 17 mm x 8 mm;
9. Frag. of a fibula foot with a J-shaped section and an upward tongue-shaped terminal, L 27 mm;
10. Frag. of a pin, L 78 mm;
11. Frag. of a pin, L 56 mm;
12. Frag. of a pin, L 34 mm;
13. Frag. of a pin, L 18 mm;
14. Frag. of a pin, L 36 mm;
15. Frag. of a pin with a bent end, L 37 mm;
16. The pin of a fibula with one part of a spiral loop, L 40 mm;
17. A finger ring with a disc-shaped bezel with impressed concentric circles. The rim of the bezel is damaged, D 22 mm;
18. Frag. of a fibula foot with an elevated terminal, L 29 mm;
19. Frag. of a fibula bow (?) with two transverse ribs, L 34 mm;
20. Frag. of a curved bronze band of uneven width, L 36 mm;
21. The foot of a fibula of J-shaped section with part of the bow, L 37 mm;
22. Frag. of a fibula foot with an upward terminal, L 22 mm;
23. A pin from a fibula with a fragment of spiral loop, L 95 mm;

24. A bronze band with two groups of transverse incisions, L 30 mm;
25. A Baška type fibula. A part of the leaf-shaped foot terminal is broken off. There are four segments with transverse incisions on the bow, L 107 mm;
26. Frag. of a trapezoidal slightly curved band with a diagonal net pattern. Possibly a fibula of the Alesia type, L 18 mm;
27. An oval ring bezel with an impressed human motif (?), L 21 mm;
28. A fragmentary ribbed rod with a D-shaped section and a hemispherical knob. It could be a fragment of a La Tène fibula foot, L 21 mm;
29. A coiled and broken piece of bronze band, L 22 mm;
30. Frag. of a curved bronze band, L 19 mm;
31. Frag. of a pin bent into a hook, L 21 mm;
32. A hook with a triangle-shaped plaque covered with randomly impressed concentric circles. There are two perforations in each corner and one in the middle of the plaque, L 69 mm.

Grave 18, Pl. 12, 1-10. Pl. 17, 11-20.
The bones from the grave were extremely badly preserved. No detailed analysis was possible. Nevertheless, based on the quantity and morphology of the bones, it was assumed that at least two adults and two children were buried in the grave.
1. Frag. of a Baška type fibula, L 62 mm;
2. Frag. of a fibula bow with a flat lenticular section, L 42 mm; W 7 mm;
3. Frag. of a curved bronze rod with a lenticular section, L 38 mm; W 4 mm;
4. Frag. of a curved bronze rod with an oval section, L 28 mm;
5. Frag. of half a ring with a square-shaped section, D 24 mm;
6. A shapeless piece of corroded bronze. The actual purpose cannot be established, L 18 mm;
7. Frag. of a pin, L 20 mm;
8. Frag. of pin, L 40 mm;
9. Frag. of a smooth convex disc with a protrusion, D 7 mm; L of protrusion 4 mm;
10. Frag. of a spirally coiled bronze band, D 12 mm; W of band 2 mm;
11. Frag. of the spiral coil of a bronze band, L 10 mm;
12. Frag. of the spiral coil of a bronze band, L 11 mm;
13. Frag. of a bronze rod with a D-shaped section, L 21 mm;
14. Frag. of a curved rod with an oval section, L 20 mm;
15. A short piece of a pin, L 12 mm;
16. Frag. of a wire ring, L 10 mm;
17. An open-ended ring, D 11 mm;
18. Five blue annular glass beads, D 6 mm;
19. Twelve glass beads, D 6-4 mm;
20. A pale blue glass bead of the Adria type, L 5 mm; D 6 mm; D of perforation 3 mm.

Grave 20, Pl. 13a, 1-19; Pl. 13b, 20-38
The bones from the grave were extremely badly preserved. No detailed analysis was possible. According to the amount and morphology of the bones, it can be

concluded that at least three adults and two children had been buried.

1. A fragment of a Certosa fibula foot, L 20 mm;
2. A pin and part of a loop from a fibula, L 57 mm;
3. A pin with a flattened and coiled end, L 52 mm;
4. A pin of a fibula with a fragment of a loop, L 56 mm;
5. A deformed pin from a fibula, L 55 mm;
6. A fragment of a fibula bow with a D-shaped section and a part of a loop, L 21 mm;
7. A multiply bent wire. The terminals have flattened spherical mouldings ending in a conical or pyramidal pointed part, L 27 mm;
8. A multiply bent wire ending in small hemispherical mouldings and conical terminals, L 27 mm;
9. Frag. of a spiral coil of a bronze band, L 25 mm;
10. An open-ended ring with a lenticular section, D 8 mm;
11. A small open-ended ring, D 3 mm;
12. Frag. of a fibula bow with a loop, L 27 mm;
13. A fibula foot of J-shaped section with a bent back leaf-shaped terminal, L 33 mm;
14. A pin from a two-part serpentine fibula with a hole on the neck and a globular head with a pointed protrusion, L 69 mm;
15. A thin bent wire with a spiral end, L 13 mm;
16. A deformed and fragmented open-ended arm ring made of thick wire ending with stylized palmetto (?), L 28 mm;
17. Frag. of bent wire, L 26 mm;
18. A large bronze bead with a biconical cross-section. The outline is pentagonal. The perforation is broad and surrounded by a rib, L 18 mm; D of perforation 8 mm;
19. Frag. of a ring with a lenticular bezel and a star-pattern impression, L 20 mm;
20. A finger ring with a lenticular bezel with an impressed bull's head, D 19 mm;
21. A finger ring with a lenticular bezel with an impressed bird motif, D 20 mm;
22. Frag. of the lenticular bezel of a finger ring, L 16 mm;
23. A spiral ring, L 13 mm; D 8 mm;
24. An open-ended ring, D 14 mm;
25. A piece of jewellery, L 24 mm;
26. Frag. of a curved pin, L 18 mm;
27. An amber bead with an oval outline, D 16 mm;
28. An amber bead, round and flattened, D 19 mm;
29. An amber bead with an oval outline, D 18 mm;
30. A flat amber bead or pendant with a perforation in the middle and a tubular longitudinal perforation at the edge, D 20 mm;
31. A cylindrical amber bead, D 13 mm;
32. A flat amber bead, D 15 mm;
33. Frag. of a rusted iron rod, L 66 mm;
34. Frag. of a pin with an oval section, L 53 mm;
35. An amber bead, D 11 mm;
36. Frag. of a hook with an oval enlarged plaque with a rivet hole, L 36 mm;
37. A vessel-shaped pendant. The loop for suspension is broken off, L 17 mm; W 14 mm;
38. A Certosa fibula with a rhomboid bow, L 74 mm.

Grave 21, Pl. 14a, 1-26; Pl. 14b, 27-43; Pl. 14c, 44-51; Pl. 14d, 52-59.

The light brown bones from grave 21 were in a very poor state of preservation. Several bones have stains from metal oxidation. On the basis of seven right hip bones, it was assumed that at least seven individuals – three male, one female, and three children – had been buried.

1. A ring with an oval bezel and lenticular section, D 16 mm;
2. Frag. of a large ring with an oval section, L 45 mm;
3. The thin pin of a fibula with a hammered end, L 42 mm;
4. Frag. of a rounded bronze band, L 40 mm;
5. A thick wire bent into a hook, L 22 mm;
6. Frag. of a pin, L 19 mm;
7. Frag. of a spiral spring from a fibula, L 8 mm;
8. Frag. of a spiral coil, L 6 mm;
9. Frag. of thick wire with a loop, L 16 mm;
10. A part of a spiral loop from a fibula, L 9 mm;
11. Frag. of a spiral coil, L 6 mm;
12. An omega fibula arranged like a pendant with a hanging pin and a fragment of a La Tène fibula, D 28 mm; L of pin 46 mm; L of fibula 43 mm;
13. Frag. of a rod with a D-shaped section, ribbed at one end, L 51 mm;
14. Frag. of a pin with a loop, D 14 mm;
15. A thin wire with a triangular section, bent into an oval ring, L 24 mm;
16. A fragment of a La Tène fibula, L 15 mm;
17. Frag. of a fibula foot with a J-shaped section, L 25 mm;
18. A small fragment of spiral wire, D 6 mm;
19. Frag. of a pin, L 30 mm;
20. Frag. of bronze wire, L 16 mm;
21. Frag. of a pin, L 40 mm;
22. Frag. of a curved pin, L 13 mm;
23. Frag. of a curved pin, L 14 mm;
24. A short fragment of spiral coil, L 4 mm;
25. Frag. of spiral coil, L 3 mm;
26. Thick wire coiled into a ring, D 11 mm;
27. Frag. of a fibula with a large external loop, L 42 mm;
28. Tweezers, L 56 mm;
29. Frag. of an astragaloid pendant with an oval section, L 22 mm;
30. Frag. of a small hook with a square rivet hole on the oval plaque, L 23 mm;
31. Frag. of a spring from a fibula, L 13 mm;
32. Frag. of a spring from a fibula, L 14 mm;
33. Frag. of a spiral coil of a bronze band, L 14 mm;
34. Frag. of a spring from a fibula, L 9 mm;
35. Frag. of a spring from a fibula, L 9 mm;
36. Frag. of a spiral coil of a bronze band, L 14 mm;
37. Frag. of a spiral coil of a bronze band, L 9 mm;
38. Frag. of a spiral coil of a bronze band, L 18 mm; W of band 5 mm;
39. Frag. of a spiral coil of a bronze band, L 50 mm;
40. Frag. of a spiral coil of a bronze band, L 26 mm;
41. A spiral coil made from a thick bronze band with a D-shaped section, L 19 mm;
42. Part of a spring from a fibula, L 17 mm;
43. Frag. of a spring from a fibula, L 19 mm;

44. Part of a fibula with a fragment of a one-sided spring, L 58 mm;
45. Frag. of a fibula with a triangular section bow and a double spiral loop, L 44 mm;
46. Frag. of a fibula bow and a long symmetrical spring with an inserted wire axis, L 36 mm, L of spiral 32 mm;
47. Frag. of a deformed fibula made of thick wire, L 55 mm;
48. Part of a fibula with a rectangular section bow, a double loop, and part of the pin, L 43 mm;
49. Frag. of a La Tène fibula, L 39 mm;
50. Frag. of a La Tène fibula bow, L 29 mm;
51. Frag. of a fibula with a large external loop, L 39 mm;
52. Frag. of a fibula bow and part of a loop, L 41 mm;
53. A loop from a fibula, D 15 mm;
54. A loop and part of a fibula bow, L 22 mm;
55. A loop from a fibula, D 6 mm;
56. A loop from a fibula, D 9 mm;
57. Frag. of a small fibula bow with a spiral spring, L 24 mm;
58. Frag. of a fibula bow, L 32 mm;
59. Frag. of an Aucissa fibula, L 28 mm;
60. An iron nail with a square section, L 72 mm;
61. An iron nail with a square section, L 43 mm;
62. A large clay bead, possibly a spindle-whorl, D 35 mm;
63. A necklace consisting of fifty-some glass beads of different colours and sizes. In the middle is a poly-chromous bead with a *Reticella* decoration, D 20 mm;
64. A melon-shaped bead made of translucent blue glass, D 19 mm;
65. A melon-shaped glass bead of translucent greenish colour, D 25 mm.

Grave 22, Pl. 15, 1-12; Fig. 11.
The light brown bones were fragmented and poorly preserved. There were two right femurs, one of an adult and one of a child. Hence, it is assumed that two persons were buried in this grave.
1. A base fragment of a green glass vessel, L 52 mm;
2. A fragment of bluish glass, dim. 16 x 25 mm;
3. A fragment of white translucent glass, dim. 20 x 16 mm;
4. A thin pin bent into a hook, L 26 mm;
5. A small piece of bronze sheet metal, L 9 mm;
6. Frag. of bronze sheet metal, S 16 x 21 mm;
7. Frag. of a spiral coil of a bronze band, L 17 mm; W of band 4 mm;
8. A fragmentary pin, curved at the point, L 34 mm;
9. A rim fragment of grey fine pottery, dim. 34 mm x 25 mm;
10. A handle with a rib, fine pale grey pottery, L 38 mm; W 19 mm;
11. A neck fragment of fine light red pottery, W 36 mm; L 23 mm;
12. A pottery wall fragment with grooves and traces of black slip inside, dim. 38 x 38 mm;
13. A small cylindrical dark blue glass bead, D 5 mm;
14. A cobalt blue glass bead, D 6 mm;
15. A blue glass bead, D 5 mm;
16. A small blue glass bead, D 4 mm;

17. A white melon-shaped glass bead made from two layers of glass, D 9 mm;
18. A bead of the Adria type, light green opaque glass, L 6 mm; D 5 mm, D of the perforation 3 mm.

Grave 23, Pl. 18, 1-11.
1. Frag. of a banded bow of a fibula (?), L 60 mm; W 4 mm;
2. Frag. of a fibula bow, L 40 mm;
3. Frag. of a broken Certosa fibula bow, L 28 mm; W 9 mm;
4. Frag. of a spiral coil of a bronze band, L 8 mm;
5. Frag. of a spiral coil of a bronze band, L 16 mm;
6. A ring with knobs, D 16 mm;
7. Frag. of a fibula foot with a raised short tongue at the terminal, L 30 mm;
8. Frag. of a bronze band with transverse incisions, L 19 mm;
9. Frag. of a bronze band, L 14 mm;
10. Frag. of a curved band, L 11 mm;
11. Frag. of a pin, L 19 mm.

Grave 24, Pl. 19, 1-11.
The light brown bones were fragmented. At least two persons were buried, based on the two left premolars of part of the mandibles found among the bones.
1. Frag. of a flat part of a fibula foot, L 31 mm;
2. Frag. of a bronze band, L 20 mm;
3. Frag. of a bronze rod with a diamond-shaped section, L 17 mm;
4. A piece of a deformed bronze band, L 20 mm;
5. An open-ended ring with flattened and bent ends, D 12 mm;
6. A vessel-shaped pendant, with the loop broken off, L 16 mm;
7. A deformed fragment of a fibula foot with a leaf-shaped terminal, L 51 mm;
8. A pin and part of a spiral loop from a fibula, L 83 mm;
9. A piece of bronze sheet metal with a rivet, dim. 12 x 9 mm;
10. Frag. of a fibula foot, L 26 mm;
11. A glass bead of opaque blue with stratified white-blue eyes, D 13 mm, D of perforation 4 mm.

Grave 25, Pl. 20, 1-7.
The light brown bones were fragmented and badly preserved. There were three frontal bones, two of adults and one of a child. It is safe to assume that at least three persons were buried in the grave.
1. 1 a-d. Four small beads made of blue glass, D 7 mm;
2. A spherical blue glass bead, D 9 mm;
3. Frag. of translucent glass, dim. 25 x 18 mm;
4. Frag. of a spiral spring from a fibula, L 25 mm;
5. Frag. of a spiral spring, L 11 mm;
6. Frag. of a pin, L 35 mm;
7. Frag. of a hollow pin, L 20 mm.

Grave 26, Pl. 21a, 1-31; Pl. 21b, 32-47.
The pale brown bones were fragmented and very poorly preserved. At least eleven persons were

buried, calculated on the basis of eight adult right *humeri* and three right shin-bones (*tibiae*) of children, thus there were eight adults and three children in this grave.

1. A deformed double pin, L 33 mm;
2. Frag. of a pin and large loop from a fibula, L 65 mm; D of loop 10 mm;
3. Frag. of a fibula, i.e. the spring and part of the inner crossbow, L 26 mm;
4. a. Frag. of a curved bronze band, L 33 mm; 4b. Frag. of a bronze band, L 21 mm;
5. Frag. of a corroded pin, L 20 mm;
6. A hook with a pierced plaque, L 33 mm;
7. Frag. of a spiral coil of wire, L 11 mm;
8. Frag. of a La Tène fibula bow, L 28 mm;
9. A bronze band, broken and bent, L 65 mm;
10. Frag. of a bronze band, L 24 mm;
11. Frag. of a pin, L 49 mm;
12. Frag. of a thin pin, L 45 mm;
13. Frag. of a pin with a loop, L 31 mm;
14. Frag. of a bent pin, L 27 mm;
15. Frag. of a pin with a square section, L 22 mm;
16. Two fragments of small tubes made of tinned sheets, L 22 mm and 21 mm;
17. Frag. of a La Tène fibula foot (?), L 22 mm;
18. A deformed and bent piece of wire, L 20 mm;
19. A thin bent bronze band, L 38 mm;
20. A distorted roll-headed pin, L 70 mm;
21. Frag. of a pin, hammered at one end, L 27 mm;
22. Frag. of a spring from a fibula, L 15 mm;
23. Frag. of a small hook with a C-shaped section, possibly part of a fibula foot (?), L 19 mm;
24. Frag. of a silver rod with a small sphere affixed to it. One half of the sphere is missing. It is a part of a Liburnian plate fibula, L 11 mm;
25. Frag. of a thin wire with a D-shaped section, L 44 mm;
26. Frag. of a small hook with a C-shaped section, part of a fibula foot (?), L 24 mm;
27. Frag. of a bronze rod with spherical moulding, L 11 mm;
28. A small piece of silver-plated ornamented sheet metal, L 20 mm;
29. Frag. of a small fibula (?), L 21 mm;
30. Frag. of a spring from a fibula, L 9 mm;
31. Frag. of a pin, L 15 mm;
32. A hinge of a fibula and part of a pin, W of hinge 16 mm;
33. A jewellery fragment consisting of a rod made of silver small spheres joined together in the shape of a cross, L 14 mm;
34. Frag. of a finger ring with an oval bezel, L 15 mm;
35. Frag. of a small piece of bronze sheet metal, dim. 14 x 11 mm;
36. Frag. of a silver earring, L 14 mm;
37. Frag. of an iron nail, L 22 mm;
38. Frag. of an iron nail with a square section and mushroom-shaped head, L 36 mm;
39. Frag. Of a rusted iron rod, L 45 mm;
40. A hemispherical rivet head, D of head 11 mm;
41. An amorphous mass of bronze patina, S 14 mm;
42. A silver Aucissa fibula. One of the lateral knobs is missing, L 45 mm;
43. A Roman coin, Aes, copper/bronze (?), weight 9.7 g, D 26 mm; Obv. Augustus, laur., ↓ CAESAR ↑ RO...; Rev. Altar of Lyons, ROMET...;
44. A string of small blue beads. In the centre is a large melon-shaped bead made of opaque blue glass with a rough surface, D 20 mm;
45. Frag. of a small glass handle of white colour, L 11 mm; W 7 mm;
46. A fragmentary rim of a green-blue glass balsamarium, dim. 28 x 32 mm;
47. A fragment of the rim of a pale green glass vessel, dim. 28 x 32 mm.

Grave 27, Pl. 16, 1-19, Fig. 12.
The taphonomy and weight of the osteological sample: Evenly fragmented remains of burnt bones, mostly white without brown stains. Weight: 48.3 g. Most probably this was a woman over 20 years of age.

1. An iron nail with a square section, L 54 mm;
2. An iron nail with a square section, L 60 mm;
3. An iron nail with a square section, L 56 mm;
4. Frag. of an iron nail, L 45 mm;
5. Frag. of an iron nail, L 30 mm;
6. An iron nail, L 29 mm;
7. The square head of an iron nail, L 15 mm;
8. Frag. of an iron nail with a square section, L 24 mm;
9. Frag. of an iron nail, L 16 mm;
10. The point of an iron nail, L 45 mm;
11. Frag. of an iron nail, L 18 mm;
12. A small fragment of an iron nail, L 11 mm;
13. Frag. of a bent iron nail, L 21 mm;
14. Frag. of a small iron nail without the head, diamond-shaped section, bent at a right angle, L 16 mm;
15. A small iron nail without the head, square section, bent at a right angle, L 30 mm;
16. A small iron nail, bent in the middle, L 20 mm;
17. An iron nail with square section, bent at a right angle, L 23 mm;
18. A piece of dark green glass slag, L 40 mm;
19. Two rim fragments of a light green translucent glass urn, dim. 36 mm x 65 mm; W of rim 10 mm.

Grave 28.
The light brown bones were fragmented and very poorly preserved. There were at least two persons, as based on the first right maxillary incisor and first right maxillary milk-tooth incisor found among the bones, thus one adult and one child had been buried.

1. A small cylindrical bead made of opaque blue glass, L 5 mm;
2. A fragment of dark brown glass, L 4 mm;
3. A dark glass bead, L 5 mm.

Grave 30, Pl. 22a, 1-28; Pl. 22b, 29-31.
The light brown bones were fragmented and poorly preserved. There were three frontal bones, one from an adult and two from children. Hence, at least three persons were buried.

1. A thick hollow pin, bent and broken, L 56 mm;
2. A thin U-shaped wire with a hook at one end, L 29 mm;

3. Frag. of a tube with a flattened and rolled end, L 66 mm; W 3 mm;
4. Frag. of a thick wire with a loop at one end, L 42 mm;
5. Frag. of a spiral band, L 17 mm;
6. Frag. of a small ring, D 4 mm;
7. Frag. of a pin and a spiral spring from a fibula, L 13 mm;
8. A hook with a fragmentary rectangular wide plaque with an incised concentric circle, dim. 17 mm x 23 mm;
9. Frag. of a ring with a flat oval section, L 22 mm;
10. Frag. of a pin with a fragment of the spring and crossbow from a fibula, L 60 mm;
11. Frag. of bronze sheet metal with a boss, dim. 24 mm x 24 mm;
12. A solid open-ended earring, D 16 mm;
13. A small fragment of a ring, L 14 mm;
14. Frag. of an earring made of thin silver wire, L 30 mm;
15. Frag. of an iron nail, L 2 mm;
16. Frag. of an iron nail, L 21 mm;
17. Piece of an iron nail, L 13 mm;
18. A large ring with a lenticular section with a rectangular indentation, D 31 mm; W 6 mm;
19. Frag. of bronze sheet metal, dim. 14 mm x 20 mm;
20. Frag. of a small curved bronze sheet, dim. 16 mm x 25 mm;
21. Frag. of thin bronze sheet metal decorated with a net-pattern, dim. 23 mm x 17 mm;
22. A small rectangular fragment of bronze sheet metal, L 18 mm;
23. A small shapeless fragment of bronze sheet meta, L 20 mm;
24. Frag. of bronze sheet, dim. 19 mm x 20 mm;
25. a, b. Two fragments of thin bronze sheet metal, dim. 36 mm x 20 mm; 17 mm x 21 mm;
26. Frag. of elongated bronze sheet metal, L 37 mm;
27. A short string of blue glass beads, several cylindrical, D 5 mm – 3 mm;
28. Frag. of curved greenish glass, dim. 20 mm x 16 mm;
29. A pottery fragment of terra sigillata from the base of a plate, dim. 63 mm x 33 mm;
30. Frag. of a pottery vessel with an everted rim and vertical handle, black shiny slip, H 48 mm; W 34 mm;
31. A grey pottery sherd of fine fabric, the foot of a bowl or krater, H 40 mm; W 42 mm.

Grave 32, Pl. 23, 1-10.
The light brown bones were poorly preserved. Based on the three adult temple bones and two right femurs of children, it was assumed that at least five individuals were buried.
1. Frag. of wire, L 16 mm;
2. Frag. of a wire hook, L 20 mm;
3. A bronze convex button, D 13 mm;
4. A short fragment of wire with a banded clamp, L 12 mm;
5. A deformed nail with a spherical head, L 28 mm;
6. Frag. of a Jezerine type fibula, L 42 mm; W of bow 10 mm;
7. Frag. of the rim of a green glass vessel, L 22 mm;
8. Frag. of a glass balsamarium of greenish colour, H 41 mm;

9. A blue glass bead, D 8 mm;
10. One half of a blue glass bead with white eyes, D 10 mm.

Grave 34, Pl. 24, 1-39.
The pale brown bones were poorly preserved. At least two individuals were buried, one adult and one child, based on two third lumbar vertebrae (L3) among the bones.
1. An iron nail with a square section, bent in the middle, L 73 mm;
2. Frag. of an iron pin, L 124 mm;
3. The point of a bronze pin, flattened at the top, L 33 mm;
4. Frag. of a pin, L 18 mm;
5. Frag. of a pin, L 21 mm;
6. Frag. of a curved bronze band, L 16 mm;
7. Frag. of a small open-ended ring with a diamond section, L 8 mm;
8. Frag. of bronze sheet, dim. 18 mm x 14 mm;
9. Frag. of T-shaped bronze sheet metal, L 16 mm;
10. A rounded fragment of bronze wire, L 19 mm;
11. Frag. of a solid ring, L 36 mm;
12. A piece of bronze, L 12 mm;
13. A bent and rusted iron nail, L 18 mm;
14. Frag. of a fibula foot, L 18 mm;
15. A small convex button, D 8 mm;
16. A convex button with a conical protrusion and the loop in the inner side, D 20 mm; H of protrusion 8 mm;
17. A large bronze bead, moulded around the perforation, ext. D 23 mm; D of perforation 12 mm;
18. One half of a hollow lenticular pendant with a hole in the middle, D 18 mm;
19. A small ring made of wire, D 10 mm;
20. a, b. Two pieces of longitudinally broken iron tube, L 28 mm; D 10 mm;
21. Frag. of an amber bead, L 10 mm;
22. Frag. of an amber bead, L 8 mm;
23. Frag. of an amber bead, L 6 mm;
24. A cylindrical amber bead with a diagonal perforation, L 9 mm; D 10 mm;
25. An amber bead, D 11 mm;
26. Frag. of an amber ring, L 21 mm;
27. Frag. of a spindle-shaped amber bead with a hemispherical indentation, L 21 mm;
28. A blue opaque glass bead with white eyes, D 13 mm;
29. Frag. of a blue glass bead with white eyes, L 9 mm;
30. Frag. of a blue glass bead with empty hollows for eyes that have fallen out and remains of bronze wire inside the bead's tube, L 8 mm;
31. An annular blue glass bead, D 9 mm;
32. A small annular blue glass bead, D 3 mm;
33. An annular blue glass bead, D 8 mm;
34. A vase-shaped glass bead made of transparent colourless glass, damaged, L 14 mm;
35. A vase-shaped bead made of transparent colourless glass, L 14 mm;
36. A thick rim of a pale green glass plate, L 22 mm;
37. Frag. of a glass bottle made from transparent greenish glass, S 35 mm;
38. Frag. of thin glass, L 38 mm;
39. A piece of rounded glass, L 40 mm.

ABBREVIATIONS

BAR IntSer   British Archaeological Reports, International Series (Oxford)

GZM   Glasnik Zemaljskog muzeja Bosne i Hercegovine (Sarajevo)

PBF   Prähistorische Bronzefunde (Stuttgart – München)

PJZ   Praistorija jugoslavenskih zemalja (Sarajevo)

PZ   Praehistorische Zeitschrift (Berlin – New York)

SPH   Starohrvatska prosvjeta (Split)

VAHD   Vjesnik za arheologiju i historiju Dalmatinsku (Split)

VAMZ   Vjesnik Arheološkog muzeja (Zagreb)

VHAD   Vjesnik Hrvatskog arheološkog društva (Zagreb)

WMBH   Wissenschaftliche Mitteilungen aus Bosnien und Herzegowina (Sarajevo)

BIBLIOGRAPHY

ADAM / FEUGERE 1982 – Anna Marie Adam, Michel Feugère, Un Aspect de L'Artisanat du Bronze dans L'Arc Alpin oriental et en Dalmatie au Ier s.av. J.-C.: Les Fibules du Type dit "de Jezerine", *Aquileia Nostra* 53, 130-188.

ARSENIJEVIĆ 1998 – Slavica Arsenijević, Pokušaj sinteze nalaza gvozdenodobnih astragaloidnih pojaseva, *Balcanica* 29, 7-33.

ARTE E CULTURA 1993 – *Arte e cultura in Croazia, Dalle Collezioni del Museo archeologico di Zagabria*, Archaeological Museum in Zagreb (catalogue of the exhibition in Arezzo).

BABIĆ 2004 – Staša Babić, *Poglavarstvo i polis, Starije gvozdeno doba centralnog Balkana i grčki svet*, Posebna izdanja 81, Srpska akademija nauka i umetnosti, Balkanološki institut (Beograd).

BAKARIĆ 1989 – Lidija Bakarić, Grob 154 iz Kompolja, *VAMZ, 3. ser.*, 22, 5-17.

BAKARIĆ 2006 – Lidija Bakarić, Pretpovijesni Prozor, in: *Pretpovijesni jantar i staklo iz Prozora u Lici i Novog Mesta u Dolenjskoj* (catalogue of the exhibition in Zagreb), 48-82; 62-186.

BALEN-LETUNIĆ 1986 – Dubravka Balen-Letunić, Revizijska iskopavanja tumula starijeg željeznog doba u Dugoj Gori, in: *Arheološka istraživanja na karlovačkom i sisačkom području*, Izdanja Hrvatskog arheološkog društva 10, 45-58.

BALEN-LETUNIĆ 1996 – Dubravka Balen-Letunić, Figuralno ukrašene trapezoidne pojasne kopče tipa Prozor, *VAMZ, 3. ser.*, 28-29, 23-39.

BALEN-LETUNIĆ 2006 – Dubravka Balen-Letunić, *Japodi* (Ogulin).

BALEN-LETUNIĆ 2010 – Dubravka Balen-Letunić, Dvije liburnske fibule iz Trošenj-grada, *Prilozi Instituta za arheologiju u Zagrebu* 27, 135-145.

BARBARIĆ 2006 – Vedran Barbarić, Nekropola u Vičoj Luci i gradina Rat na otoku Braču – nova razmatranja, *VAHD* 99, 43-62.

BATOVIĆ A 2001 – Ante Batović, *Helenistički grobovi iz Nadina u okviru V. (zadnje) faze liburnske kulture* (unpublished BA thesis), Faculty of Arts, Zadar.

BATOVIĆ Š 1958 – Šime Batović, Plattenfibeln aus Kroatien (Hrvatska), *Germania, Anzeiger RGK*, Heft 3/4, Jhr. 36, 361-372.

BATOVIĆ Š 1959 – Šime Batović, Predmeti osobitih oblika s područja Liburna, *Radovi Instituta Jugoslavenske akademija znanosti i umjetnosti u Zadru*, Sv. IV-V, 425-452.

BATOVIĆ Š 1962 – Šime Batović, Sepulture de la peuplade Illyrienne des Liburnes, *Inventaria Archaeologica, Jugoslavija*, Fasc. 4.

BATOVIĆ Š 1965 – Šime Batović, Die Eisenzeit auf dem Gebiet des illyrischen Stammes der Liburner, *Archaeologia Iugoslavica* 6, 55-77.

BATOVIĆ Š 1968 – Šime Batović, Nin u prapovijesti, in: *Nin, Problemi arheoloških istraživanja* (Zadar), 7-38.

BATOVIĆ Š 1974 – Šime Batović, Ostava iz Jagodnje Gornje u okviru zadnje faze liburnske kulture, *Diadora* 7, 159-245.

BATOVIĆ Š 1976 – Šime Batović, La Relazioni culturali tra le sponde adriatiche nell'età del ferro, in: *Jadranska obala u protohistoriji* (Zagreb) 11-93.

BATOVIĆ Š 1980 – Šime Batović, Istraživanje prapovijesti u Bribiru, *Diadora* 9, 55-95.

BATOVIĆ Š 1981 – Šime Batović, Nakit u prapovijesti sjeverne Dalmacije, in: *Nakit na tlu sjeverne Dalmacije od prapovijesti do danas* (catalogue to the exhibition in Zadar) 7-31; 89-150.

BATOVIĆ Š 1982 – Šime Batović, Kultura starih Liburna, *Dometi* 12, 7-40.

BATOVIĆ Š 1983 – Šime Batović, Kasno brončano doba na istočnom Jadranskom primorju, in: *PJZ IV, Bronzano doba* (Sarajevo) 271-374.

BATOVIĆ Š 1985 – Šime Batović, Zaton kod Nina – istraživane arheoloških nalazišta od brončanog doba do srednjeg vijeka, *Arheološki pregled* 24, 32-39.

BATOVIĆ Š 1986 – Šime Batović, Dalmatska kultura željeznog doba, *Radovi filozofskog fakulteta u Zadru* 25, 15-75.

BATOVIĆ Š 1987 – Šime Batović, Liburnska grupa, in: *PJZ V, Željezno doba* (Sarajevo) 339-391.

BATOVIĆ Š 1990 – Šime Batović, Benkovački kraj u prapovijesti, *Radovi Filozofskog fakulteta u Zadru* 29, 5-142.

BATOVIĆ Š 2011 – Šime Batović, Predrimski novci iz južne Italije na istočnom jadranskom primorju, *Diadora* 25, 7-46.

BENAC / ČOVIĆ 1957 – Alojz Benac, Borivoj Čović, *Glasinac II, Željezno doba* (Sarajevo).

BERTONCELJ-KUČAR 1977 – Mira Bertoncelj-Kučar, Nakit iz stekla in jantarja, *Arheološki vestnik* 30, 254-293.

BLEČIĆ 2002 – Martina Blečić, Kastav u posljednjem tisućljeću prije Krista, *VAMZ, 3. ser.* 35, 67-131.

BLEČIĆ 2005 – Martina Blečić, Grobnik u željezno doba, *VAMZ, 3. ser.* 37, 47-106.

BLEČIĆ 2007 – Martina Blečić, Reflections of Picens Impacts in the Kvarner Bay, in: *Piceni ed Europa, Atti del Convegno*, Ed. Mitja Guštin, Peter Ettel, Maurizio Buora, Archeologia di Frontiera 6 (Udine), 109-123.

BONAČIĆ-MANDINIĆ 2003 – Maja Bonačić-Mandinić, Nekoliko primjeraka novca 2. i 1. stoljeća prije Krista s Brača – uz razmišljanje o keltskim nalazima u Dalmaciji, *Opuscula Archaeologica* 27, 435-441.

BOUZEK 1997 – Jan Bouzek, *Greece, Anatolia and Europe: Cultural Interrelations during the Early Iron Age*, Studies in Mediterranean Archaeology 122 (Göteborg).

BOŽIČ 1981 – Drago Božič, Kasnolatenski astragalni pojasevi tipa Beograd, *Starinar N.S.* 32, 47-56.

BOŽIČ 1987 – Drago Božič, Zapadna grupa, in: *PJZ V, Željezno doba* (Sarajevo), 855-815.

BOŽIČ 1998 – Drago Božič, Neues über die Kontakte längs der Bernsteinstrasse während der Spätlatènezeit, *Arheološki vestnik* 49, 141-156.

BOŽIČ 2009 – Drago Božič, *Poznolatensko – rimsko grobišče v Novom Mestu, Ljubljanska cesta in Okrajno glavarstvo*, Katalogi in Monografije 39 (Ljubljana).

BRUNŠMID 1902 – Josip Brunšmid, Prethistorijski predmeti iz srijemske županije, *VHAD, N.S.* 6, 68-86.

BRUSIĆ 1976 – Zdenko Brusić, Gradinska utvrđenja u šibenskom kraju, in: *Materijali 12*, IX Kongres arheologa Jugoslavije (Zadar), 113-128.

BRUSIĆ 1980 – Zdenko Brusić, Tehnike grobne i stambene arhitekture na nekim gradinskim naseljima južne Liburnije, in: *Materijali, tehnike i strukture predantičkog i antičkog graditeljstva na istočnom Jadranskom prostoru* (Zagreb) 9-14.

BRUSIĆ 1988 – Zdenko Brusić, Helenistička reljefna keramika u Liburniji, *Diadora* 10, 19-65.

BRUSIĆ 1989 – Zdenko Brusić, Reljefna sjevernoitalska terra sigillata iz Liburnije, *Diadora* 11, 93-158.

BRUSIĆ 1999 – Zdenko Brusić, *Hellenistic and Roman Relief Pottery in Liburnia (North-East Adriatic, Croatia)*, BAR Int. Ser. 817 (Oxford)

BRUSIĆ 2000 a – Zdenko Brusić, Nekropola gradine kod Dragišića, *Radovi Filozofskog fakulteta u Zadru* 25, 1-15.

BRUSIĆ 2000 b – Zdenko Brusić, *Arauzona, Velika Mrdakovica, Liburnski grad i nekropola* (exhibition catalogue, Šibenik), 2000.

BRUSIĆ 2002 – Zdenko Brusić, Nekropole liburnskih naselja Nina i Kose kod Ljupča, *Histria Antiqua* 8, 213-242.

BRUSIĆ 2005 – Zdanko Brusić, Ostaci liburnske nekropole ispred zapadnog bedema Aserije, in: *Asseria 3* (Zadar) 7-24.

BRUSIĆ 2010 a – Zdenko Brusić, Izbor iz liburnskog nakita, *Prilozi Instituta za arheologiju u Zagrebu* 27, 241-249.

BRUSIĆ 2010 b – Zdenko Brusić, Antička plovidba i trgovina s autohtonim zajednicama, in: *Antički Grci na tlu Hrvatske* (catalogue of exhibition in Zagreb) 102-106.

BUDJA 1979 – Miha Budja, Kovinske zapestnice v rimskih grobovih Slovenije, *Arheološki vestnik* 30, 234-250.

BULJEVIĆ 1998 – Zrinka Buljević, Stakleni inventar s lokaliteta Sv. Vid u Vidu kod Metkovića, *VAHD* 87-89, 123-162.

BULJEVIĆ 2003 – Zrinka Buljević, Stakleni inventar, in: *Mirjana Sanader, Tilurium I* (Zagreb) 271-341.

BULJEVIĆ 2004 – Zrinka Buljević, Stakleni balzamariji iz Salone, in: *Dropci antičkega stakla* (Koper), 81-95.

BULJEVIĆ 2005 – Zrinka Buljević, Tragovi staklara u rimskoj provinciji Dalmaciji, *VAHD* 98, 93-106.

BUORA 1999 – Maurizio Buora, Osservazioni sulle Fibule dei Tipi Alesia e Jezerine. Un Esempio di Contatti comerciali e culturali tra l'Età di Cesare e quella di Augusto nell'Arco alpino orientale, *Aquileia Nostra* 70, 106-144.

BUSULADŽIĆ 2008 – Adnan Busuladžić, Zbirka fibula iz Mogorjela, *Opuscula Archaeologica* 32, 21-55.

ČAČE 1990 – Slobodan Čače, Blandona i susjedna središta, Prilog antičkoj topografiji biogradskog područja, *Biogradski zbornik* 1, 197-212.

ČAČE 1993 a – Slobodan Čače, Broj liburnskih općina i vjerodostojnost Plinija (Nat. hist. 3, 130; 139-141), *Radovi Filozofskog fakulteta u Zadru* 32, 1-36.

ČAČE 1993 b – Slobodan Čače, *Civitates Dalmatiae* u "Kozmografiji" Anonima Ravenjanina, *Diadora* 15, 347-442.

ČAČE 2005 – Slobodan Čače, Liburnski pirati: Mit i stvarnost, *Bakarski zbornik* 10, 169-181.

ČAČE / KUNTIĆ-MAKVIĆ 2010 – Slobodan Čače / Bruna Kuntić Makvić, Pregled povijesti jadranskih Grka, in: *Antički Grci na tlu Hrvatske* (catalogue of exhibition in Zagreb) 64-65; 68-71.

ČOVIĆ 1987 a – Borivoj Čović, Srednjodalmatinska grupa, in: *PJZ V, Željezno doba* (Sarajevo) 442-481.

ČOVIĆ 1987 b – Borivoj Čović, Grupa Donja Dolina – Sanski Most, in: *PJZ V, Željezno doba* (Sarajevo) 232-289.

CRISMANI / RIGHI 2002 – Anna Crismani, Guliano Righi, La sepolture protostoriche e ili catalogo dei materiali, in: *La necropoli di San Servolo, Veneti, Istri, Celti e Romani nel territorio di Trieste* (Trieste), 65-89.

ĆUS-RUKONIĆ 1981 – Jasminka Ćus-Rukonić, Neki prapovijesni nalazi u Arheološkoj zbirci Osor, *Histria Archaeologica* 11-12, 5-15.

DEMETZ 1999 – Stefan Demetz, *Fibeln der spälatène- und frühen römischen Kaiserzeit in den Alpenländern*, Frühgeschichtliche und provinzialrömische Archäologie, Materialien und Forschungen 4 (Rahden/Westf.)

DIE PICENER 1999 – *Die Picener, Ein Volk Europas* (exibition catalogue) Frankfurt.

DIZDAR 1999 – Marko Dizdar, Željezno doba, in: *Vinkovci u svijetlu arheologije* (exhibition catalogue, Vinkovci) 39-51, 101-123, 151-159.

DIZDAR 2001 – Marko Dizdar, Nalazišta latenske kulture na vinkovačkom području, *Prilozi Instituta za arheologiju u Zagrebu* 18, 103-135.

DIZDAR 2007 – Marko Dizdar, Bikonični lonci sa stepeničasto raščlanjenim ramenom s groblja Zvonimirovo – Veliko Polje, *Prilozi Instituta za arheologiju u Zagrebu* 24, 121-145.

DOBIAT 1987 – Claus Dobiat, Perlen mit konzentrischen Ringen, in: *Glasperlen der Vorrömischen Eisenzeit II*, Marburger Studien zur Vor-und Frühgeschichte 9, 15-35.

DRECHSLER-BIŽIĆ 1958 – Ružica Drechsler-Bižić, Naselje i grobovi preistorijskih Japoda u Vrepcu, *VAMZ, 3. ser.* 1, 35-60.

DRECHSLER-BIŽIĆ 1966 – Ružica Drechsler-Bižić, Les Tombes des Japodes prehistoriques a Kompolje, *Inventaria Archaeologica, Jugoslavija,* Fasc. 9.

DRECHSLER-BIŽIĆ 1968 – Ružica Drechsler-Bižić, Japodske kape i oglavlja, *VAMZ, 3. ser.* 3, 29-52.

DRECHSLER-BIŽIĆ 1973 – Ružica Drechler-Bižić, Nekropola prahistorijskih Japoda u Prozoru kod Otočca, *VAMZ, 3. ser.* 6/7, 1-45.

DRECHSLER-BIŽIĆ 1987 – Ružica Drechsler – Bižić, Japodska grupa, in: *PJZ V, Željezno doba* (Sarajevo) 391-442.

DRECHSLER-BIŽIĆ 1991 – Ružica Drechler-Bižić, Prahistorijski nakit s kaori puževima, Zbornik radova posvećenih akademiku Alozu Bencu, *Posebna Izdanja, Knjiga 95, Odjeljenje društvenih nauka, Knjiga* 27 (Sarajevo) 79-89.

v. ELES-MASI 1986 – Patrizia von Eles Masi, *Le Fibule dell'Italia settentrionale*, PBF, Abt. 14, Bd. 5 (München).

ETTLINGER 1973 – Elisabeth Ettlinger, *Die Römischen Fibeln in der Schweiz* (Bern).

FADIĆ 1982 – Ivo Fadić, Tipologija i kronologija rimskog stakla iz Arheološke zbirke u Osoru, in: *Arheološka istraživanja na otocima Cresu i Lošinju*, Izdanja Hrvatskog arheološkog društva 7, 111-137.

FADIĆ 2004 – Ivo Fadić, Antičke staklarske radionice u Hrvatskoj, in: *Dropci antičkega stakla* (Koper) 95-107.

FIALA 1889 – Franjo Fiala, Das Flachgräberfeld und die prähistorische Ansiedlung in Sanskimost, *WMBH* 4, 62-127.

GABROVEC et al. 2006 – Stane Gabrovec, Ana Kruh, Ida Murgelj, Biba Teržan, *Stična II / 1, Gomile starejše železne dobe*, Katalogi in Monografije 37 (Ljubljana).

GABROVEC / MIHOVILIĆ 1987 – Stane Gabrovec, Kristina Mihovilić, Istarska grupa, in: *PJZ V, Željezno doba* (Sarajevo) 293-339.

GLOGOVIĆ 1982 – Dunja Glogović, Predmeti starijeg željeznog doba iz grobova na Kavaneli kraj Osora, in: *Arheološka istraživanja na otocima Cresu i Lošinju*, Izdanja Hrvatskog arheološkog društva 7, 33-43.

GLOGOVIĆ 1988 – Dunja Glogović, Dvodijelne zmijaste fibule iz Jugoslavije, *Diadora* 10, 5-18.

GLOGOVIĆ 1989 a – Dunja Glogović, Nalazi iz okolice Baške na otoku Krku, in: *Arheološka istraživanja na otocima Krku, Rabu i Pagu i u Hrvatskom primorju*, Izdanja Hrvatskog arheološkog društva 13, 97-102.

GLOGOVIĆ 1989 b – Dunja Glogović, *Prilozi poznavanju željeznog doba na sjevernom Jadranu, Hrvatsko primorje i Kvarnerski otoci* (Zagreb).

GLOGOVIĆ 1998 – Dunja Glogović, Fibule iz Ljupča, *Prilozi Instituta za arheologiju u Zagrebu* 13/14, 33-40.

GLOGOVIĆ 2003 – Dunja Glogović, *Fibeln im kroatischen Küstengebiet*, PBF, Abt. 14, 13 (Stuttgart).

GLOGOVIĆ 2006 a – Dunja Glogović, The prehistoric background to Dalmatia: Dalmatia from 8th to 4th centuries BC, in: *Dalmatia, Research in the Roman Province 1970-2001, Papers in honour of J.J. Wilkes* (Ed. D. Davison, V. Gaffney, E. Marin), BAR IntSer. 1576 (Oxford).

GLOGOVIĆ 2006 b – Dunja Glogović, Novi nalazi liburnskih pločastih fibula iz Dragišića kod Šibenika, *Prilozi Instituta za arheologiju u Zagrebu* 23, 129-140.

GLOGOVIĆ 2008 – Dunja Glogović, Liburnska imitacija astragalnih pojaseva, *Archaeologia Adriatica* 2, 325-333.

GLOGOVIĆ / MENĐUŠIĆ 2007 a – Dunja Glogović, Marko Menđušić, O nalazima staklenih zrnaca tip Adria na južnoliburnskom području, in: *Scripta Praehistorica in Honorem Biba Teržan,* Situla 44, (Ljubljana) 789-796.

GLOGOVIĆ / MENĐUŠIĆ 2007 b – Dunja Glogović, Marko Menđušić, Osvrt na fibule tipa Jazerine u Hrvatskoj povodom novih nalaza iz Dragišića, *Prilozi Instituta za arheologiju u Zagrebu* 24, 145-152.

GUŠTIN 1984 – Mitja Guštin, Die Kelten in Jugosawien, Übersicht über das Archäologische Fundgut, *Jahrb. RGZM* 31, 305-363.

GUŠTIN 1987 a – Mitja Guštin, La Tène Fibulae from Istria, *Arhaeologia Iugoslavica* 24, 43-57.

GUŠTIN 1987 b – Mitja Guštin, Latenske fibule iz Istre, in: *Arheološka istraživanja u Istri i Hrvatskom primorju*, Izdanja Hrvatskog arheološkog društva 11, 33-47.

GUŠTIN 1991 – Mitja Guštin, *Posočje in der jüngeren Eisenzeit, Posočje v mlajši železni dobi*, Katalogi in monografije 27 (Ljubljana).

GUŠTIN / KNIFIC 1973 – Mitja Guštin, Timotej Knific, Halštatske in antične najdbe iz Javora, *Arheološki vestnik* 24, 831-848.

HENCKEN 1978 – Hugh Hencken, *The Iron Age Cemetery of Magdalenska Gora in Slovenia, Mecklenburg Collection, Part II* (Cambridge, Massachusetts).

HILLER 1991 – Gundula Hiller, *Zur Japodischen und Liburnischen Früheisenzeit Nordwest Jugoslawiens*, Fakultät für Orientalistik und Altertumswissenschaft der Ruprecht-Karls Universität Heidlberg (unpublished doctoral dissertation).

IVČEVIĆ 2002 – Sanja Ivčević, Fibule, in: *Longe Salona I* (Split) 268-273.

JEREM 1974 – Elizabeth Jerem, Handelbeziehungen zwichen der Balkanhalbinsel und dem Karpatenbecken im IV. und V. Jahrhundert v.u.Z., in: *Symposium zu Problemen der jüngeren Hallstattzeit in Mitteleuropa* (Bratislava) 229-242.

JOVANOVIĆ 1988 – Marija Jovanović, Astragalni pojasevi na području centralnog Balkana i jugoistočne Evrope, *Rad muzeja Vojvodine* 40, 39-95.

KLARIN 2000 – Natalija Klarin, Prapovijesni grobovi na Aseriji – istraživanja 1999. godine, *Diadora* 20, 23-71.

KLEMENC 1935 – Josip Klemanc, Ostava u Ličkom Ribniku, *VHAD*, N.S. 35, 84-125.

KOS 2002 – Peter Kos, A find of Celtic coins from the area of Balina Glavica (*Sinotion*) in Dalmatia, *VAMZ*, 3. Ser. 35, 147-157.

KOŠČEVIĆ 1980 – Remza Koščević, *Antičke fibule s područja Siska* (Zagreb).

KOŠČEVIĆ 1991 – Remza Koščević, *Antička bronca iz Siska, Umjetničko-obrtna metalna produkcija iz razdoblja rimskog carstva* (Zagreb).

KRIŽ 2005 – Borut Križ, *Novo Mesto VI, Mlajšeželeznodobno grobišče Kapiteljska njiva*, Carniola Archaeologica 6 (Novo Mesto).

KRIŽ 2006 – Borut Križ, Jantarni i stakleni nakit iz Novog Mesta, in: *Pretpovijesni jantar i staklo iz Prozora u Lici i Novoga Mesta u Dolenjskoj* (catalogue of the exhibition in Zagreb), 94-141.

KUČAR 1979 – Vladimira Kučar, Prahistorijska nekropola Beram, *Histria Archaeologica* 10, 85-131.

KUKOČ 2010 – Sineva Kukoč, Osvrt na spaljivanje pokojnika u liburnskom kulturnom kontekstu, *Prilozi Instituta za arheologiju u Zagrebu* 27, 95-111.

KUNTER 1986 – Kari Kunter, Zu den polychromen Glasperlen aus Fürstengrab von Reinheim, in: *Marburger Studien* 7, 91-128.

KUNTER 1995 – Kari Kunter, Schichtaugenperlen, Glasperlen der Vorrömischen Eisenzeit IV, *Marburger Studien* 18 (Marburg/Lahn).

LANDOLFI 2000 – Maurizo Landolfini, Die Toreutik, in: *Die Picener, Ein Volk Europas*, (exhibition catalogue) Frankfurt, 122-134.

LAZAR 2003 – Irena Lazar, *Rimsko steklo Slovenije* (Ljubljana).

LAZAR 2006 – Irena Lazar, An oil lamp from Slovenia depicting a Roman glass furnace, *VAHD* 99, 227-235.

LO SCHIAVO 1970 – Fulvia Lo Schiavo, *Il gruppo Liburnico-japodico*, Atti della Accademia Nazionale dei Lincei, classe di scienze morali, storice e filosofiche, ser. 8, vol. 14, fasc. 6 (Roma).

LOLLINI 1976 – Delia G. Lollini, Sintesi della civiltà picena, in: *Jadranska obala u protohisotriji* (Zagreb), 117-155.

LJUBIĆ 1889 – Šime Ljubić, *Popis Arkeologičkog odjela Nar. Zem. Muzeja u Zagrebu* (Zagreb).

MAJNARIĆ-PANDŽIĆ 1970 – Nives Majnarić-Pandžić, *Keltsko-latenska kultura u Slavoniji i Srijemu* (Vinkovci).

MAJNARIĆ-PANDŽIĆ 1998 – Nives Majnarić-Pandžić, Brončano i željezno doba, in: *Prapovijest* (Zagreb), 161-194.

MARCHESETTI 1924 – Carlo Marchesetti, Isole del Quarnero, *Notizie degli Scavi* 1924, 122-148.

MARCHESETTI 1993 – Carlo Marchesetti, *Scritti sulla necropoli di S. Lucia di Tolmino (Scavi 1884-1902)*, reprint 1993 (Trieste).

MARIĆ 1962 – Zdravko Marić, Vir kod Posušja, *GZM*, N.s. 17, 64-72.

MARIĆ 1964 – Zdravko Marić, Donja Dolina, *GZM*, N.s. 19, 5-83.

MARIĆ 1968 – Zdravko Marić, Japodska nekropole u dolini Une, *GZM*, N.s. 23, 5-79.

DE MARINIS 1974 – Raffaele de Marinis, La situla di Trezzo (Milano), in : *Varia Archaeologica* 1, 67-87.

MARIJAN 2001 – Boško Marijan, Željezno doba na južnojadranskom području (Istočna Hercegovina, južna Dalmacija) *VAHD* 93, 7-199.

MAROVIĆ 1959 – Ivan Marović, Iskopavanja kamenih gomila oko vrela Cetine god. 1953., 1954. i 1958. *VAHD* 61, 5-80.

MAROVIĆ 1961 – Ivan Marović, Fibeln mit Inschrift von Typus Aucissa in den archäoligischen Museen von Zagreb, Zadar und Split, *Jahrb. RGZM* 8, 1961, 96-106.

MAROVIĆ 1962 – Ivan Marović, Nekoliko nalaza iz halštatskog perioda u Dalmaciji, *VAHD* 43-64, 8-22.

MAROVIĆ 1969 – Ivan Marović, Četiri groba iz nekropole u Vičoj Luci (o. Brač) pronađena u 1908. god., *VAHD* 60-61, 5-55.

MAROVIĆ 1970 – Ivan Marović, Nekoliko neobjelodanjenih srebrnih predmeta s liburnskog područja u Arheološkom muzeju u Splitu, in: *Adriatica praehistorica et antiqua, Zbornik radova posvećen Grgi Novaku* (Zagreb), 265-284.

MAROVIĆ 1981 – Ivan Marović, Prilozi poznavanju brončanog doba u Dalmaciji, *VAHD* 75, 7-61.

MAROVIĆ 1984 – Ivan Marović, Sinjska regija u prahistoriji, in: *Cetinska krajina od prethistorije do dolaska Turaka*, Izdanja Hrvatskog arheološkog društva 8, 27-65.

MAROVIĆ 1985 – Ivan Marović, Iskopavanje kamenih gomila u Bogomolju na otoku Hvaru, *VAHD* 78, 5-35.

MAROVIĆ / NIKOLANCI 1969 – Ivan Marović, Mladen Nikolanci, Četiri groba iz nekropole u Vičoj Luci (o. Brač) pronađena u 1908. god., *VAHD* 70-71, 5-55.

MATASOVIĆ 2003 – Ranko Matasović, Jezični tragovi Kelta u Iliriku, *Latina et Graeca*, n.s. 3, 6-23.

MATTHÄUS 1987 – Hartmut Matthäus, Ringaugenperlen, in: *Glasperlen der Vorrömischen Eisenzeit II, Marburgen Studien* 9, 9-14.

MEDUNA 1996 – Jiří Meduna, Das Depot von Ptení (Kr. Prostějov) und die Handelsbeziehungen Märens während der Spätlatènezeit, in: *Kontakt lägst der Bernsteinstrasse (zwischen Caput Adriae und den Ostseegebieten) in der Zeit um Christi Geburt* (Kraków) 97-103.

MIHOVILIĆ 1979 – Kristina Mihovilić, Prstenje i naušnice rimskog doba Slovenije, *Arheološki vestnik* 30, 223-239.

MIHOVILIĆ 1983 – Kristina Mihovilić, Histri, in: *Keltoi in njihovi sodobniki na ozemlju Jugoslavije* (exhibition catalogue) 52-55.

MIHOVILIĆ 1991 – Kristina Mihovilić, L'Istria dal IV al I Secolo A.C., *Antichità Altoadriatiche* 37, 157-164.

MIHOVILIĆ 1995 a – Kristina Mihovilić, Srebrni nakit iz Nezakcija (Podaci za VI. stupanj razvoja istarske grupe), *Diadora* 16-17, 1995, 81-100.

MIHOVILIĆ 1995 b – Kristina Mihovilić, Reichtum durch Handel in der Hallstattzeit Istriens, in: *Handel, Tausch und Verkehr im Bronze- und Früheisenzeitlichen Südosteuropa* (München – Berlin), 283-329.

MIHOVILIĆ 2001 a – Kristina Mihovilić, *Nesactium, Prapovijesni nalazi 1900.-1953.*, Monografije i katalozi 11 (Pula).

MIHOVILIĆ 2001 b – Kristina Mihovilić, L'Istra tra Celti e Roma, in: *I Celti nell'Alto Adriatico*, Antichità Altoadriatiche 48 (Trieste) 261-275.

MIHOVILIĆ 2009 – Kristina Mihovilić, New Finds of La Tène fibulae from Istria, in: *Keltske študije II, Studies in Celtic Archaeology, Papers in honour of Mitja Guštin*, Ed. G. Tiefengruber, B. Kavur, A. Gaspari (Montagnac) 209-216.

MILETIĆ 1992 – Željko Miletić, Rimska cestovna mreža između Arauzone i Tragurija, *Radovi, Razdio povijesnih znanosti* (18), Sveučilište u Splitu, Filozofski fakultet – Zadar 31, 63-87.

NEDVED 1981 – Branka Nedved, Nakit rimskog razdoblja, in: *Nakit na tlu sjeverne Dalmacije od prapovijesti do danas* (exhibition catalogue, Zadar) 151-182.

OŠTRIĆ 1981 – Olga Oštrić, Narodni nakit sjeverne Dalmacije, in: *Nakit na tlu sjeverne Dalmacije od prapovijesti do danas* (exhibition catalogue, Zadar) 73-82, 205-219.

PALAVESTRA 1993 – Aleksandar Palavestra, *Praistorijski ćilibar na centralnom i zapadnom Balkanu*, Posebna izdanja 52, Srpska akademija nauka i umetnosti, Balkanološki institut (Beograd).

PALAVESTRA 2006 – Aleksandar Palavestra, Ćilibar u arheologiji, in: *Aleksandar Palavestra, Vera Krstić, Magija ćilibara*, Arheološke monografije 18 (Beograd), 32-86.

PETRIĆ 1998 – Nikša Petrić, Pretpovijest Pharosa, *Radovi Filozofskog fakulteta Zadar* 36, 23-33.

PETTARIN 2006 – Silvia Pettarin, La necropoli di San Pietro al Natisone e Dernazzacco, *Studi e ricerche di protostoria Mediterranea* 7 (Roma).

POPOVIĆ 2000 – Petar Popović, Le perle di vetro a forma di vaso o di anfora nella regione compresa tra l'Adriatico e ili Danubio, *Ocnus* 8, 269-276.

PRELOŽNIK 2008 – Andrej Preložnik, Fibula s podobo Harisa iz Nina – poreklo in pomen, in: *Srednji vek, Mittelalter, Arheološke raziskave med Jadranskim morjem in Panonsko nižijo* (Ed. Mitja Guštin) Annales Mediterranea (Ljubljana), 203-211.

PROTIĆ 1985 – Goran Protić, Prahistorijski nalazi s otoka Visa, *VAHD* 78, 37-43.

RAUNIG 2004 – Branka Raunig, *Umjetnost i religija prahistorijskih Japoda*, Djela centra za balkanološka ispitivanja, Knjiga 8 (Sarajevo).

RIECKHOFF 1975 – Sabine Rieckhoff, Münzen und Fibeln aus dem Vicus des Kastells Hüfingen (Schwarzwald-Baar-Kreis), *Saalburg Jahrbuch* 32, 5-105.

RIECKOFF-PAULI 1977 – Sabine Rieckoff-Pauli, Die Fibeln aus dem Römischen Vicus von Sulz am Neckar, *Saalburg Jahrbuch* 34, 6-28.

SAKARA SUČEVIĆ 2004 – Maša Sakara Sučević, *Kaštelir, Prazgodovinska naselbina pri Novi Vasi / Brtonigla (Istra)*, Annales Mediterranea (Koper).

ŠEPAROVIĆ 1998 – Tomislav Šeparović, *Aucissa* fibule s natpisom iz zbirke Muzeja hrvatskih arheoloških spomenika, *SHP*, III. ser. 25, 178-187.

ŠEPAROVIĆ 2003 – Tomislav Šeparović, Metalni nalazi, in: *Mirjana Sanader, Tilurium I* (Zagreb), 219-257.

ŠEPAROVIĆ / URODA 2009 – Tomislav Šeparović / Nikolina Uroda, *Antička zbirka Muzeja hrvatskih arheoloških spomenika – izbor* (Split).

ŠEŠELJ 2010 – Lucijana Šešelj, Rt Ploča, in: *Antički Grci na tlu Hrvatske* (exhibition catalogue, Zagreb), 110-113.

ŠIMIĆ / FILIPOVIĆ 1997 – Jasna Šimić, Slavica Filipović, *Kelti i Rimljani na području Osijeka*, Muzej Slavonije Osijek (exhibition catalogue, Osijek) 1997.

SIMS-WILLIAMS 2006 – Patrick Sims-Williams, *Ancient Celtic Place-Names in Europe and Asia Minor*, Publication of the Philological Society, 39 (Oxford UK, Boston USA).

ŠKOBERNE 1999 – Želimir Škoberne, *Budinjak, Kneževski tumul* (Zagreb).

ŠKOBERNE 2003 – Želimir Škoberne, Nalaz neuobičajene višeglave igle s budinjačke nekropole, *Opuscula Archaeologica* 27, 199-210.

ŠOUFEK 2006 – Marin Šoufek, Od kremena do stakla, in: *Pretpovijesni jantar i staklo iz Prozora u Lici i Novog Mesta u Dolenjskoj* (exhibition catalogue, Zagreb), 24-36.

STIPČEVIĆ 1960 – Aleksandar Stipčević, Latenski predmeti iz okolice Obrovca, *Diadora* 1, 87-94.

51

SUIĆ 2003 – Mate Suić, *Antički grad na istočnom Jadranu*, 2nd edition (Zagreb).

TERŽAN 1974 – Biba Teržan, Halštatske gomile iz Brusnic na Dolenjskem, in: *Varia Archaeologica* (Brežice), 31-67.

TERŽAN 1977 a – Biba Teržan, Certoška fibula, *Arheološki vestnik* 27, 317-443.

TERŽAN 1977 b – Biba Teržan, O horizontu bojevniških grobov med Padom in Dunavo v. 5. in 4. stol. pr.n.št., in: *Keltske študije* (Brežice), 9-21.

TERŽAN 1995 – Biba Teržan, Handl und soziale Oberschichten im Früheisenzeitlichen Südosteuropa, in: *Handel, Tausch und Verkehr im Bronze- und Früheisenzeitlichen Südosteuropa*, Ed. Bernhard Hänsel (München-Berlin), 81-158.

TERŽAN 2013 – Biba Teržan, Liburnska dvodelne fibule s stožičastimi spiralicami – označevelke stana in izobilja, in: *Batovićev zbornik,* Diadora 26/27, 241-267.

TERŽAN / LO SCHIAVO / TRAMPUŽ-OREL 1985 – Biba Teržan, Fulvia Lo Schiavo, Neva Trampuž-Orel, *Most na Soči (S. Lucia) II*, Katalogi in monografije 23 (Ljubljana).

TESSMANN 2001 – Barbara Tessmann, Schmuck und Trachtzubehör aus Prozor, Kroatien. Ein Beitrag zur Tracht im japodischen Gebiet, *Acta Praehistorica et Archaeologica* 33, 28-151.

TESSMANN 2007 – Barbara Tessmann, Körbchenanhänger im Süden – Göritzer Bommeln im Norden. Eine vergleichende Studie zu einem späthallstattzeitlichen Anhängertyp, in: *Scripta Praehistorica in Honorem Biba Teržan*, Situla 44, 667-695.

TEŽAK-GREGL 1981 – Tihomila Težak-Gregl, Certosa fibula na centralnom japodskom području, *VAMZ*, 3. ser. 14, 26-48.

TEŽAK-GREGL 1982 – Tihomila Težak-Gregl, Rimske provincijalne fibule iz arheološke zbirke u Osoru, in: *Arheološka istraživanja na otocima Cresu i Lošinju*, Izdanja Hrvatskog arheološkog društva 7, 99-111.

TODOROVIĆ 1964 – Jovan Todorović, Ein Beitrag zur stilistischen und zeitlichen Bestimmung der astragaloiden Gürtel in Jugoslawien, *Archaeologia Jugoslavica* 5, 45-48.

TOWLE *et al.* 2001 – Andrew Towle, Julian Henderson, Paolo Bellintani, Giovanna Gambacurta, Frattesina and Adria: report of scientific analyses of early glass from the Veneto, *Padusa* 37, Nuova Serie, 7-69.

TRUHELKA 1895 – Ćiro Truhelka, Prähistorische Bronzen aus Bezirke Prozor, *WMBH* 3, 510-512.

TRUHELKA 1902 – Ćiro Truhelka, Zwei prähistorische Funde aus Garica, *WMBH* 8, 4-47.

TRUHELKA 1904 – Ćiro Truhelka, Der vorgeschichtliche Phalbau im Savebette bei Donja Dolina, *WMBH* 9, 1-156.

VASIĆ 1982 – Rastko Vasić, Ein Beitrag zu den Doppelnadeln im Balkanraum, *PZ* 57, 220-257.

VASIĆ 1989 – Rastko Vasić, Jedan prilog proučavanju sremske grupe, *Godišnjak Centra za balkanološka ispitivanja* 25, (Sarajevo) 103-113.

VASIĆ 2003 – Rastko Vasić, *Die Nadeln im Zentralbalkan*, PBF, Abt. 13, Bd. 11 (Stuttgart).

VASIĆ 2007 – Rastko Vasić, Kneginje Centralnog Balkana, in: *Scripta Praehistorica in Honorem Biba Teržan*, Situla 44, (Ljubljana) 557-563.

VENCLOVÁ 1990 – Natalia Venclová, *Prehistoric Glass in Bohemia* (Praha).

VINSKI 1956 – Zdenko Vinski, Ein Liburnischer Depotfund aus Baška, *Archaeologia Iugoslavica* 2, 20-30.

VINSKI / VINSKI-GASPARINI 1962 – Zdenko Vinski / Ksenija Vinski-Gasparini, O utjecajima istočno-alpske halštatske kulture i balkanske ilirske kulture na slavonsko-srijemsko Podunavlje, *Arheološki radovi i rasprave* 2, 263-295.

WARNEKE 1999 – Thilo F. Warneke, *Hallstatt- und frühlatènezeitlicher Anhängerschmuck, Studien zu Metallanhängern des 8.-5. Jahrhunderts v.Chr. zwischen Main un Po,* Internationale Archäologie 50 (Rahden / Westf.).

WERNER 1979 – Joachim Werner, Bemerkungen zu norischen Trachtzubehör und zu Fernhandelbeziehungen der Spätlatènzeit im Salzburgerland, in: *Joachim Werner, Spätes Keltentum zwichen Rom und Germanien*, Hrsg. Ludwig Pauli (München), 138-157.

ZANINOVIĆ 2007 – Marin Zaninović, *Ilirsko pleme Dalmati* (Šibenik).

INDEX LOCI

PLATES

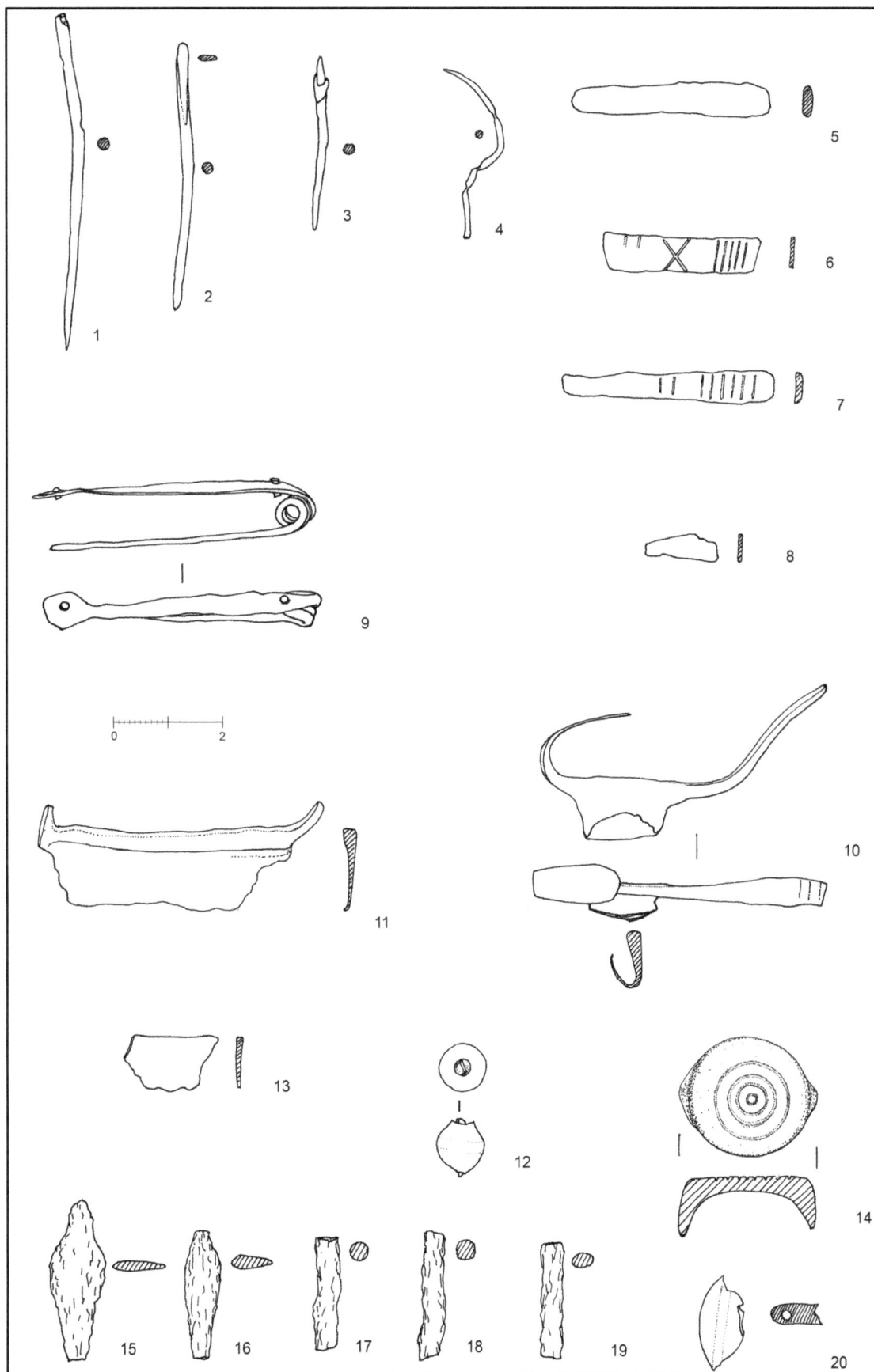

Pl. 1. Dragišić, grave 6. 1-11, 13-14 bronze; 12 silver; 15-19 iron; 20 glass

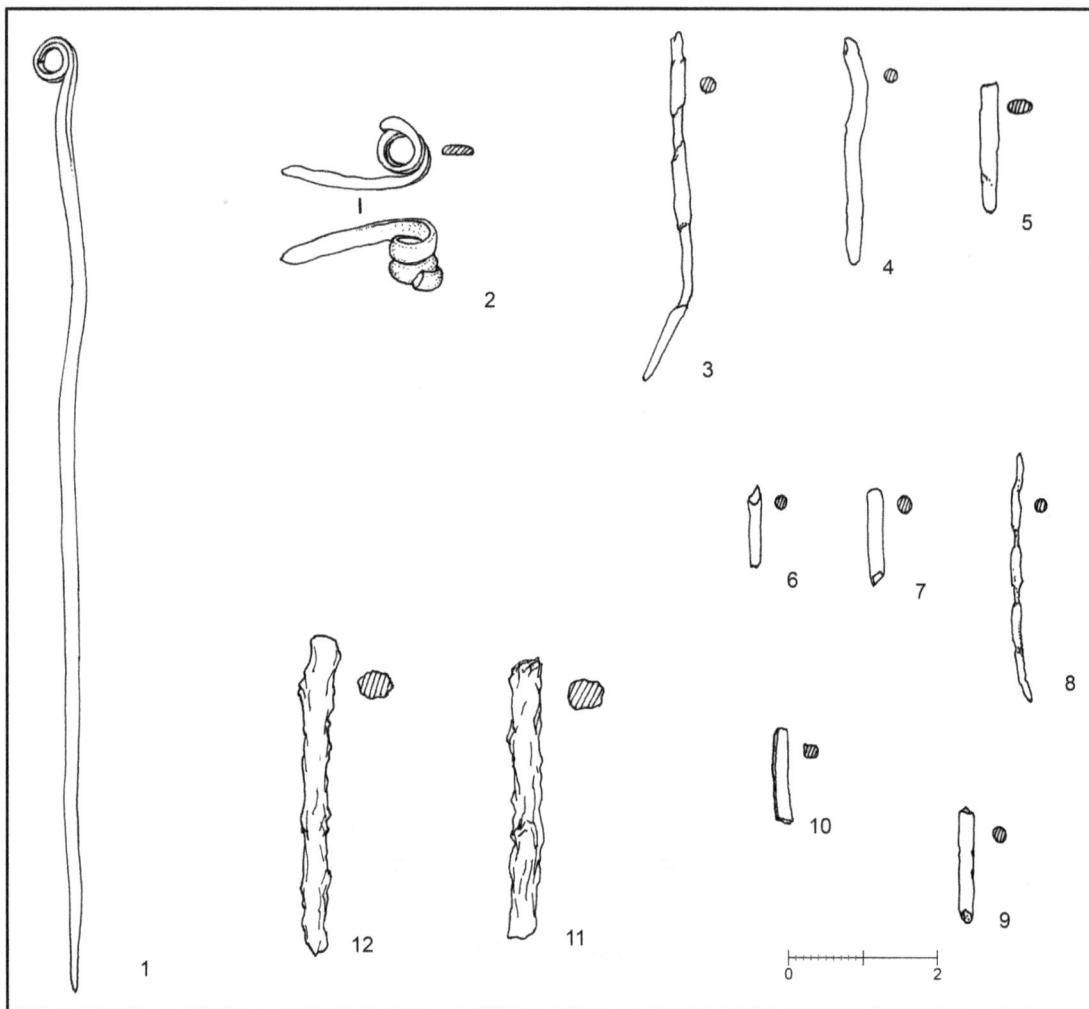

Pl. 2. Dragišić, grave 7. 1-10 bronze; 11-12 iron

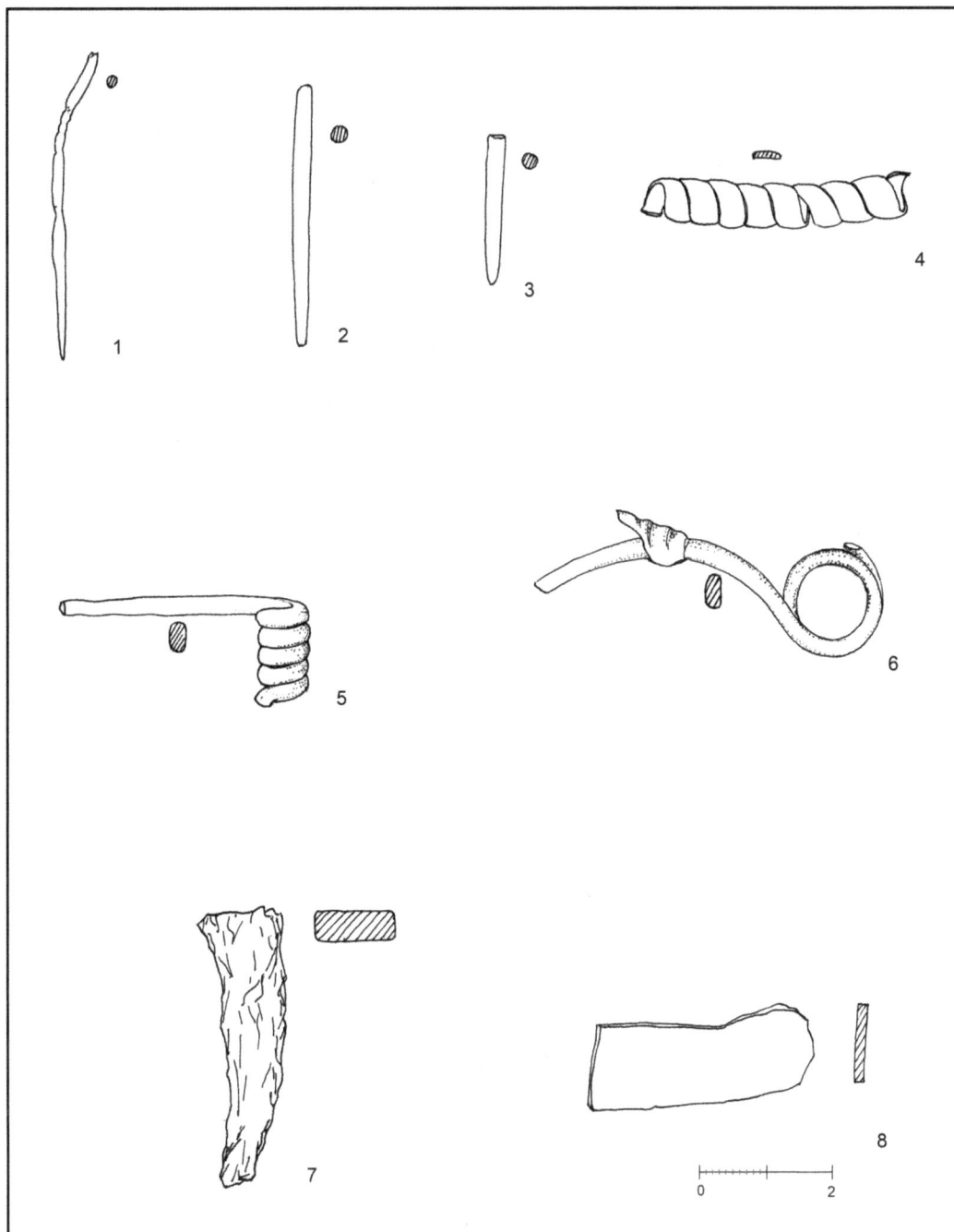

Pl. 3. Dragišić, grave 8. 1-6 bronze; 7 iron; 8 glass

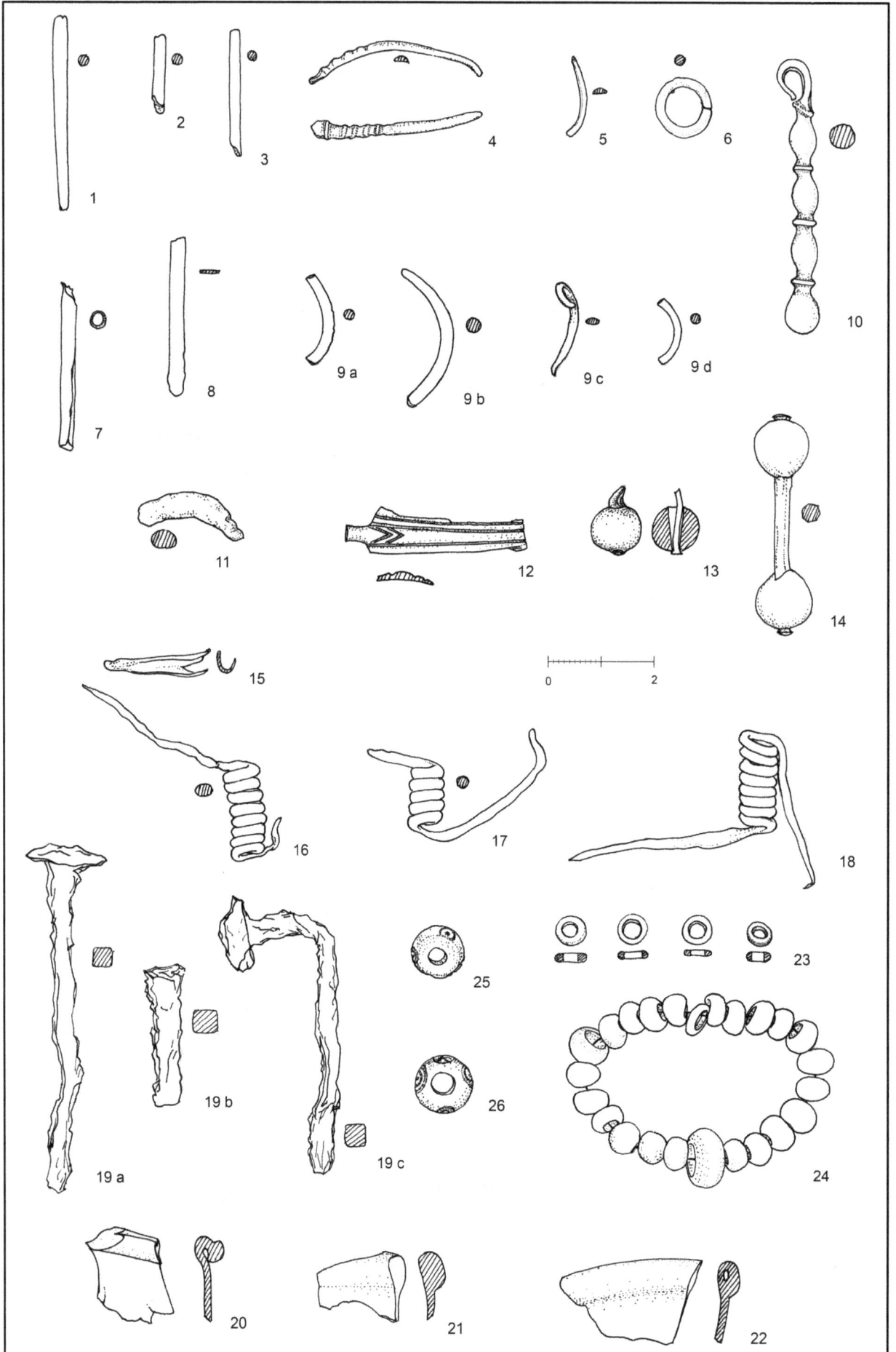

Pl. 4. Dragišić, grave 9. 1-12, 15-18 bronze; 13, 14 silver; 19 iron; 20-26 glass

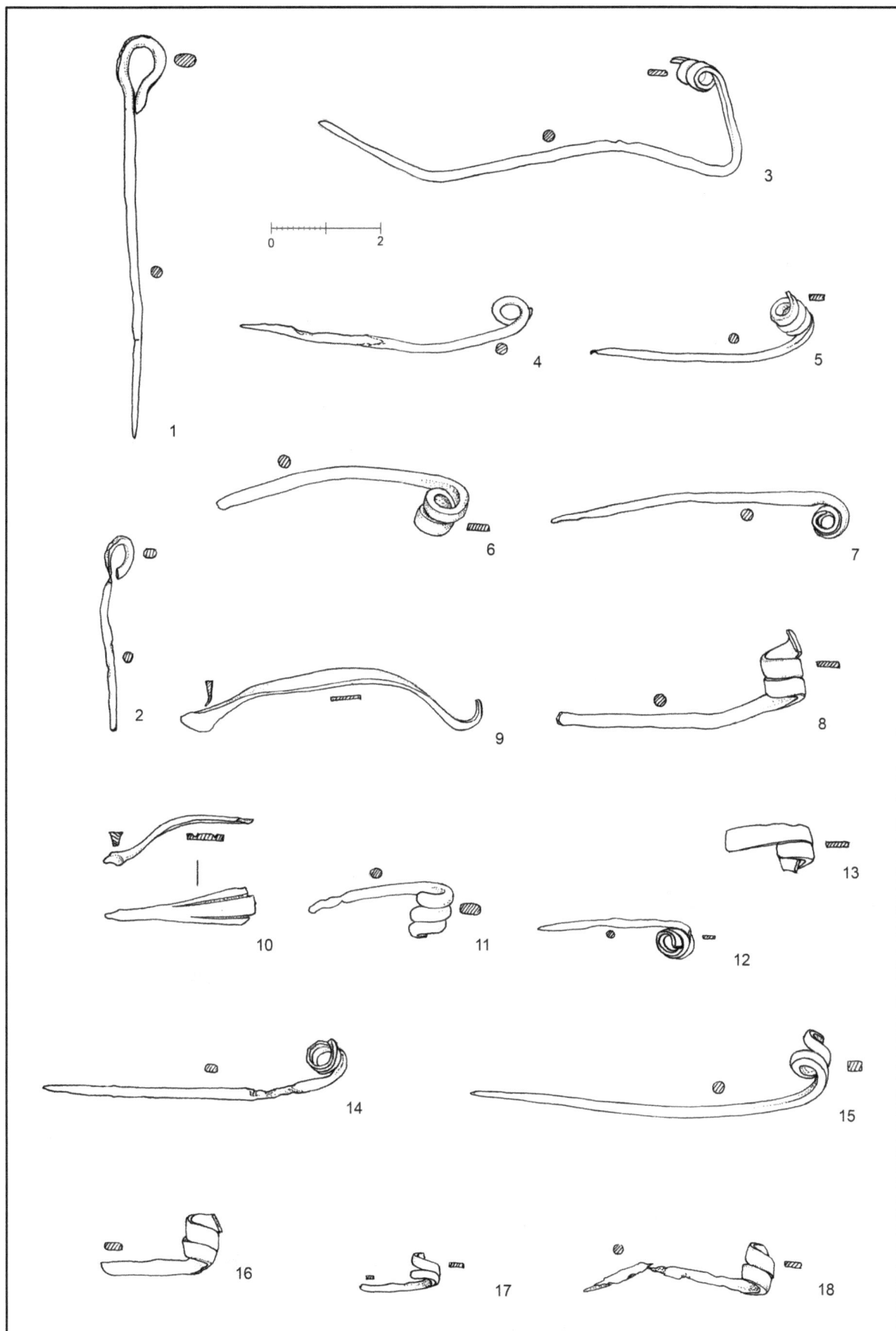

Pl. 5a. Dragišić, grave. 10, 1-18 bronze

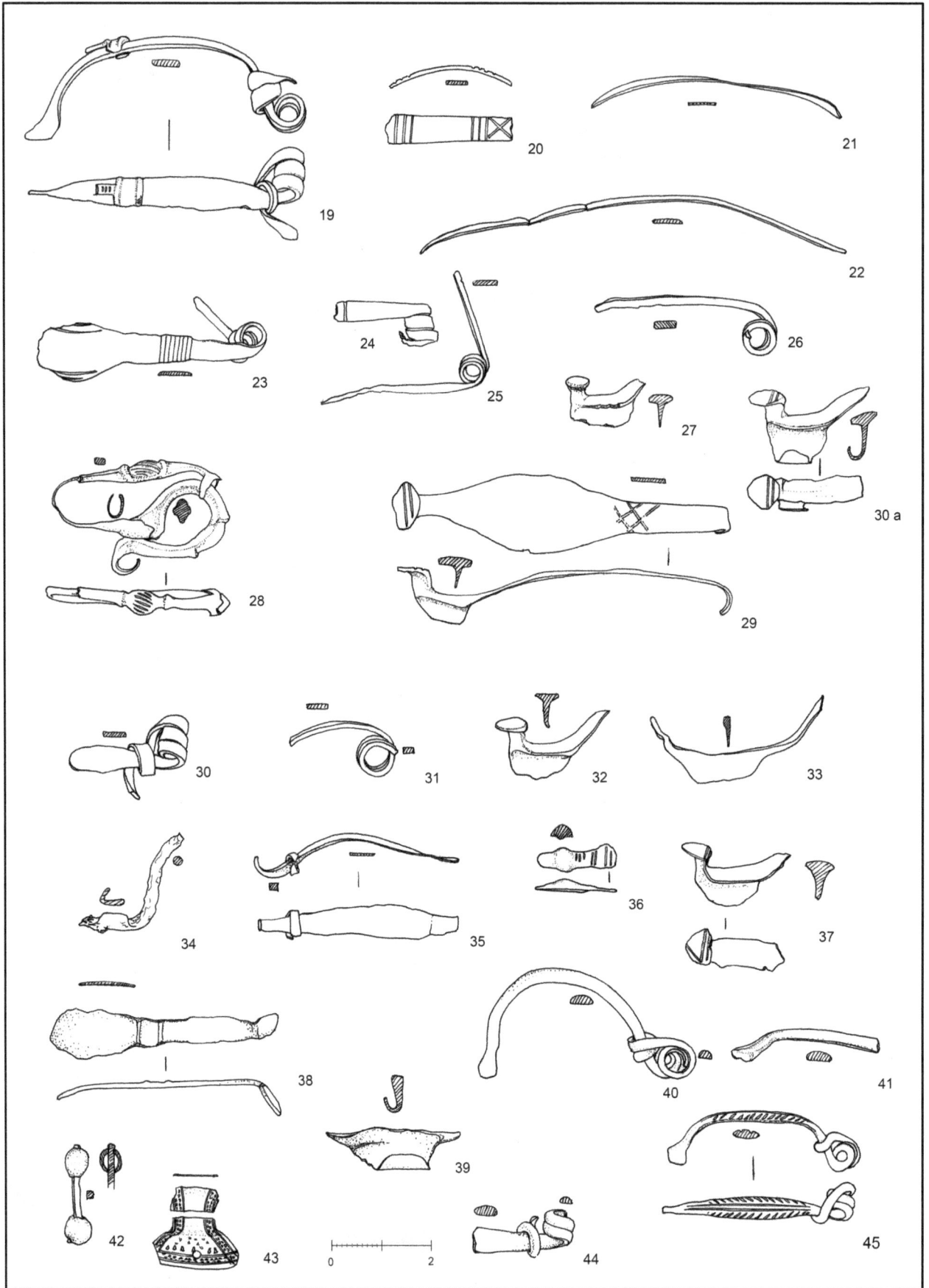

Pl. 5b. Dragišić, grave 10. 19-33, 35-41, 44, 45 bronze; 34 iron; 42-43 silver

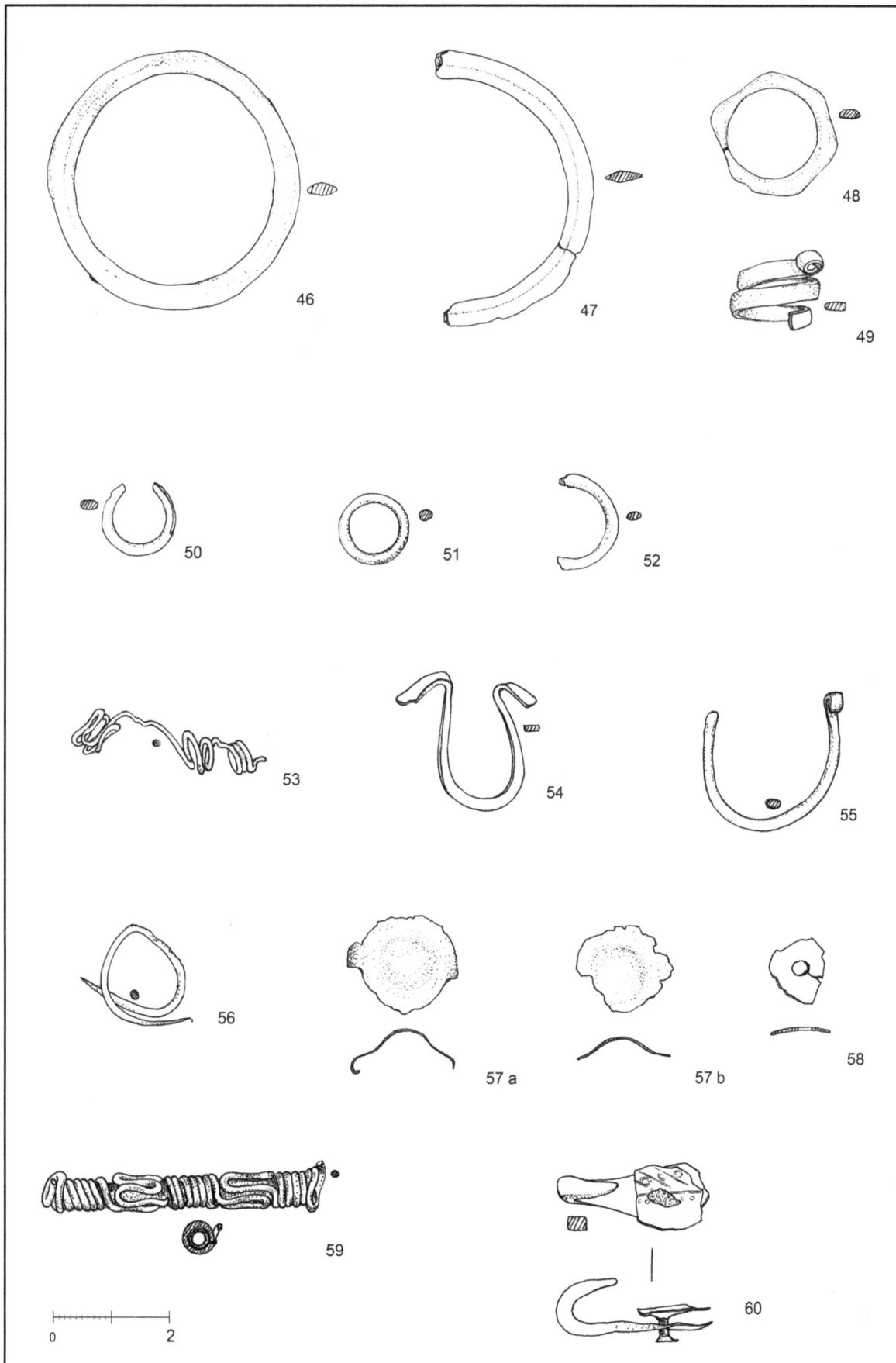

Pl. 5c. Dragišić, grave 10. 46-60 bronze

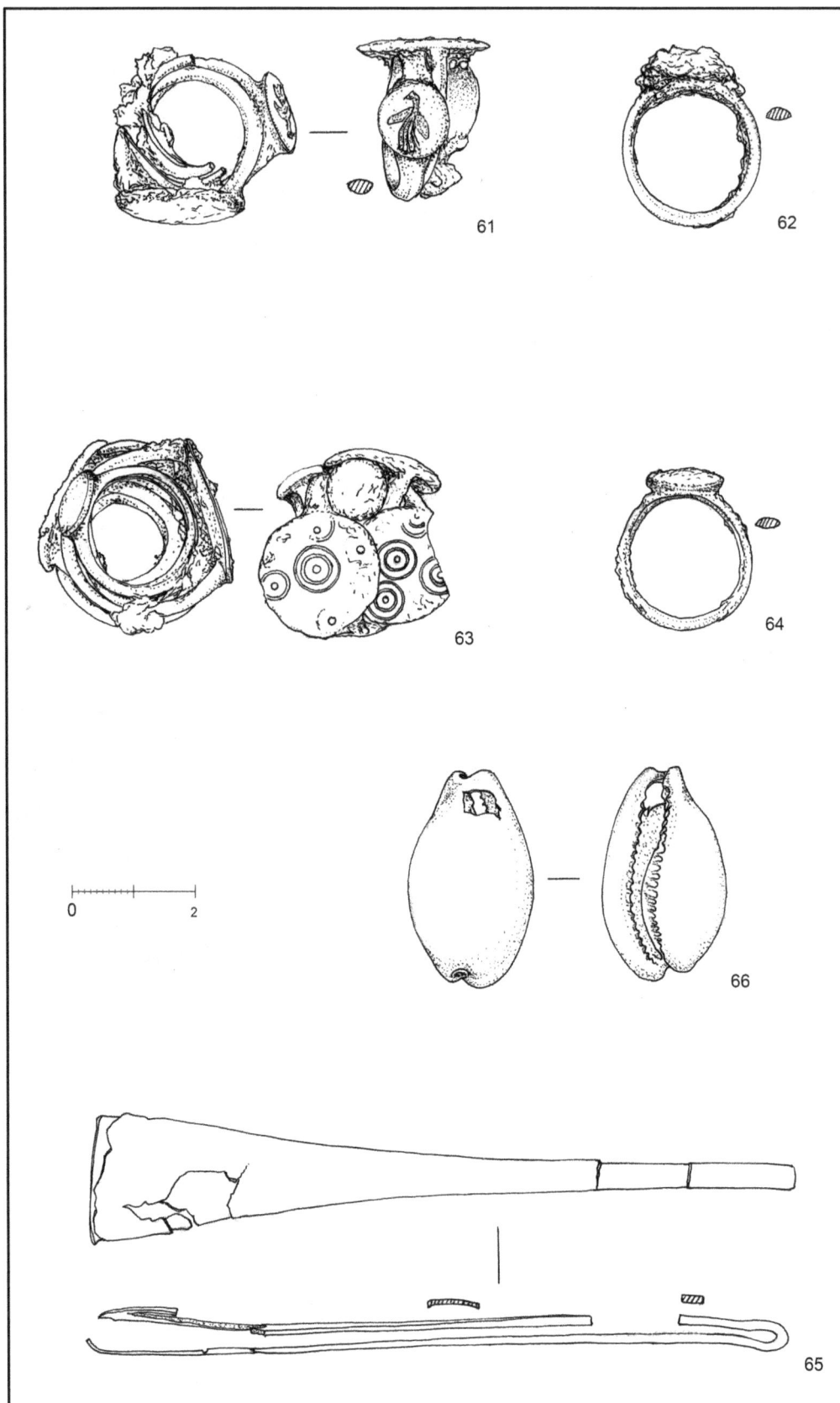

Pl. 5d. Dragišić, grave 10. 61-65 bronze; 66 cowrie shell

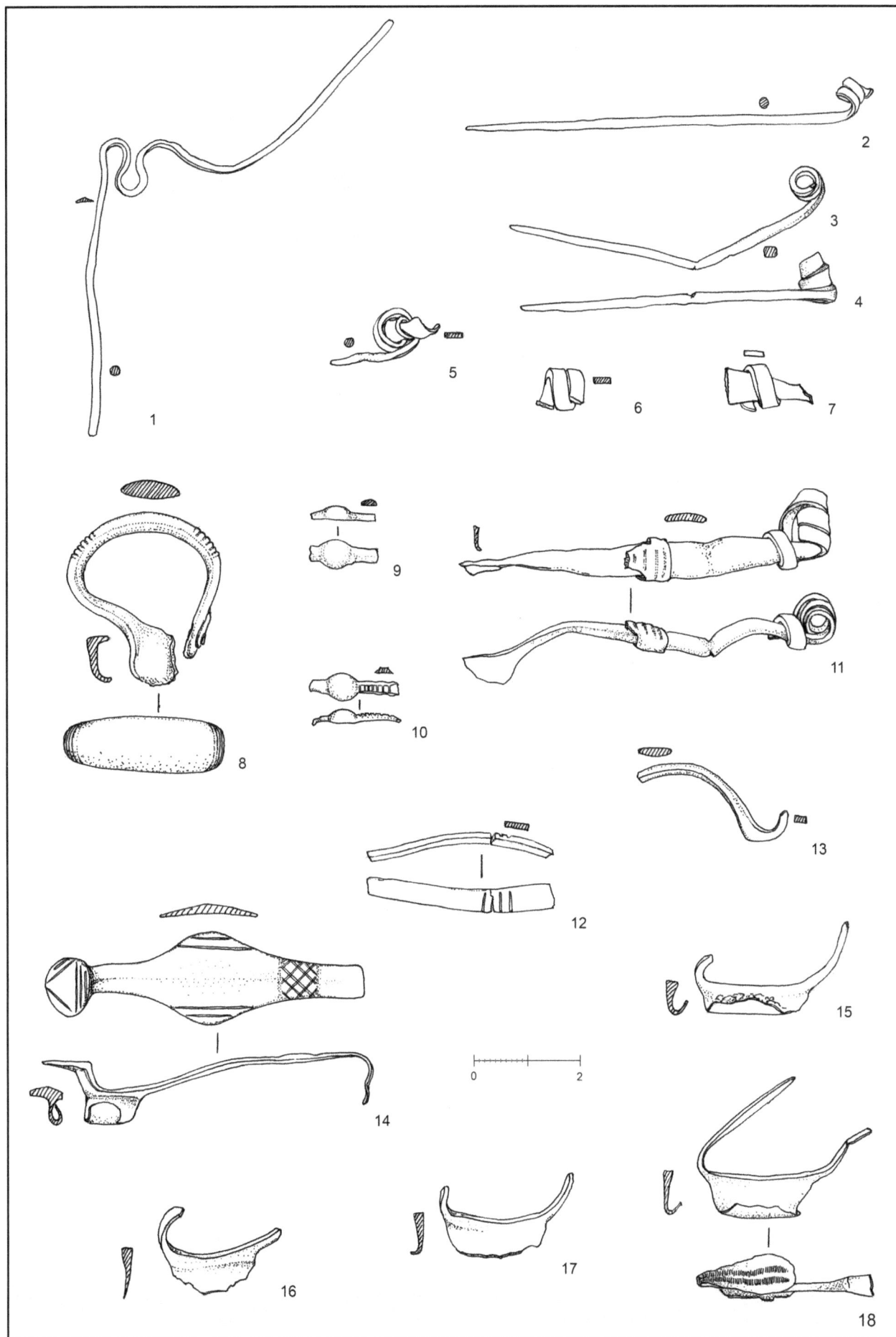

Pl. 6a. Dragišić, grave 11. 1-18 bronze

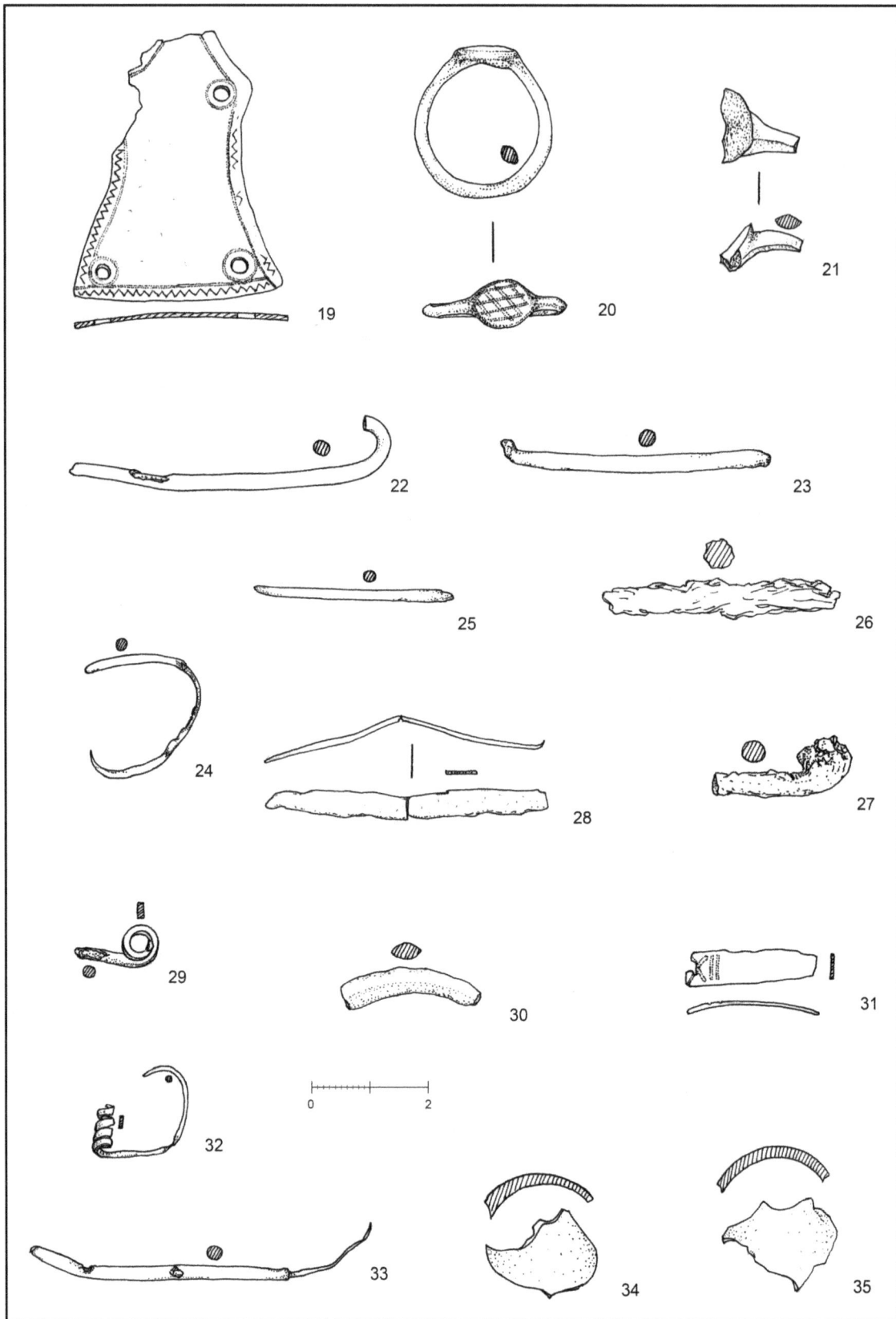

Pl. 6b. Dragišić, grave 11. 19-25, 28-33 bronze; 26, 27 iron; 34-35 glass

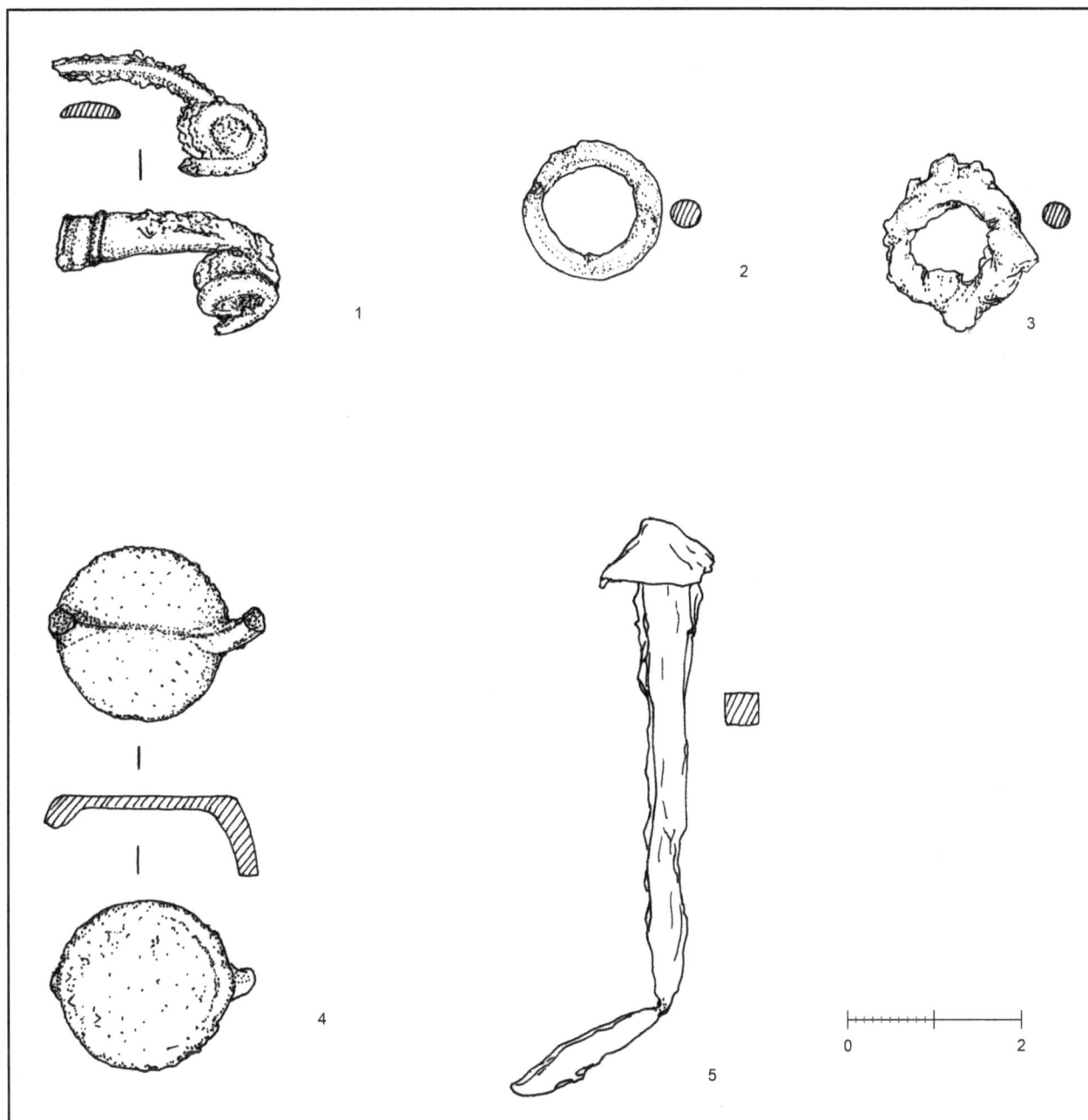

Pl. 7. Dragišić, grave 12. 1-4 bronze; 5 iron

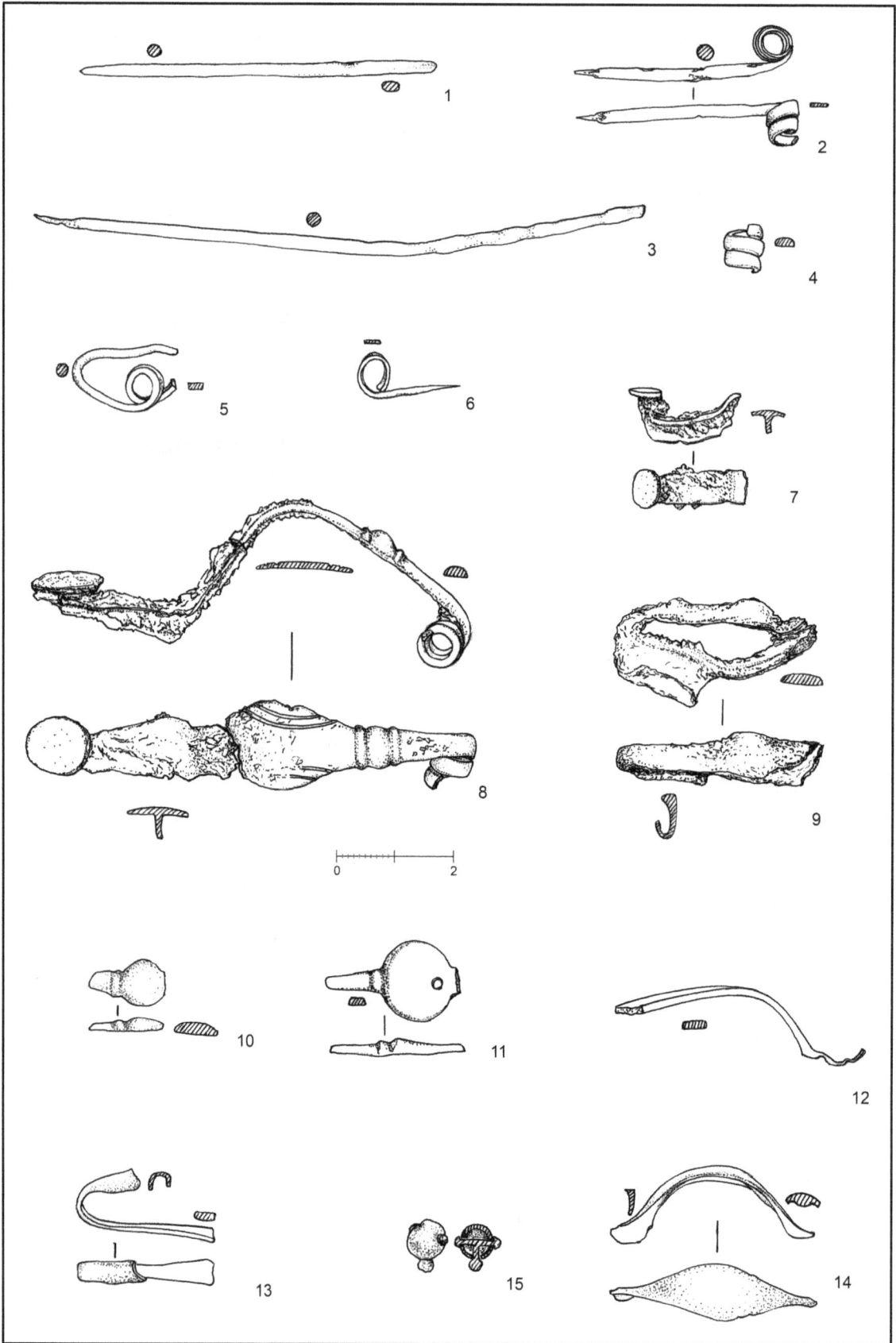

Pl. 8a. Dragišić, grave 13. 1-14 bronze; 15 silver

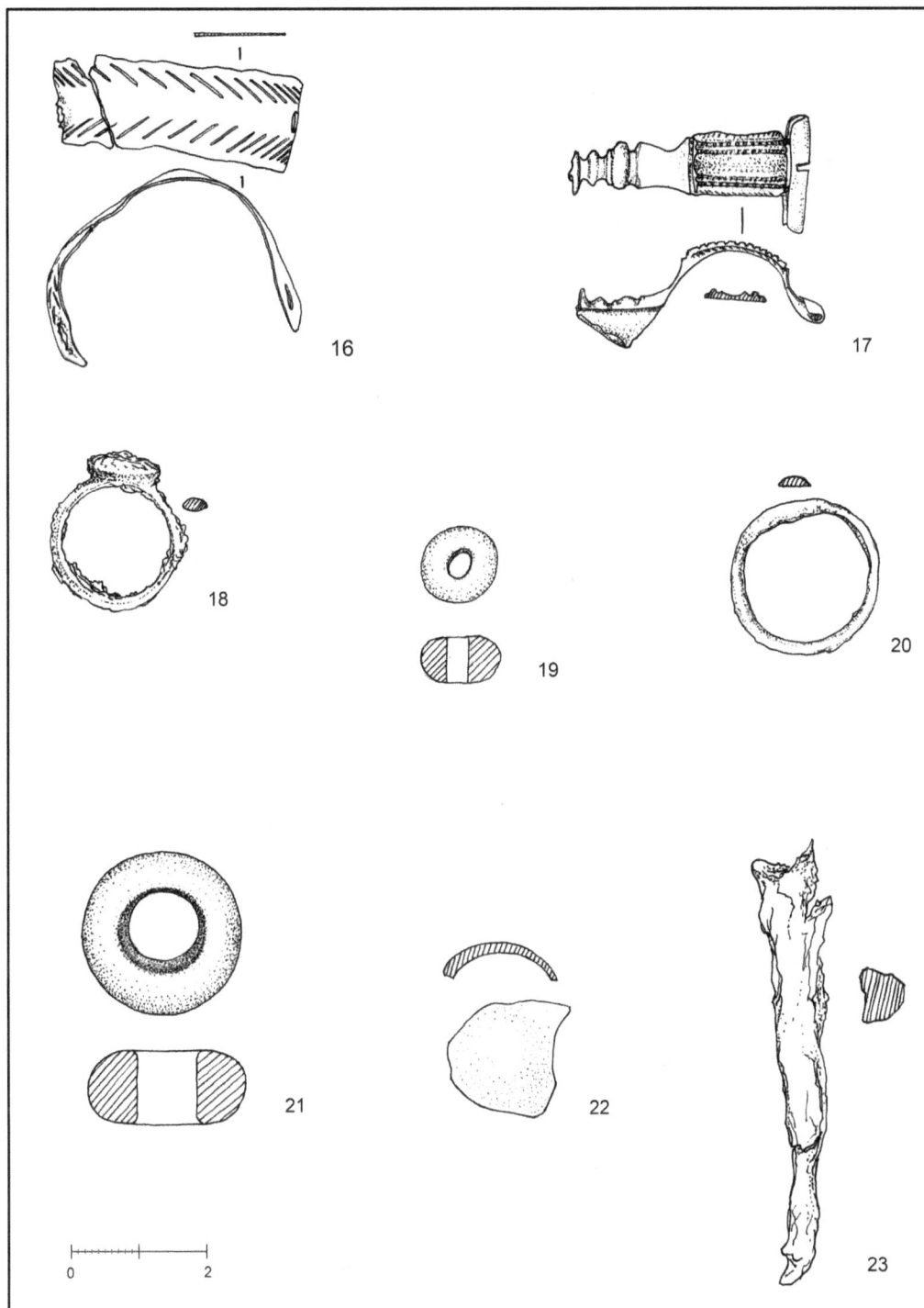

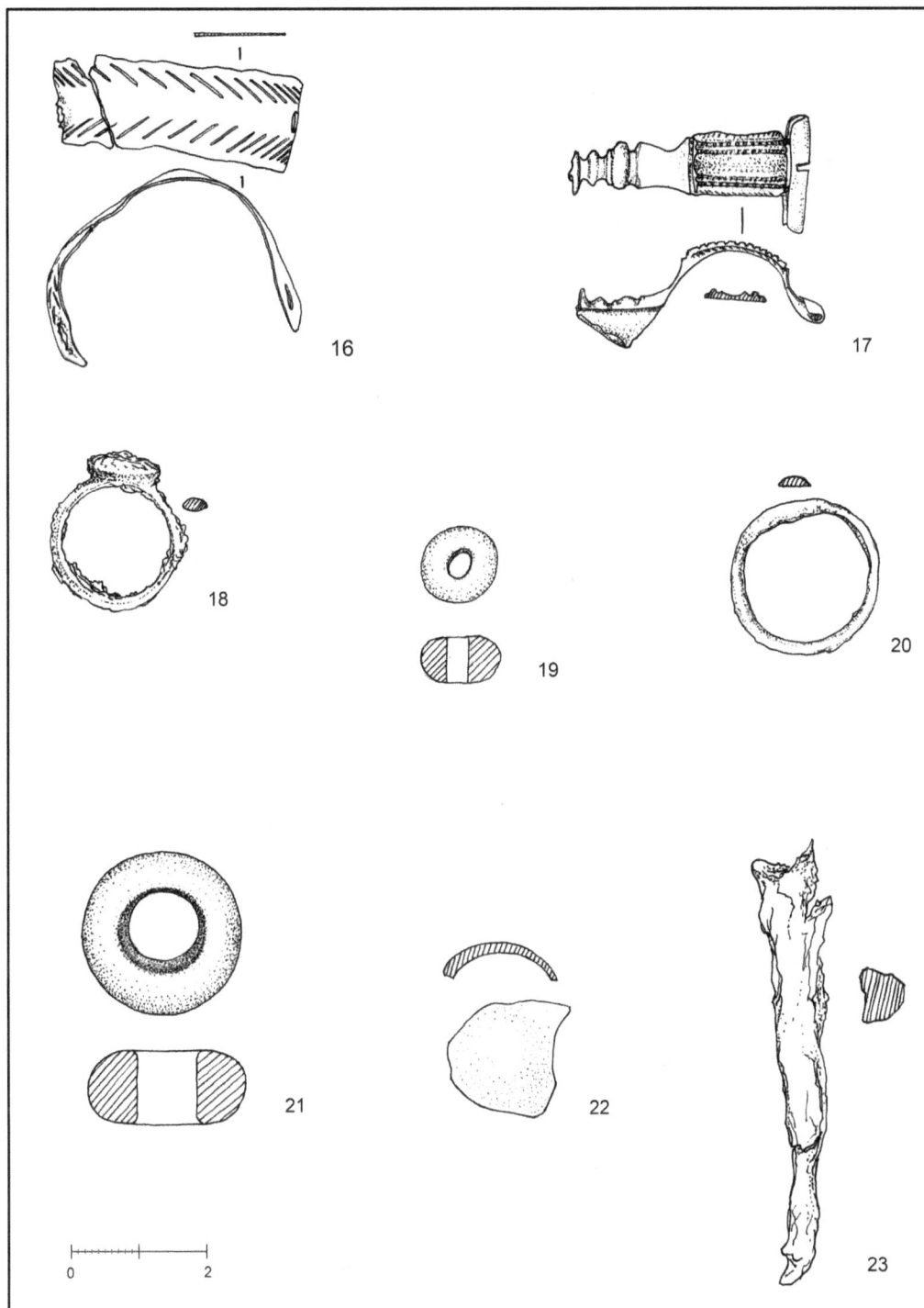

Pl. 8b. Dragišić, grave 13. 16-21 bronze; 22 glass; 23 iron

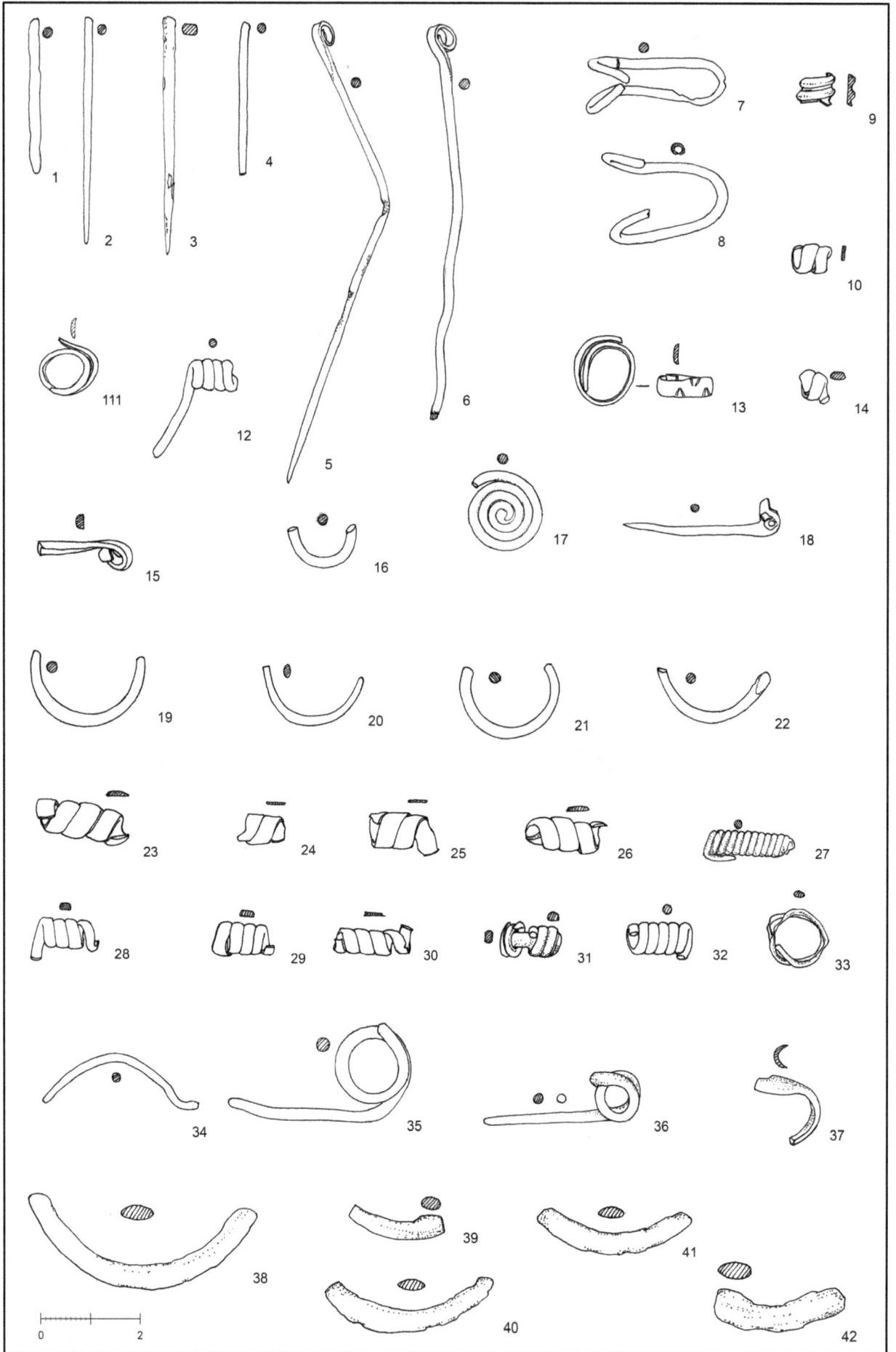

Pl. 9a. Dragišić, grave 14. 1-42 bronze

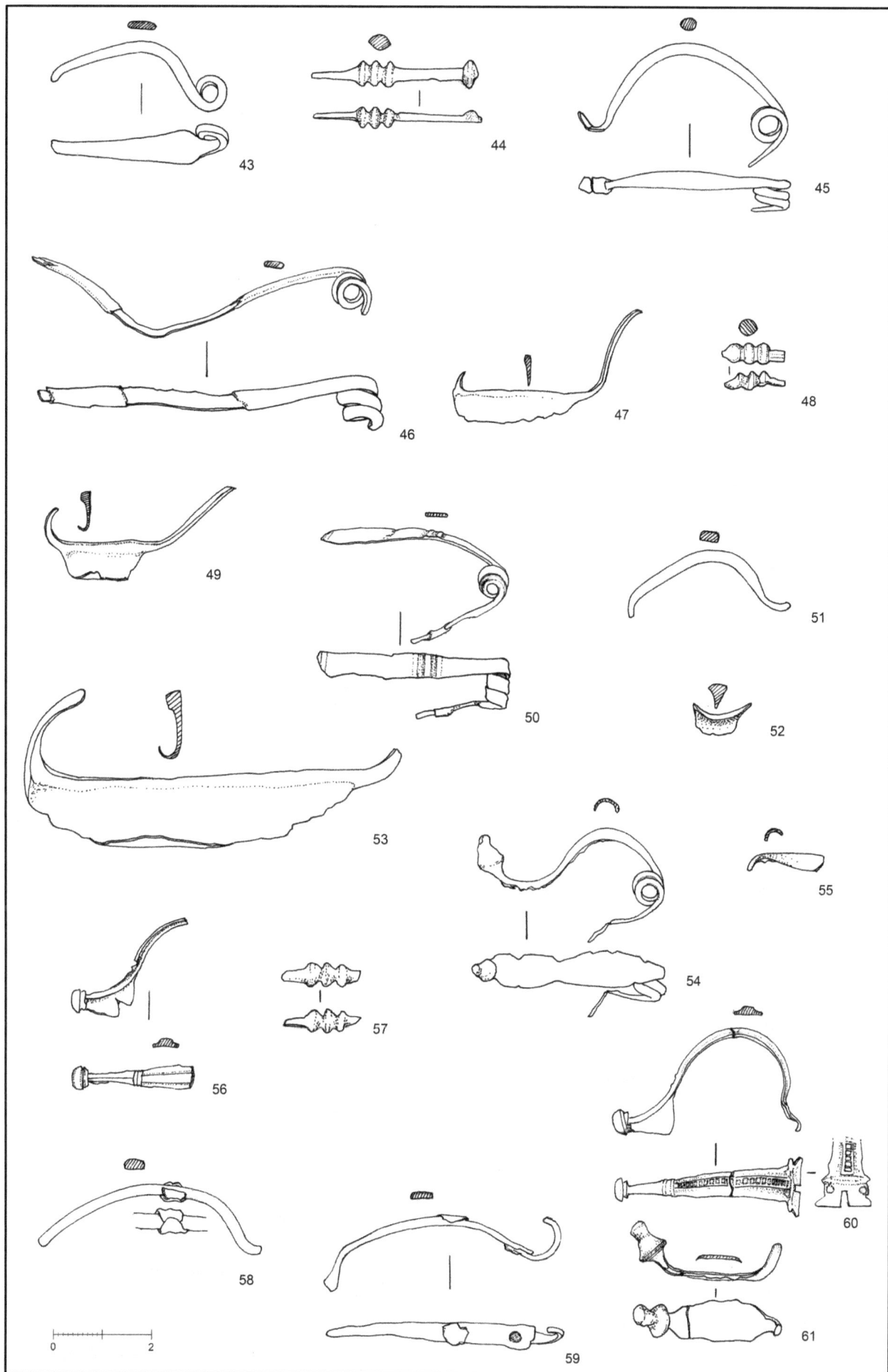

Pl. 9b. Dragišić, grave 14. 43-61 bronze

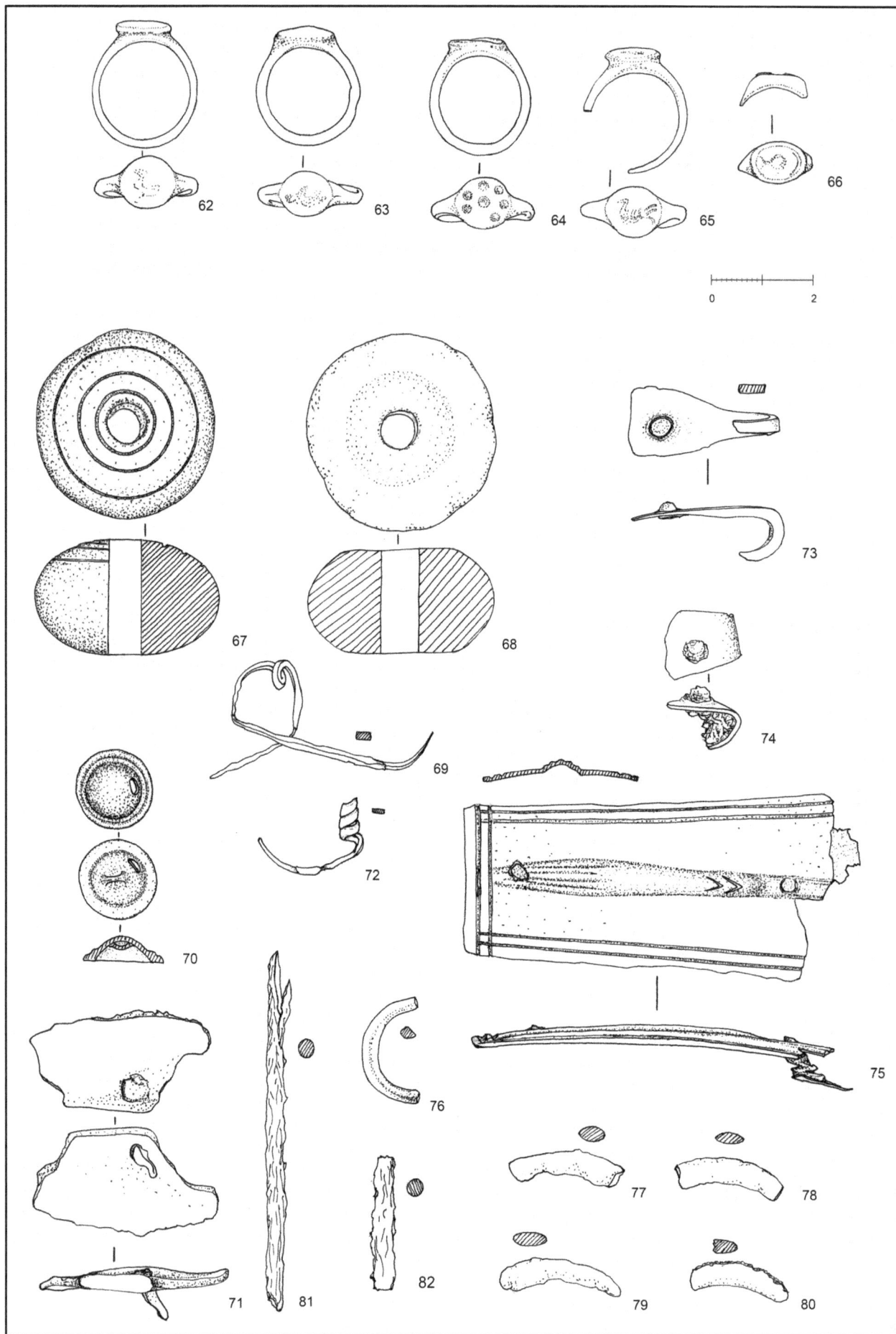

Pl. 9c. Dragišić, grave 14. 62-66, 69-80 bronze; 67 bone; 68 ceramic; 81-82 iron

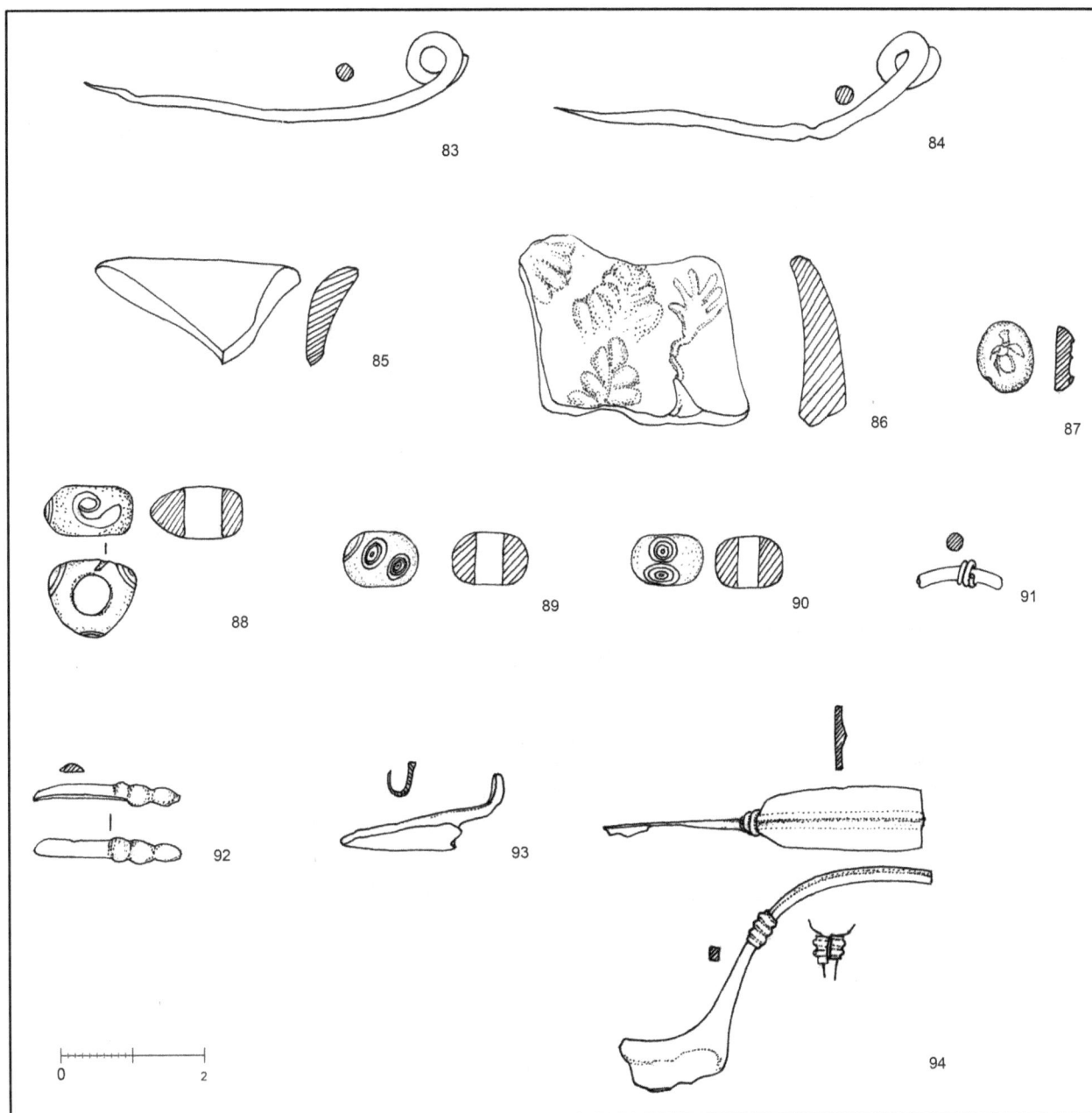

Pl. 9d. Dragišić, grave 14. 83-84, 91-94 bronze; 85, 86 pottery; 87-90 glass

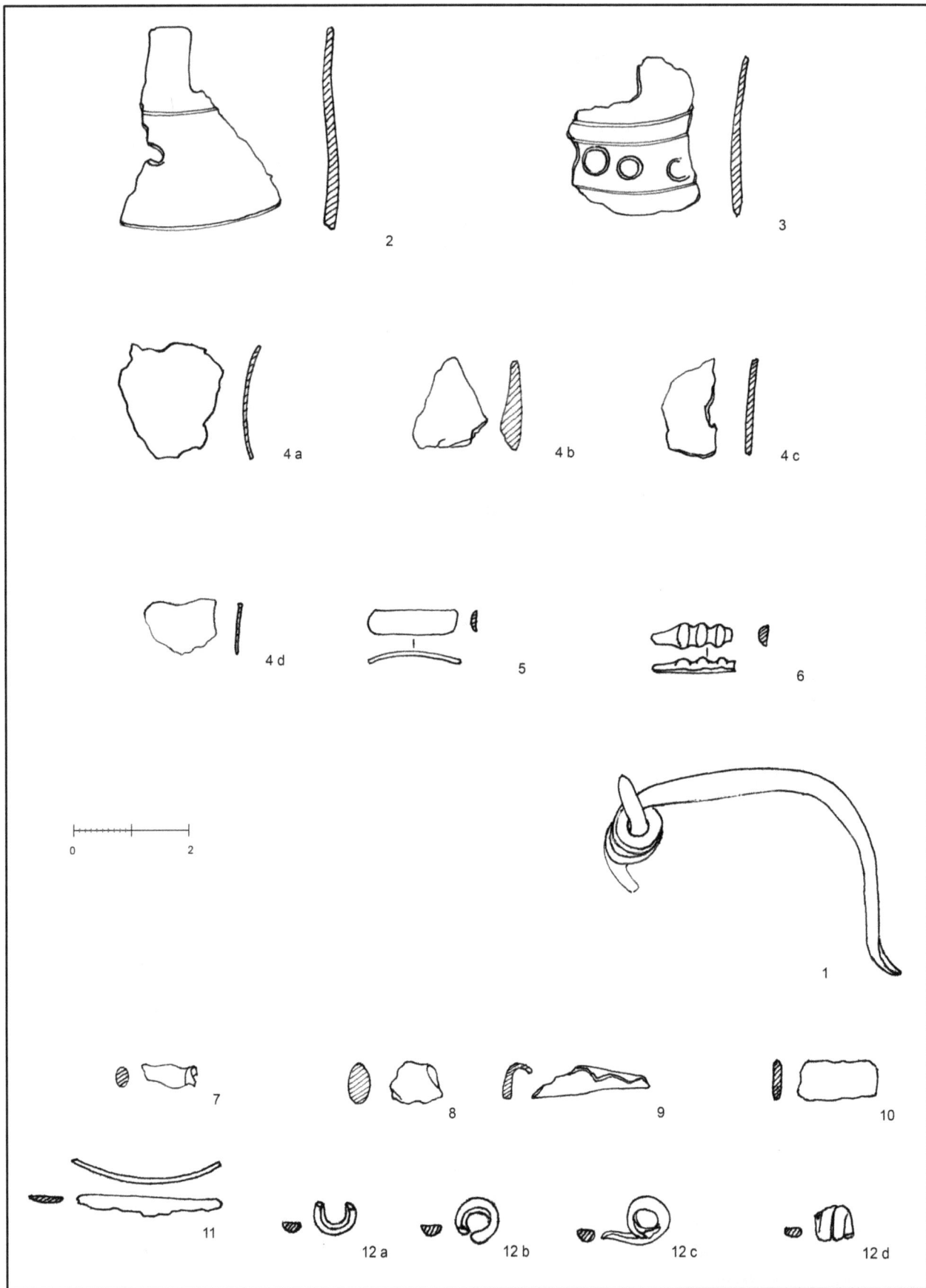

Pl. 10a. Dragišić, grave 15. 1-12 bronze

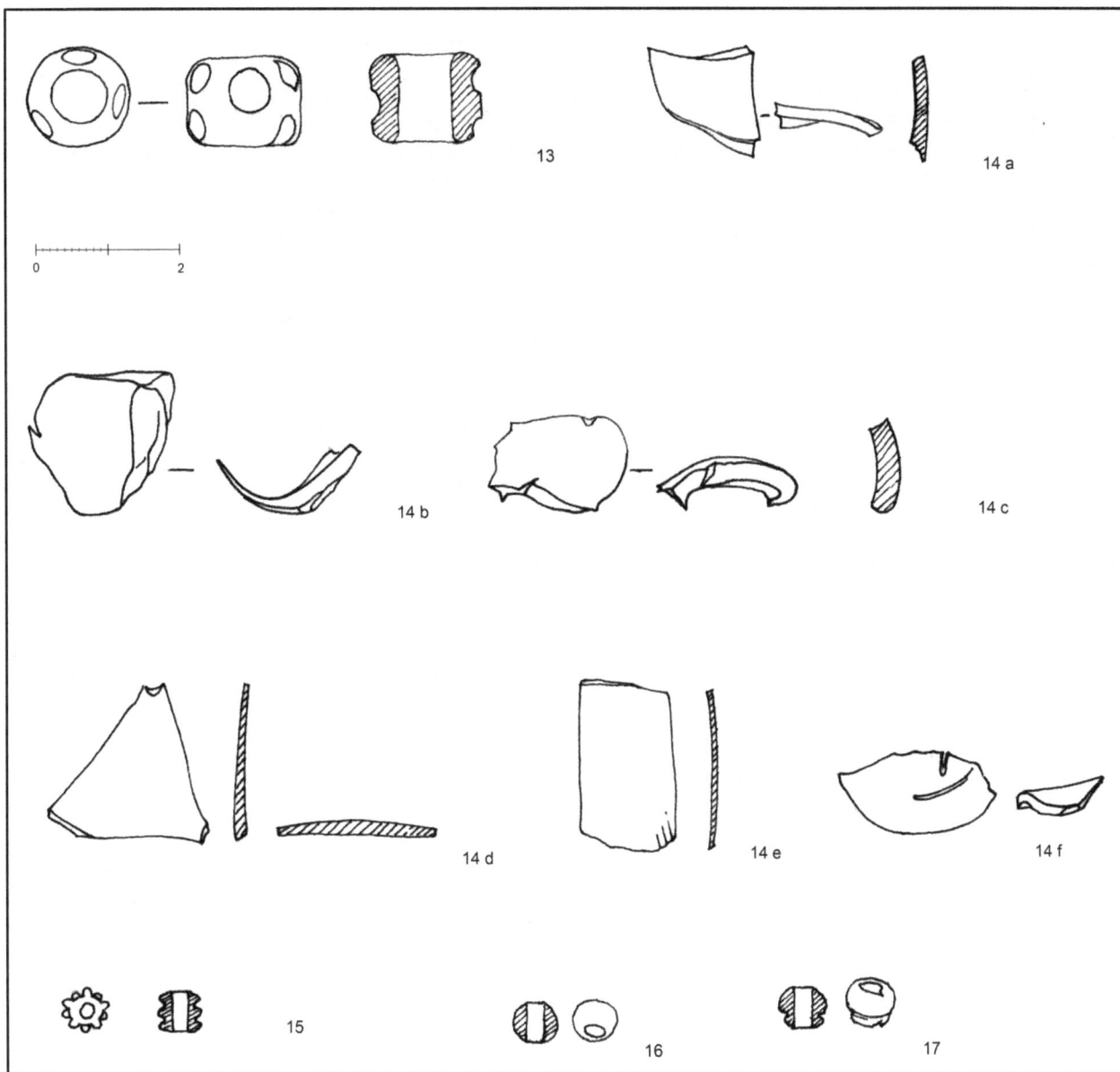

Pl. 10b. Dragišić, grave 15. 13-17 glass

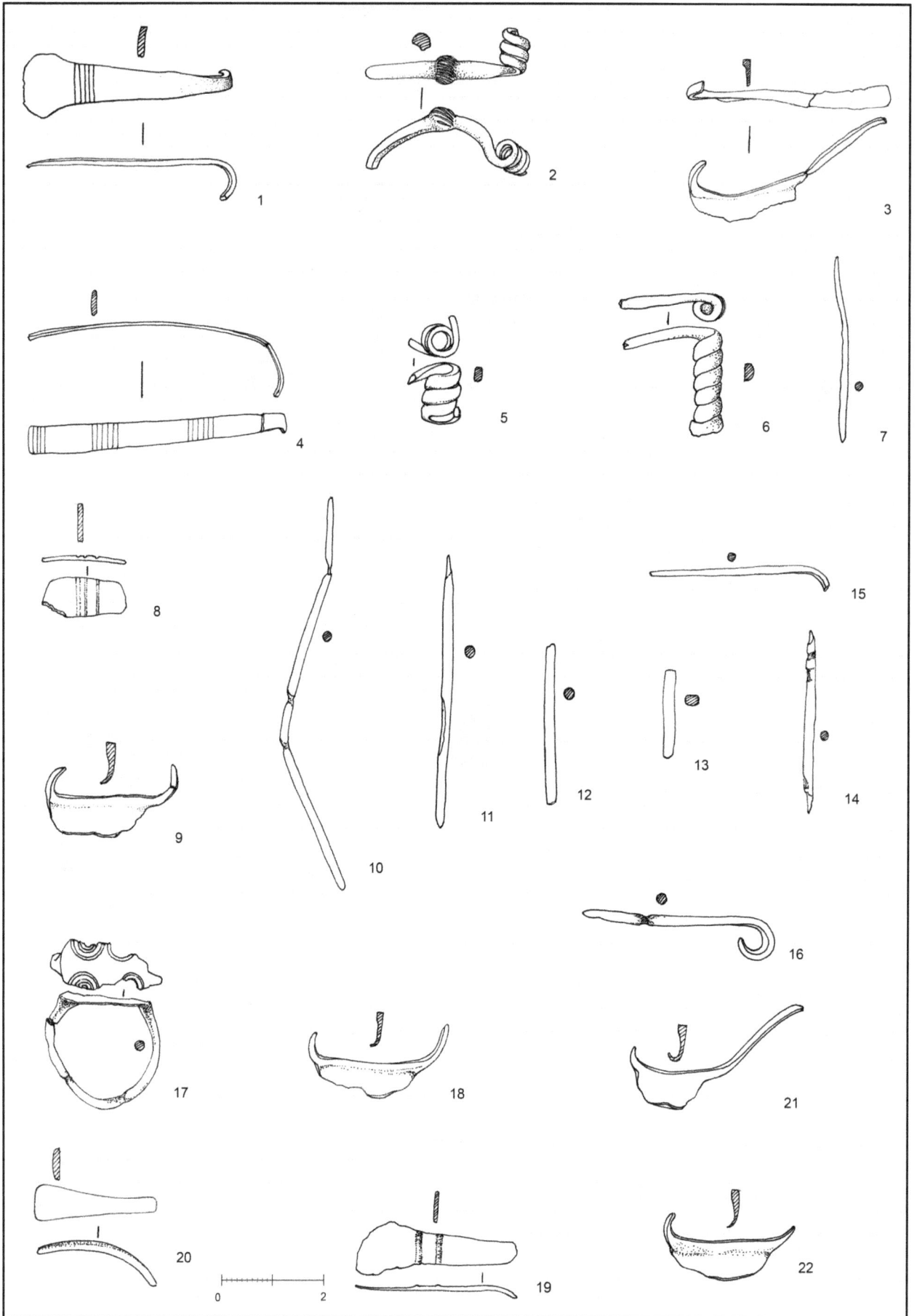

Pl. 11a. Dragišić, grave 17. 1-22 bronze

23

24

26

25

27

28

29

30

31

32

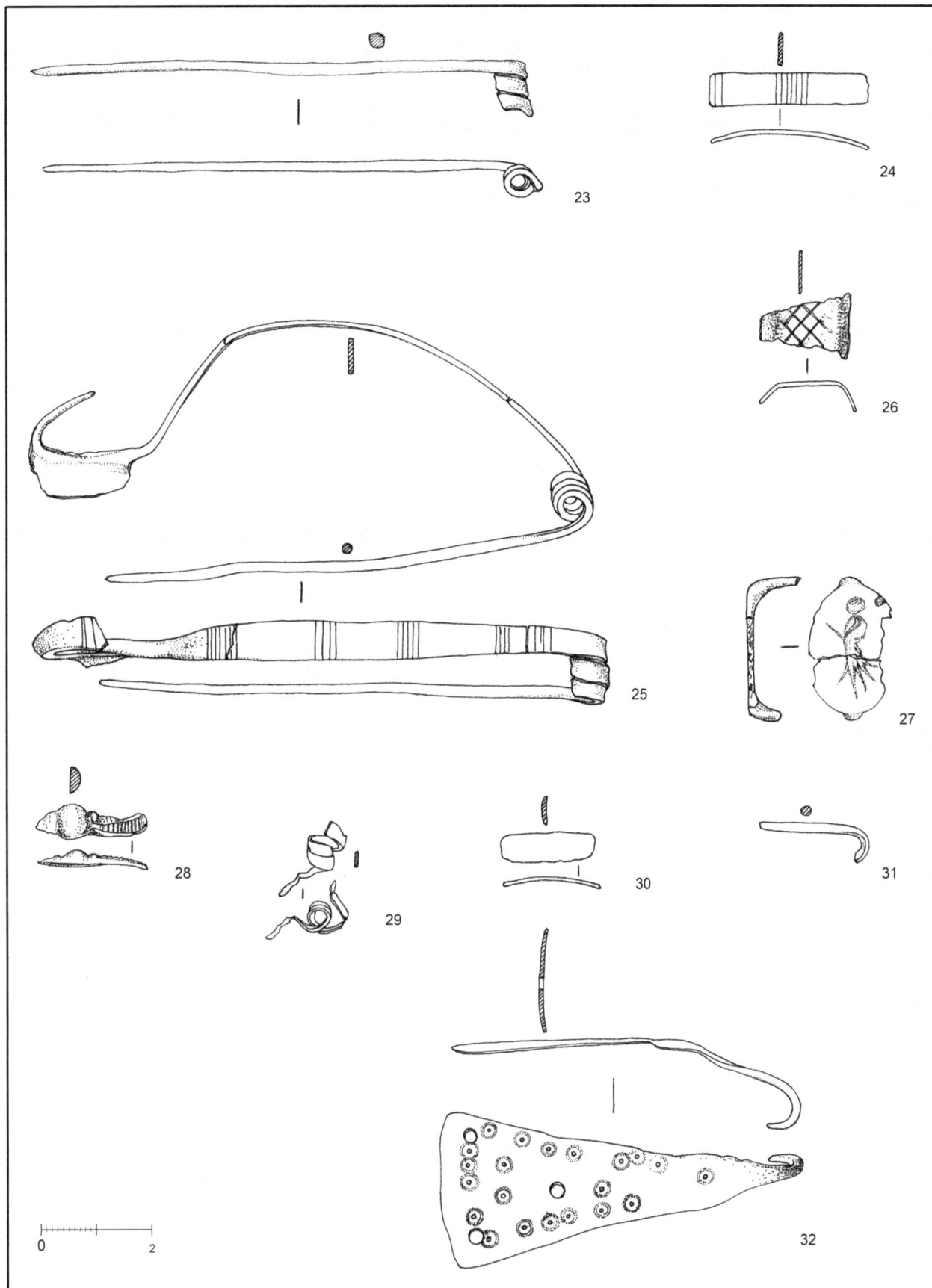

Pl. 11b. Dragišić, grave 17. 23-32 bronze

0   2

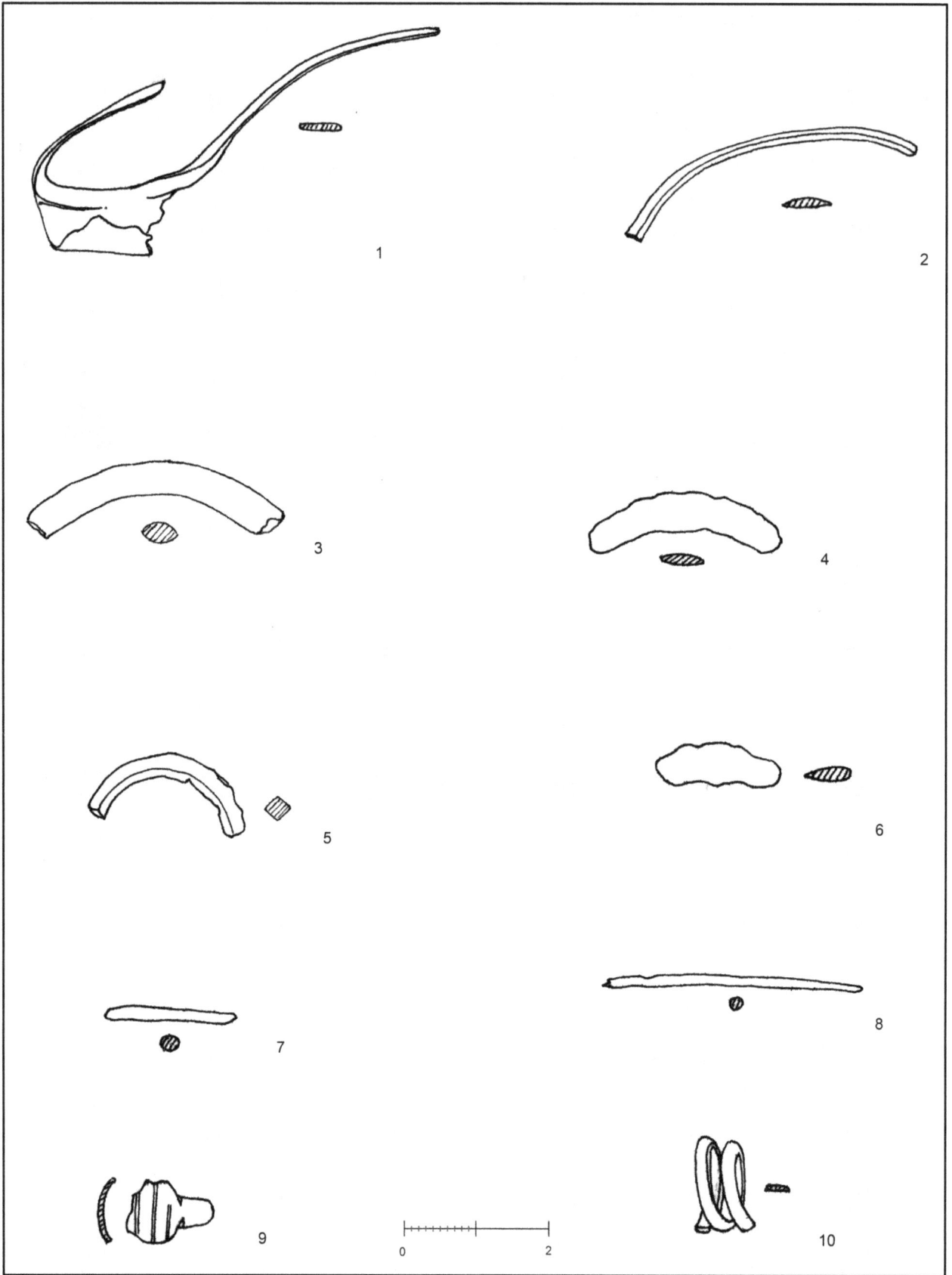

Pl. 12. Dragišić, grave 18. 1-10 bronze

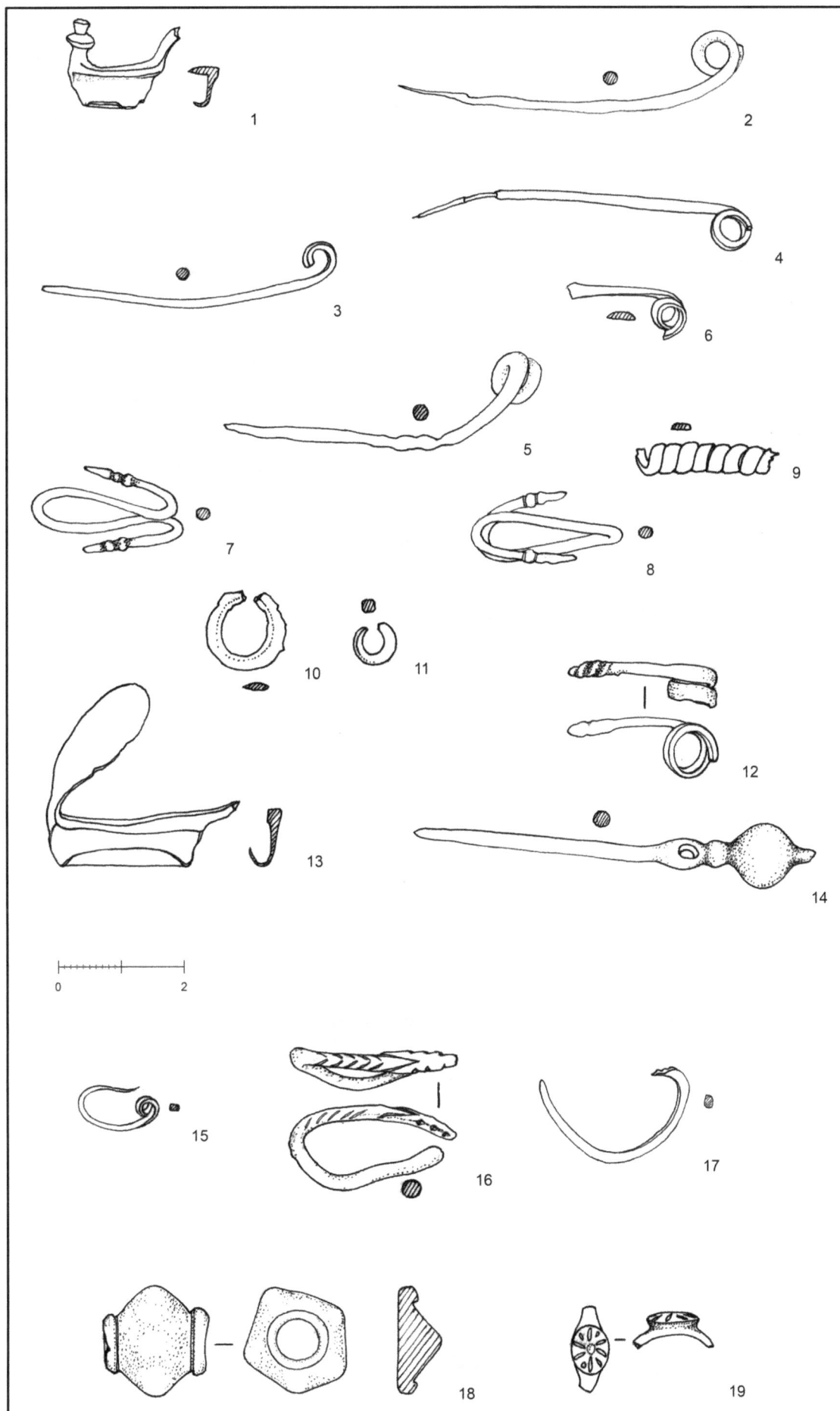

Pl. 13a. Dragišić, grave 20. 1-19 bronze

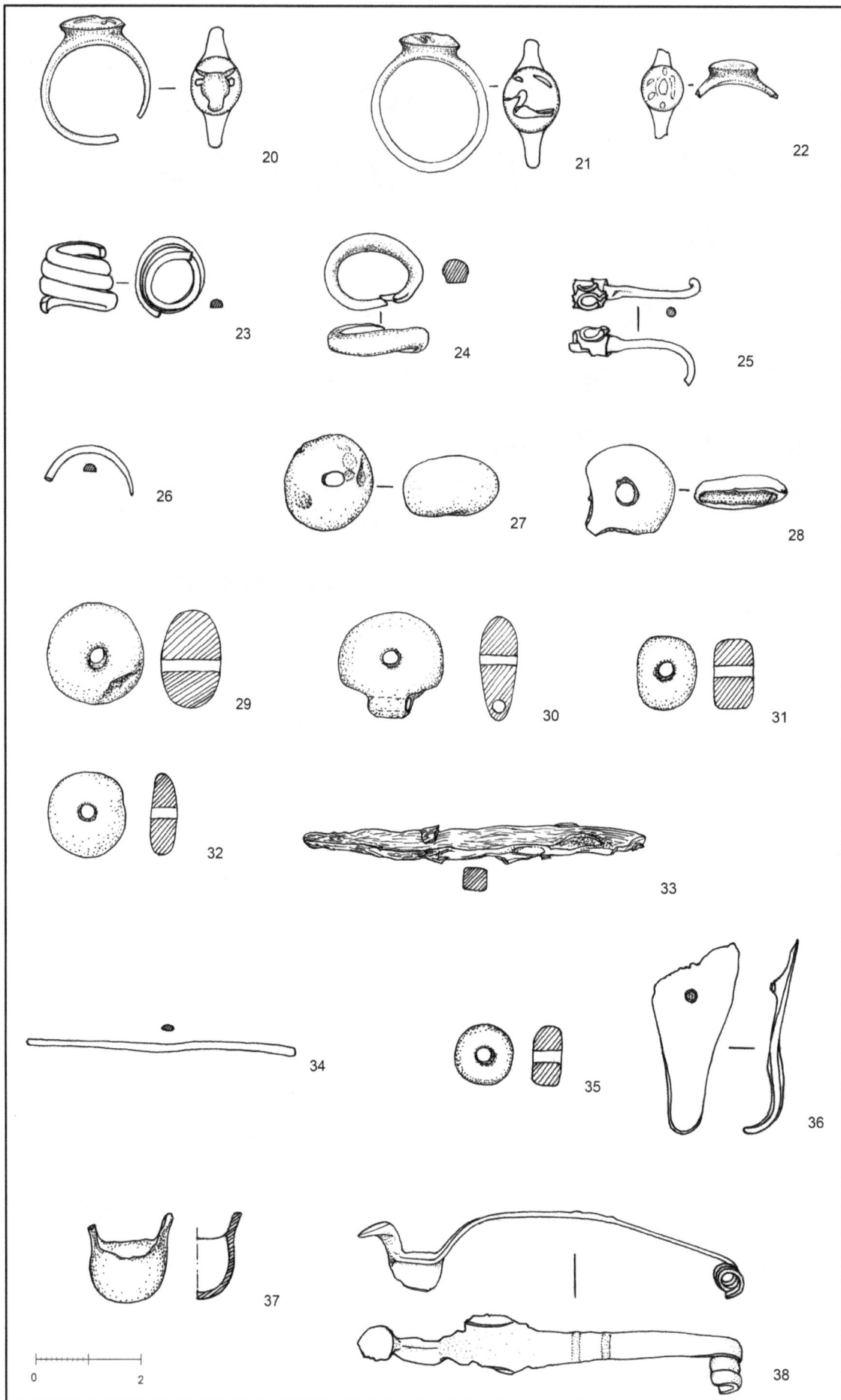

Pl. 13b. Dragišić, grave 20. 20-26, 34, 36-38 bronze; 27-32, 35 amber; 33 iron

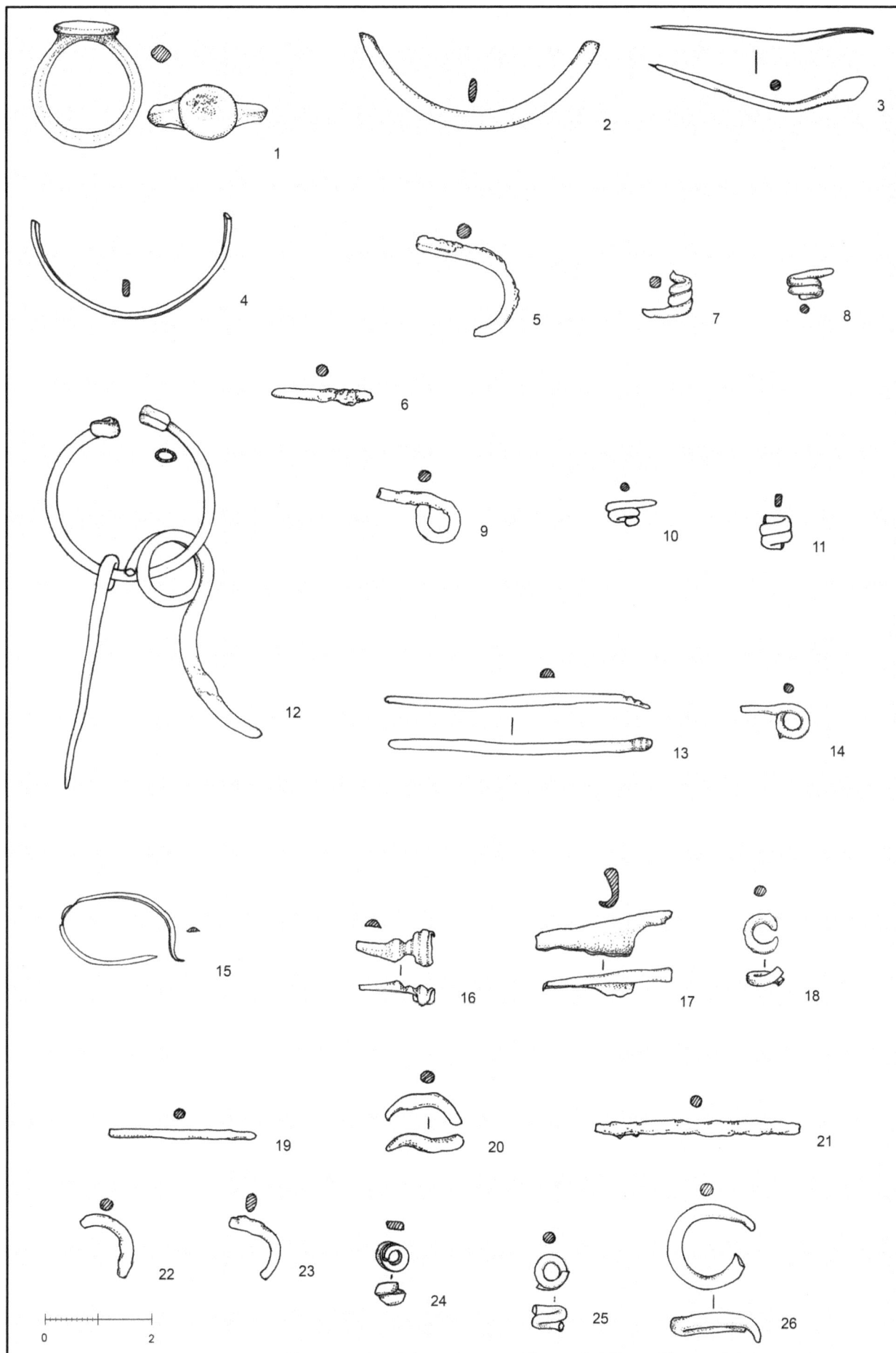

Pl. 14a. Dragišić, grave 21. 1-26 bronze

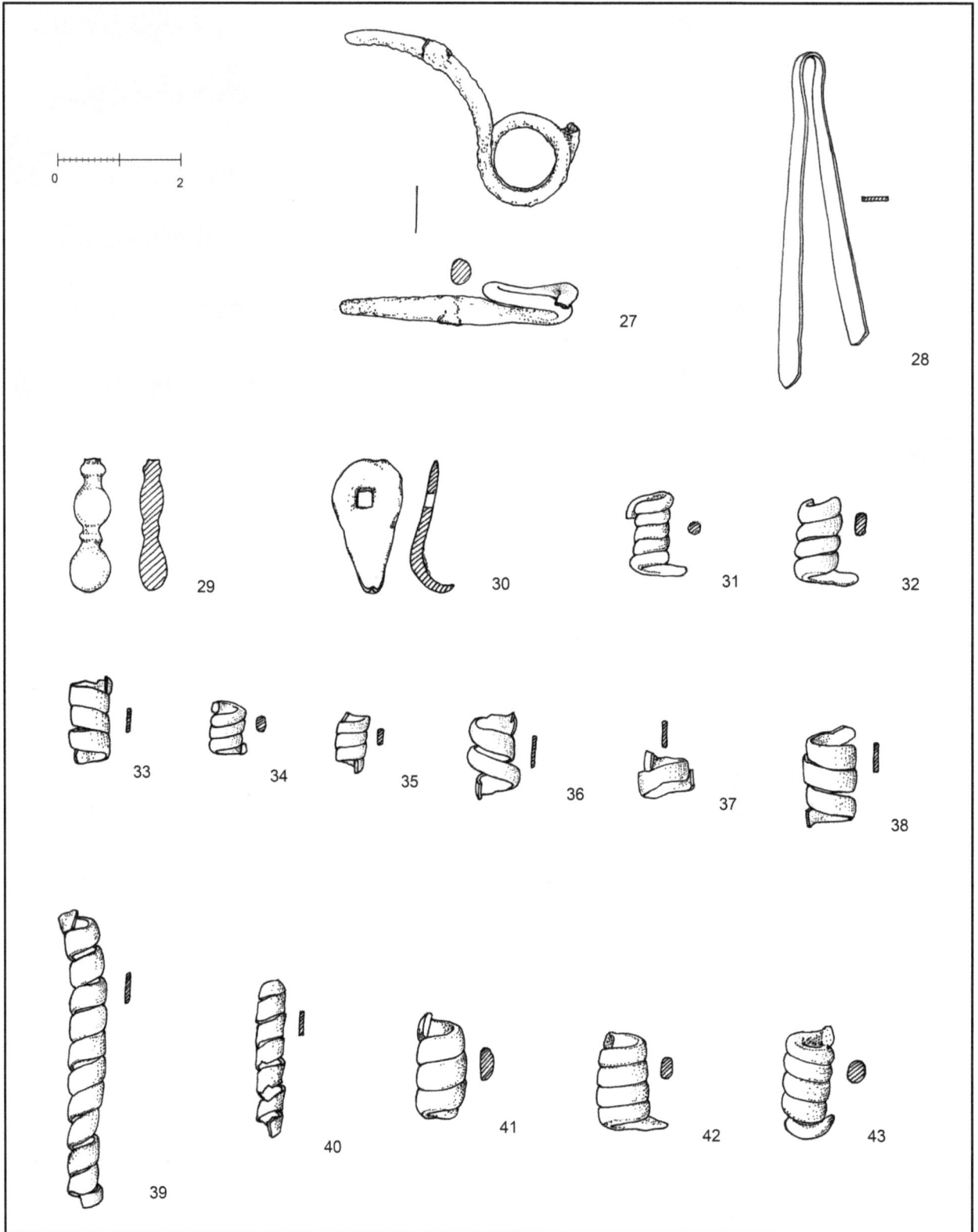

Pl. 14b. Dragišić, grave 21. 27-43 bronze

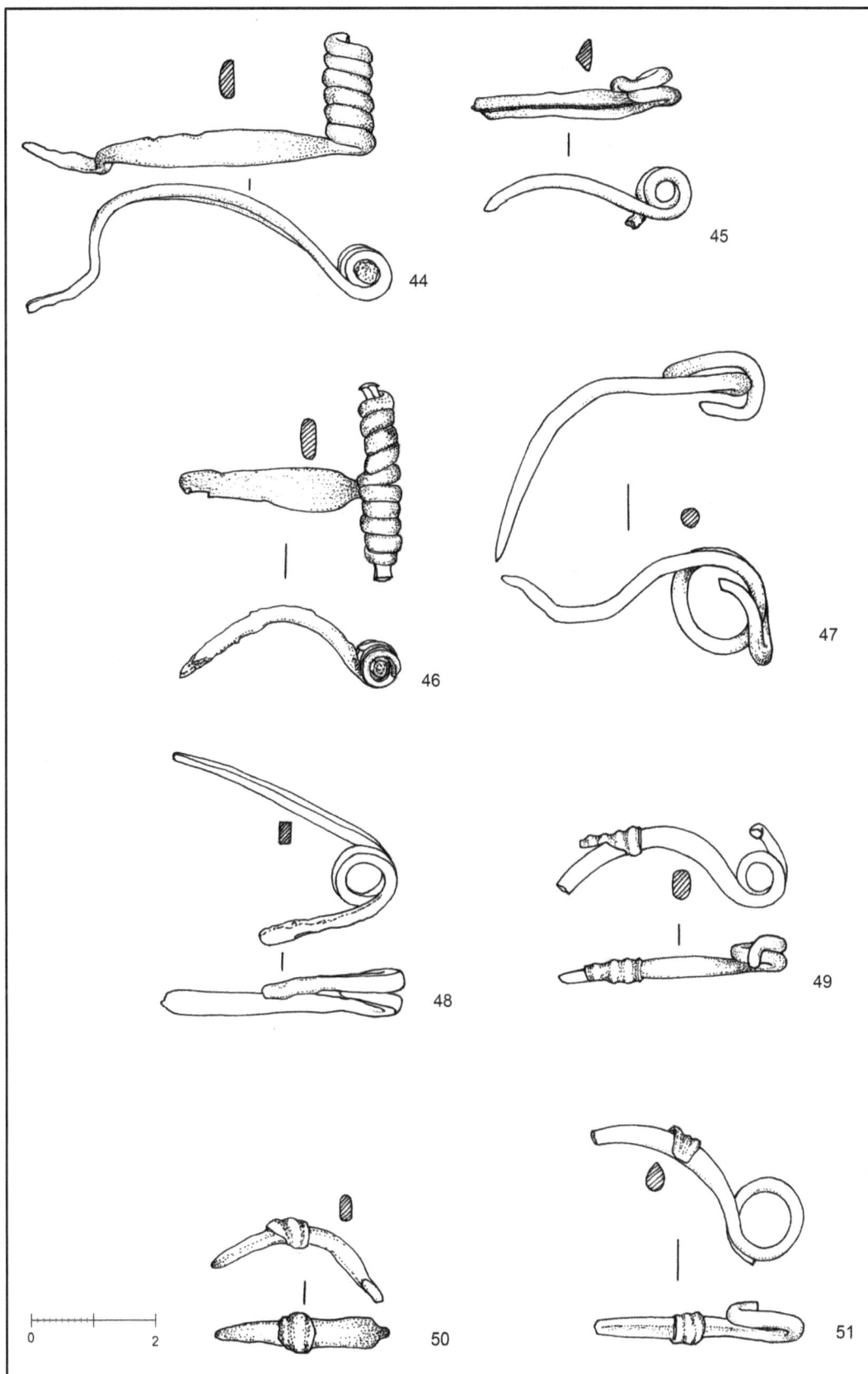

Pl. 14c. Dragišić, grave 21. 44-51 bronze

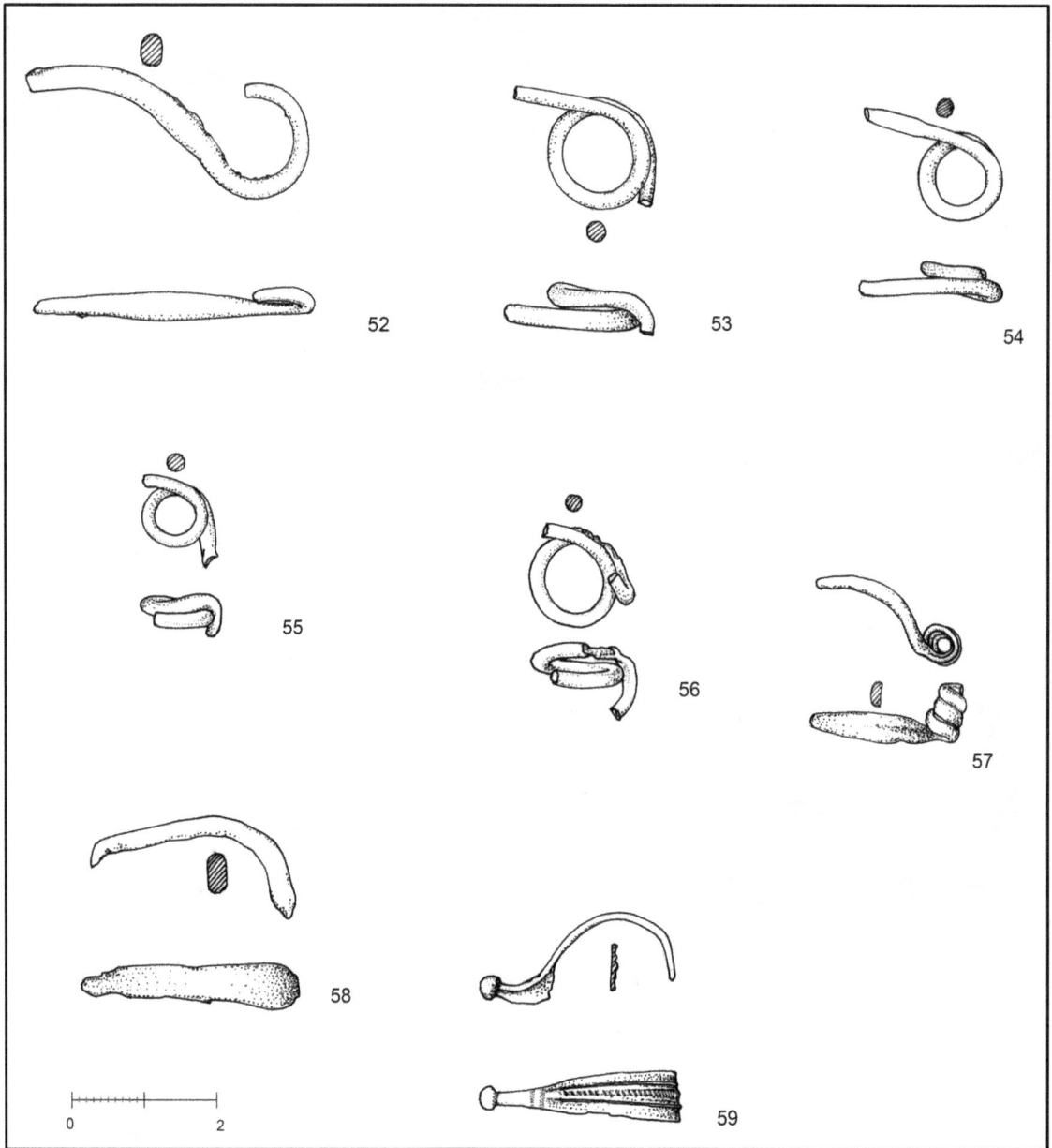

Pl. 14d. Dragišić, grave 21. 52-59 bronze

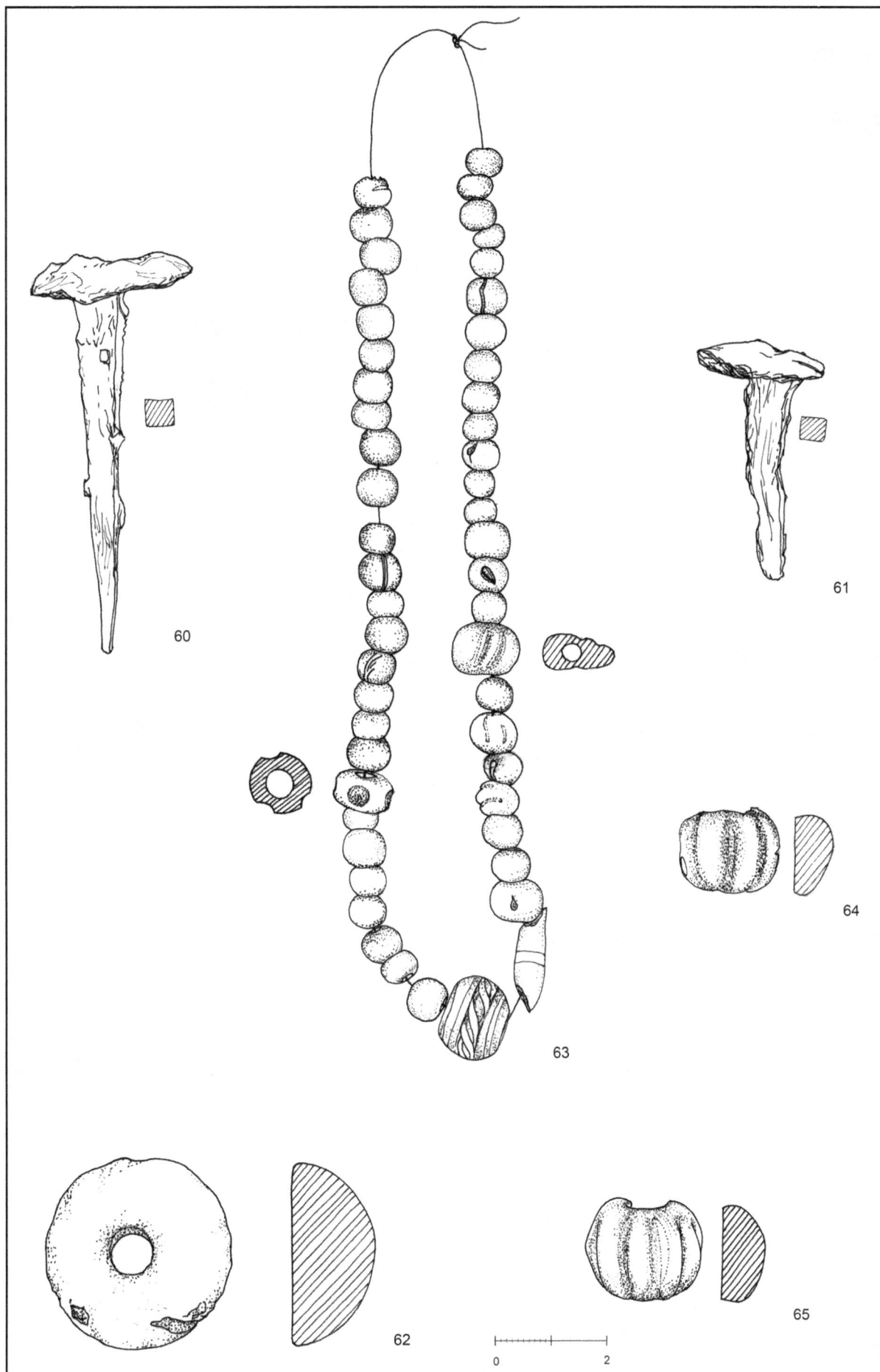

Pl. 14e. Dragišić, grave 21. 60, 61 iron; 63-65 glass; 62 ceramic

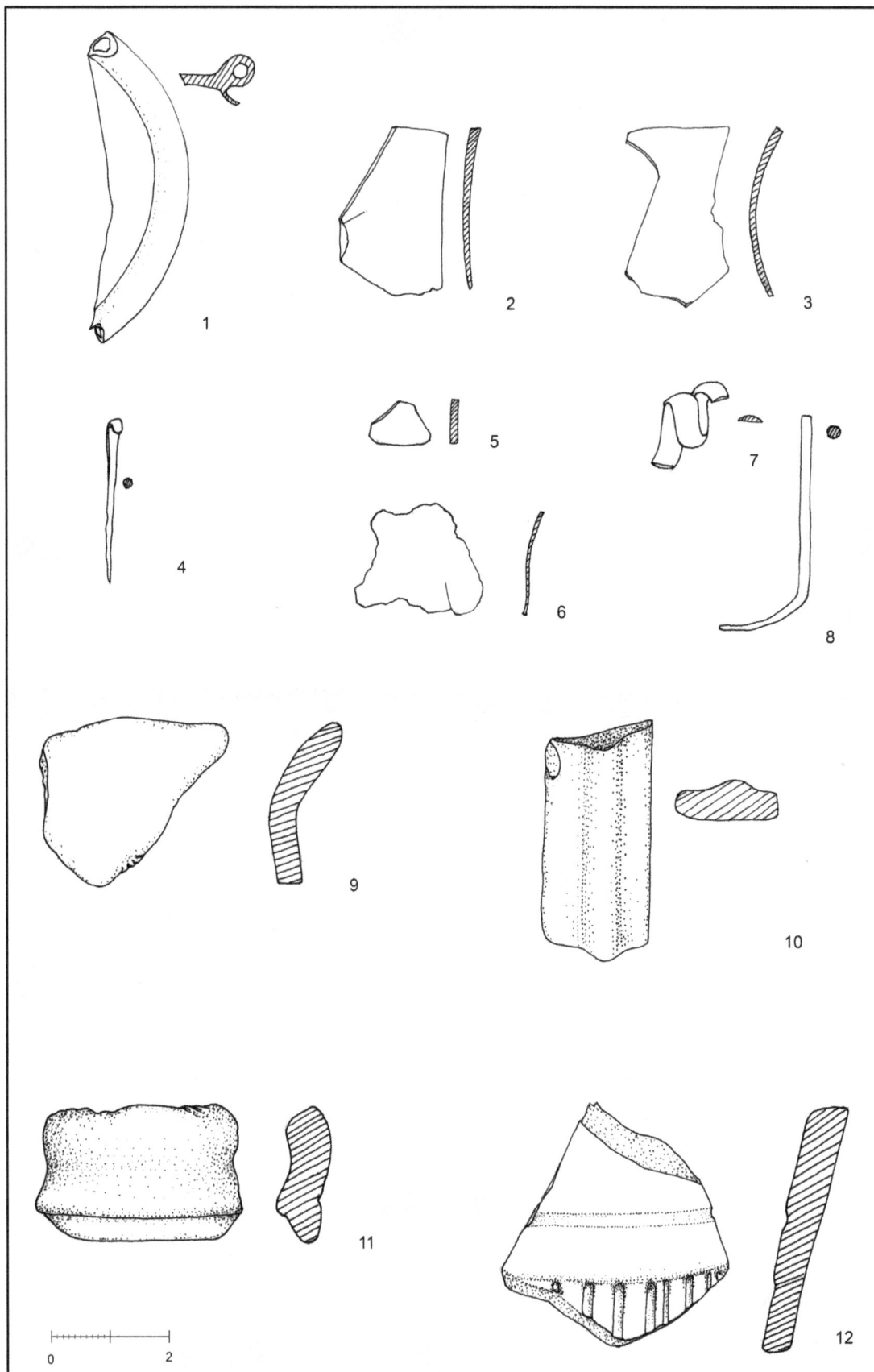

Pl. 15. Dragišić, grave 22. 1-3 glass; 4-8 bronze; 9-12 pottery

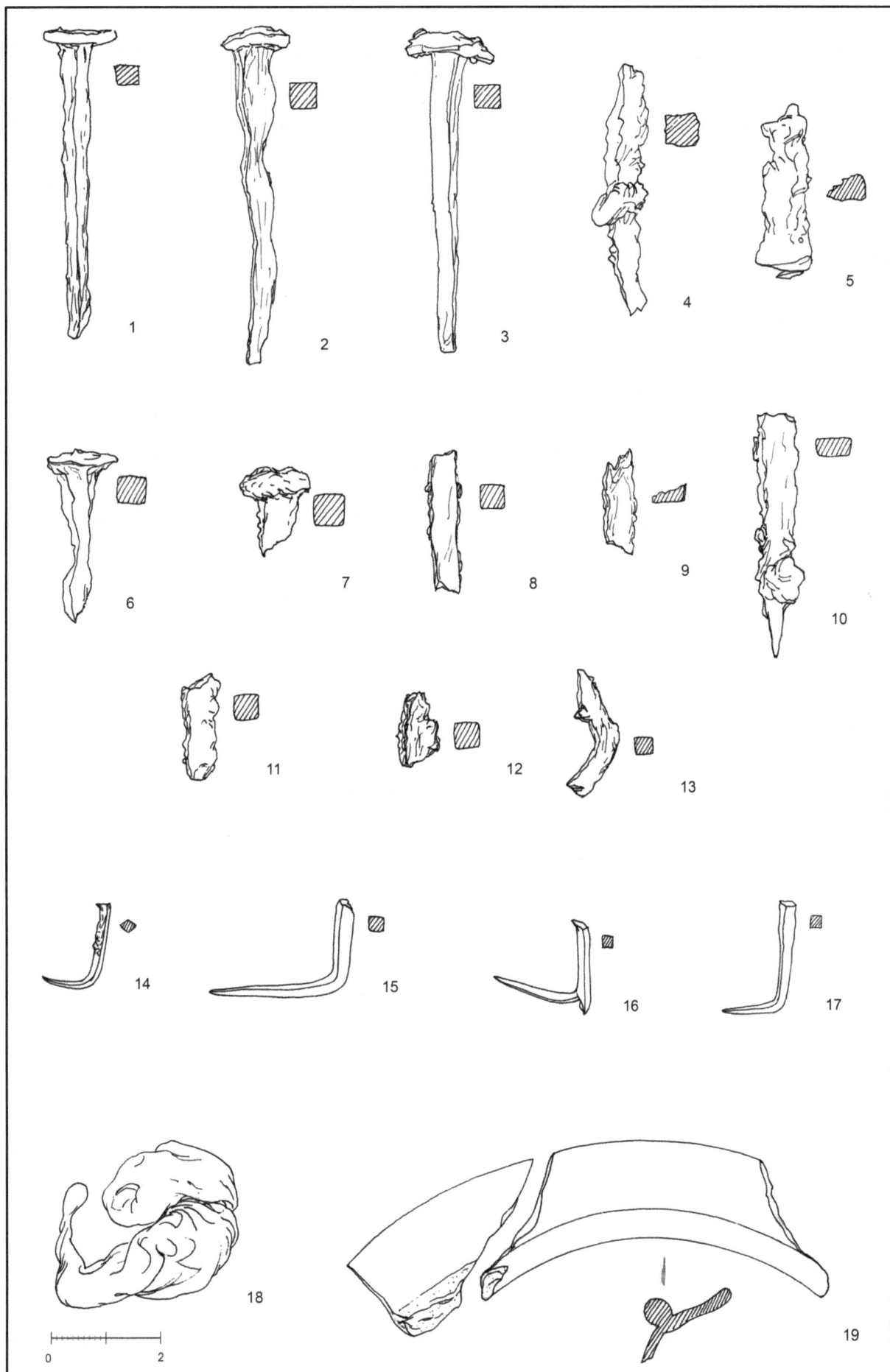

Pl. 16. Dragišić, grave 27. 1-17 iron; 18. 19 glass

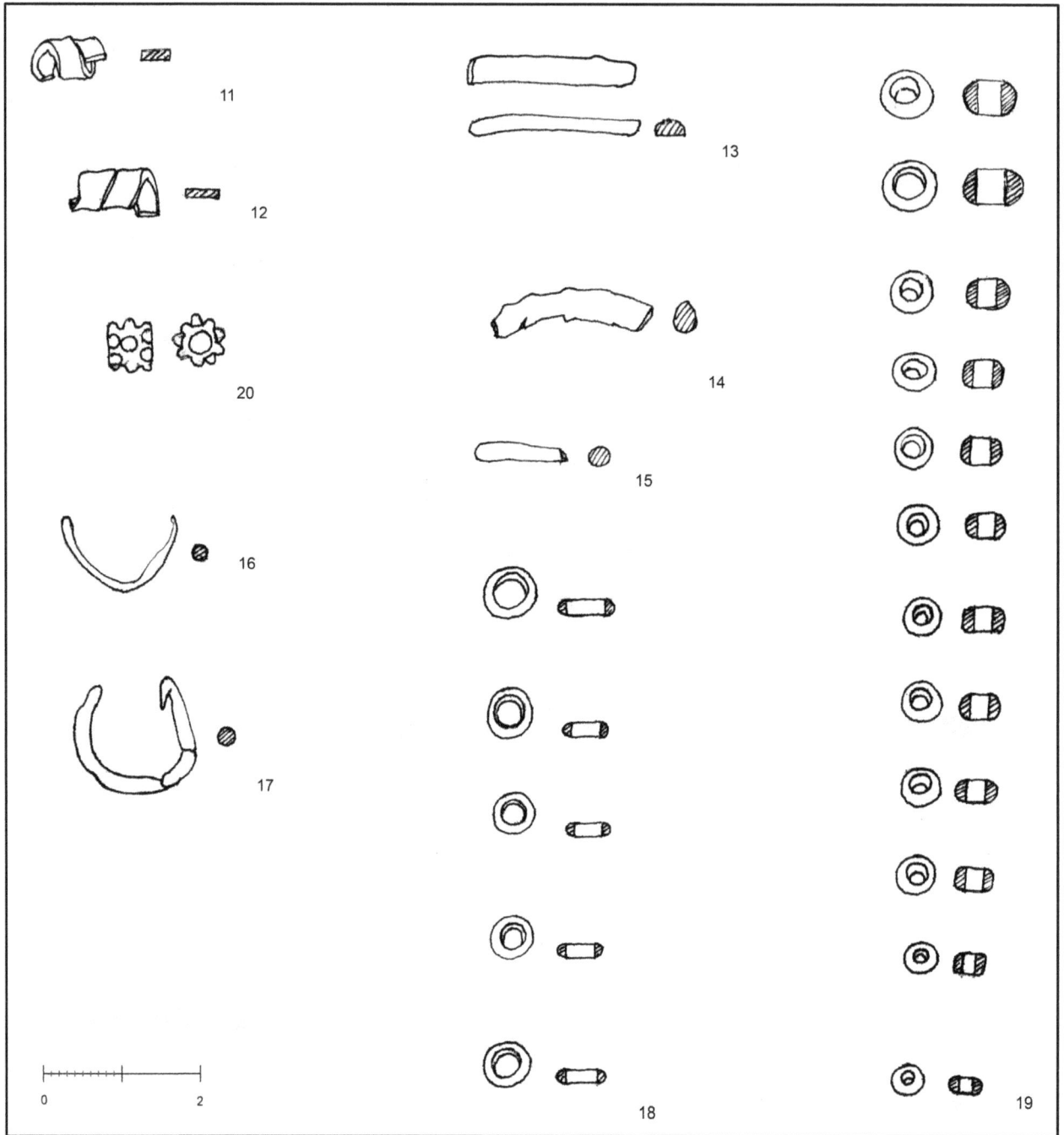

Pl. 17. Dragišić, grave 18. 11-17 bronze; 18-20 glass

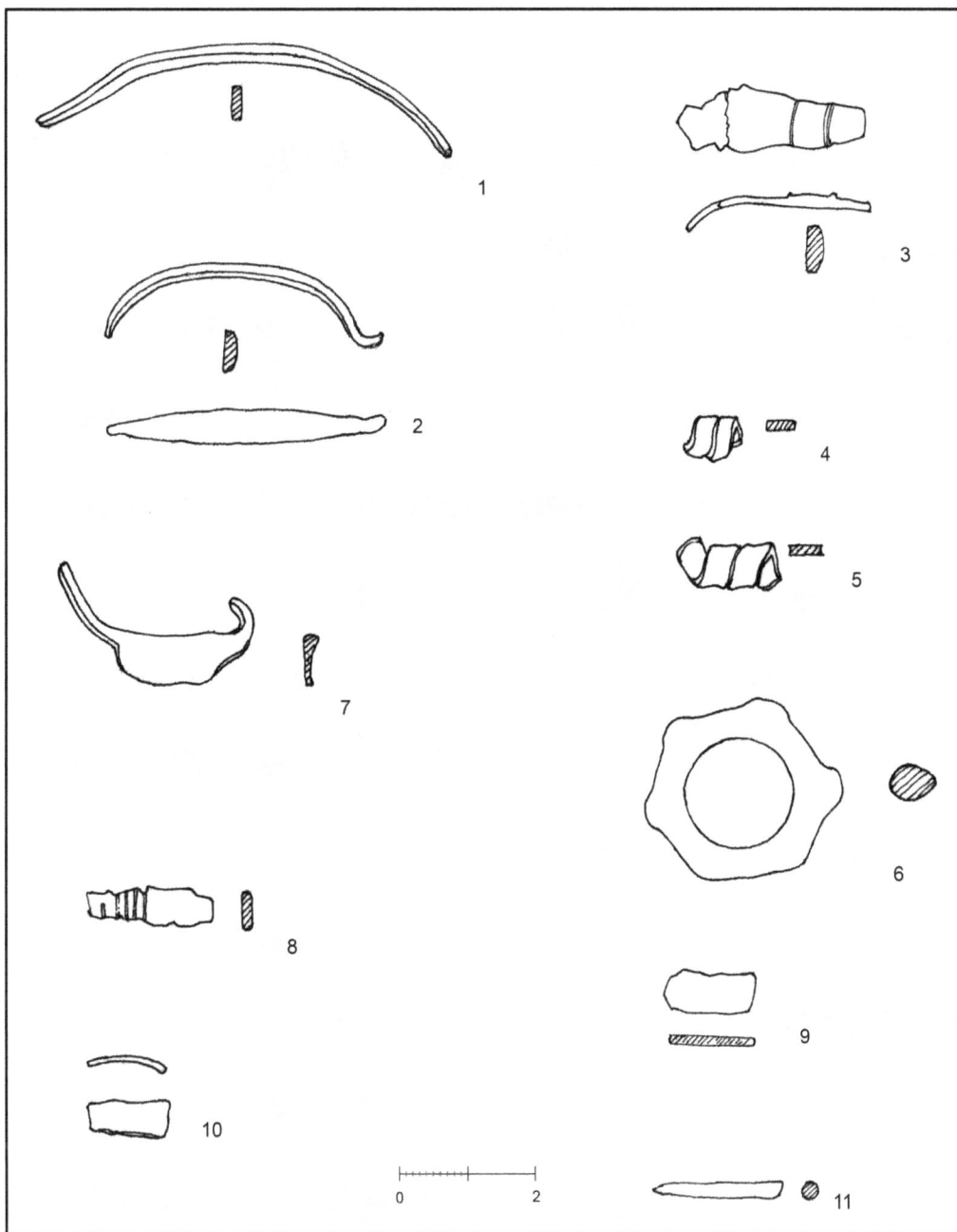

Pl. 18. Dragišić, grave 23. 1-11 bronze

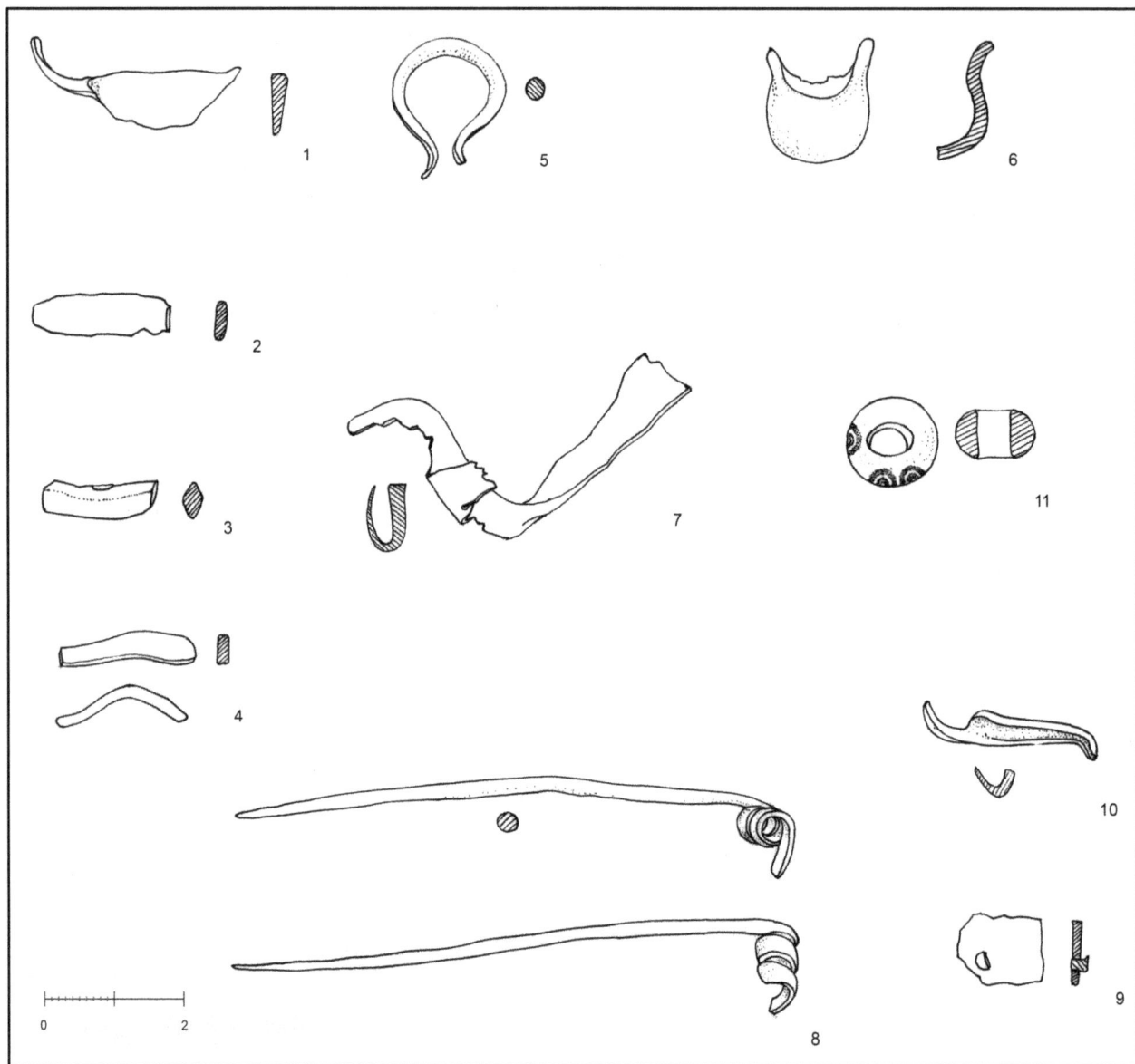

Pl. 19. Dragišić, grave 24. 1-10 bronze; 11 glass

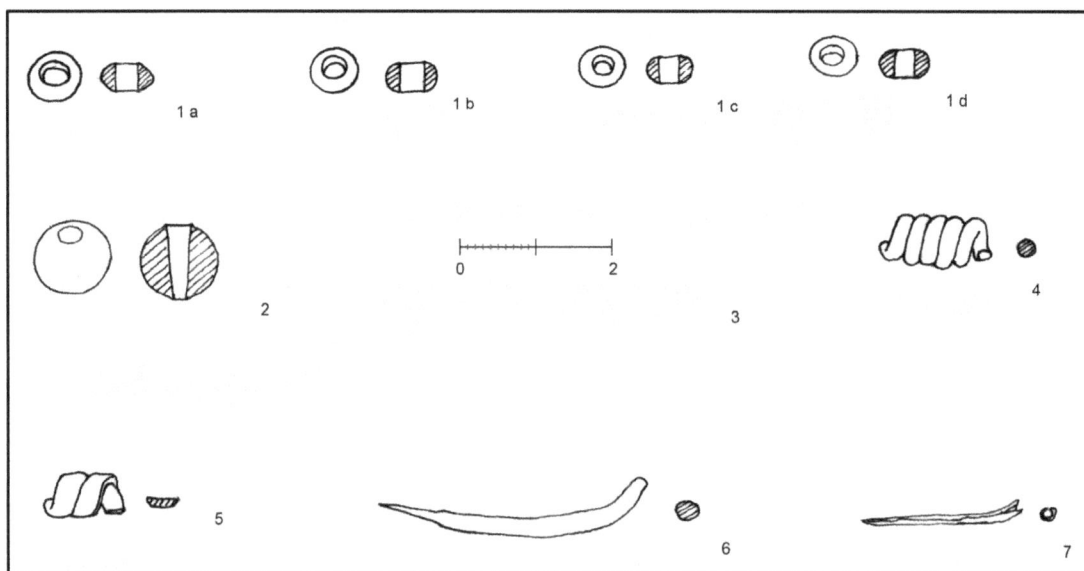

Pl. 20. Dragišić, grave 25. 1-3 glass; 4-7 bronze

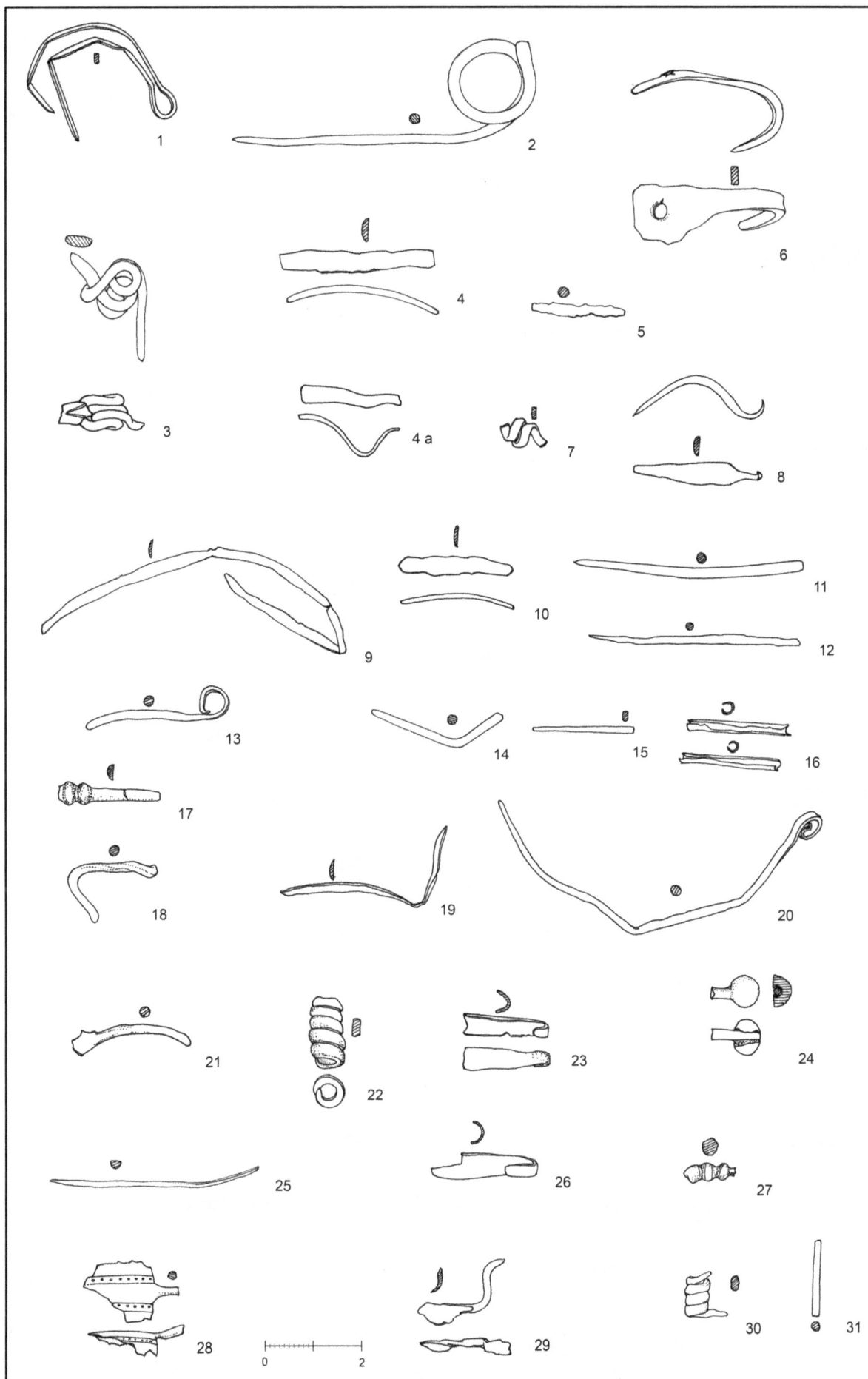

Pl. 21a. Dragišić, grave 26. 1-23, 25-31 bronze; 24 silver

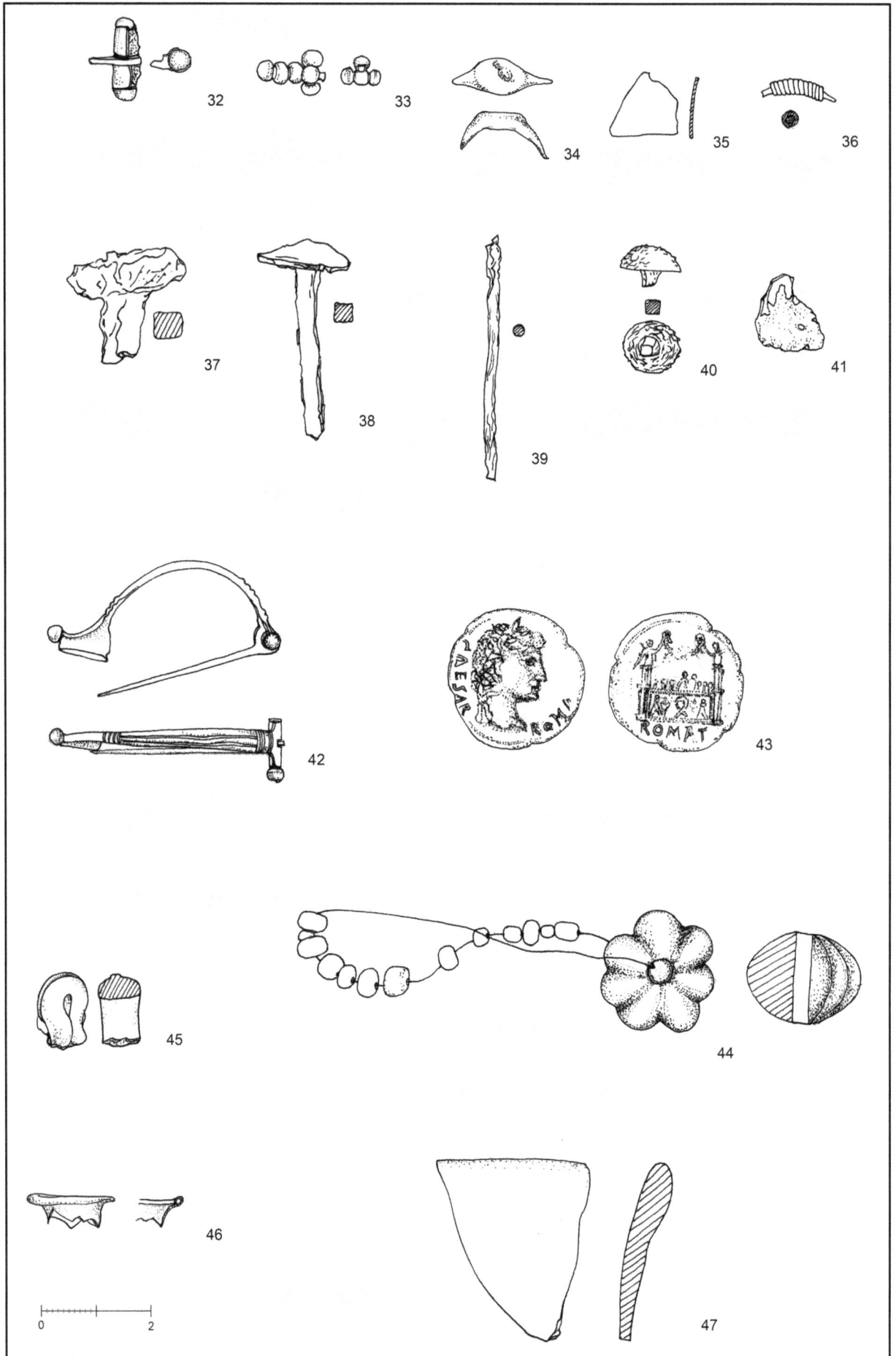

Pl. 21b. Dragišić, grave 26. 32, 34-43 bronze; 33 silver; 44-47 glass

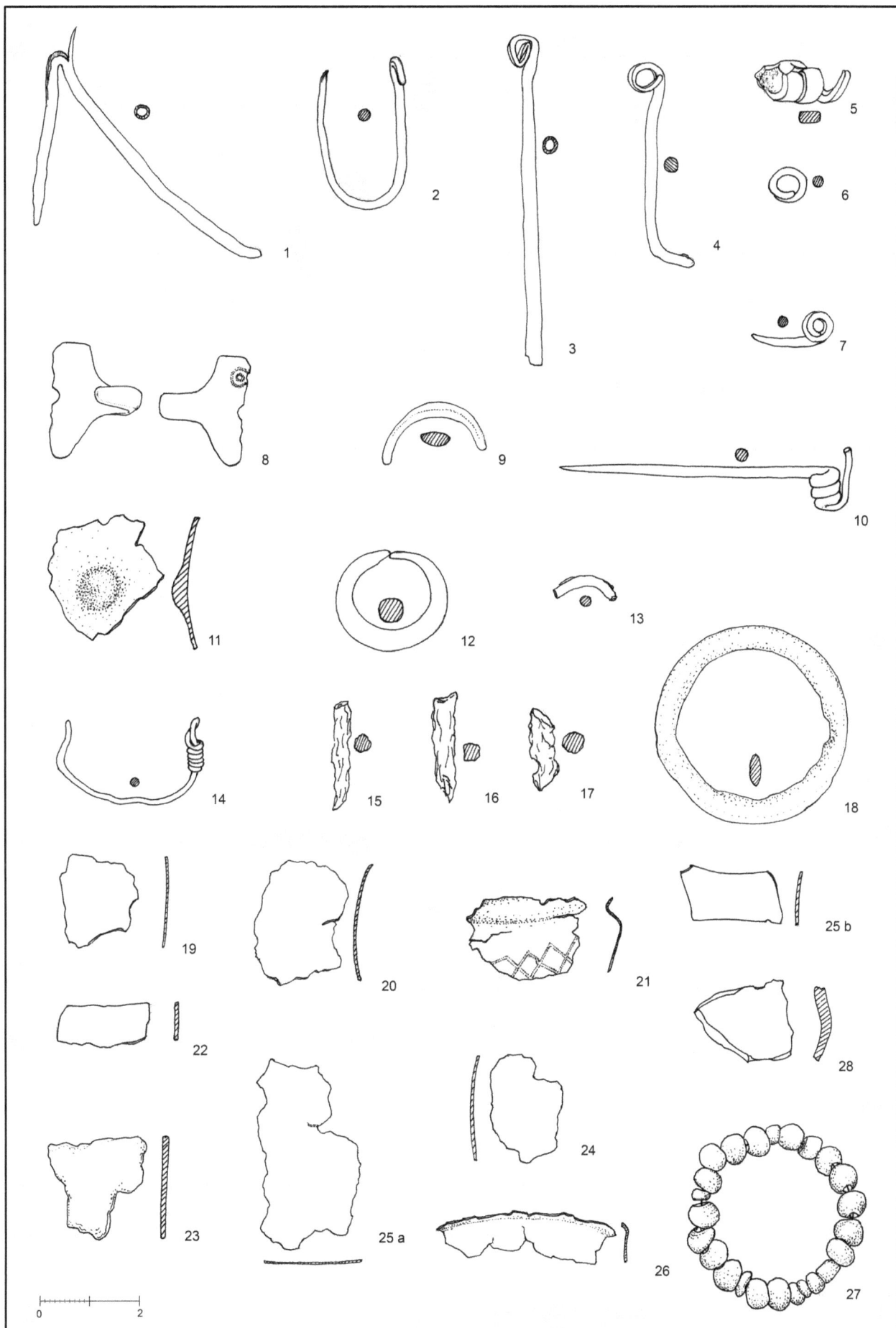

Pl. 22a. Dragišić, grave 30. 1-14, 18-26 bronze; 15-17 iron; 27. 28 glass

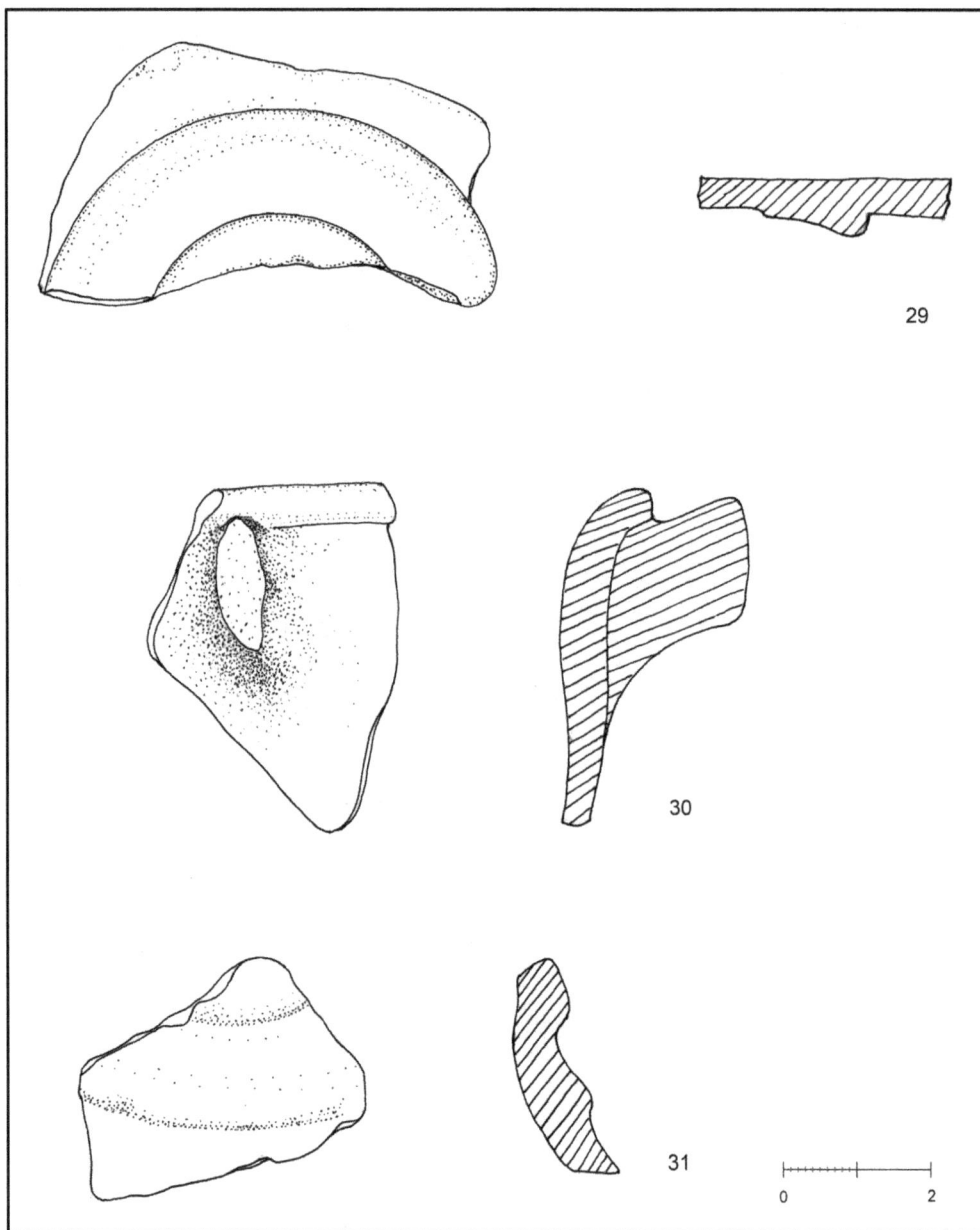

Pl. 22b. Dragišić, grave 30. 29-31. pottery

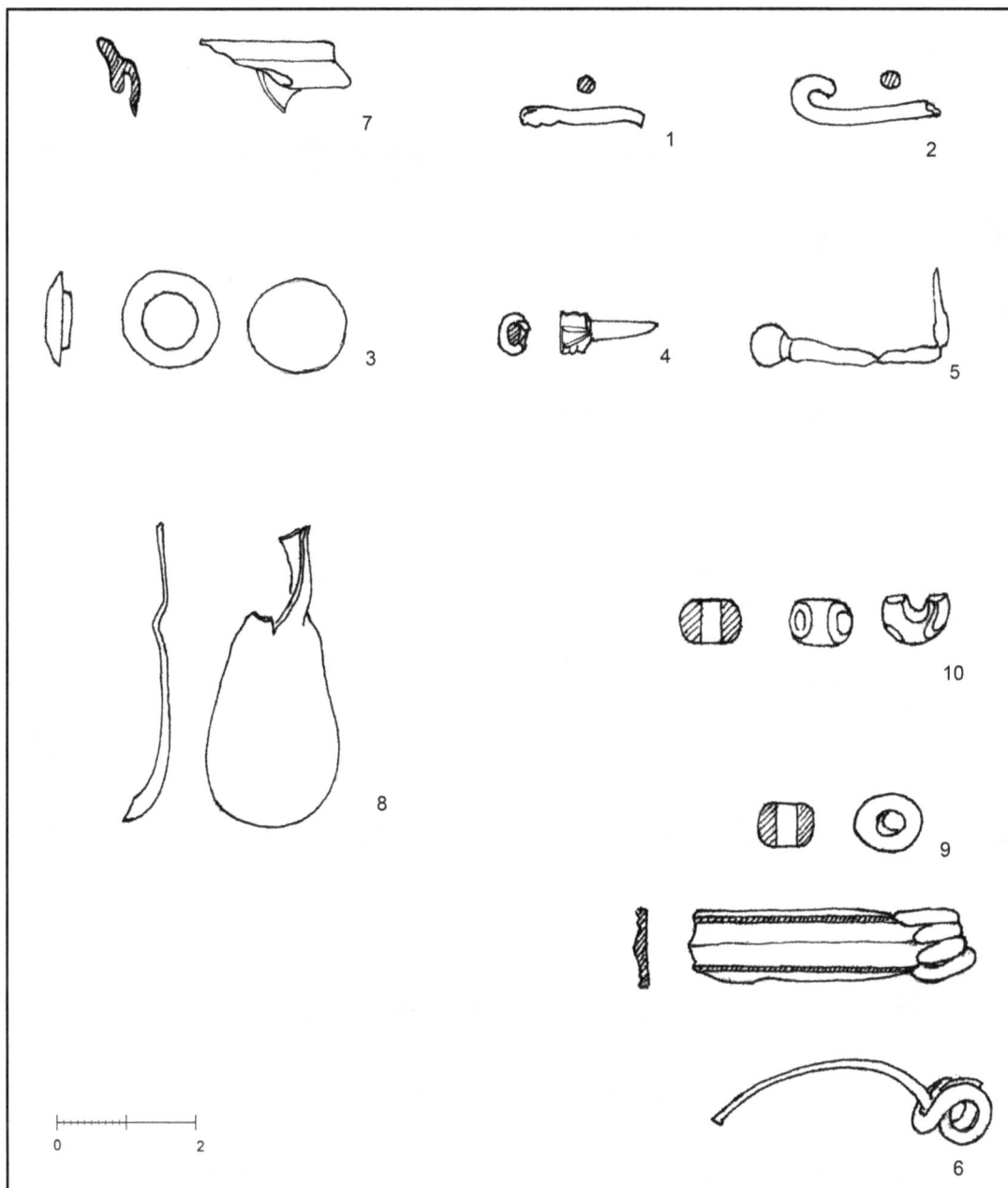

Pl. 23. Dragišić, grave 32. 1-6 bronze; 7-10 glass

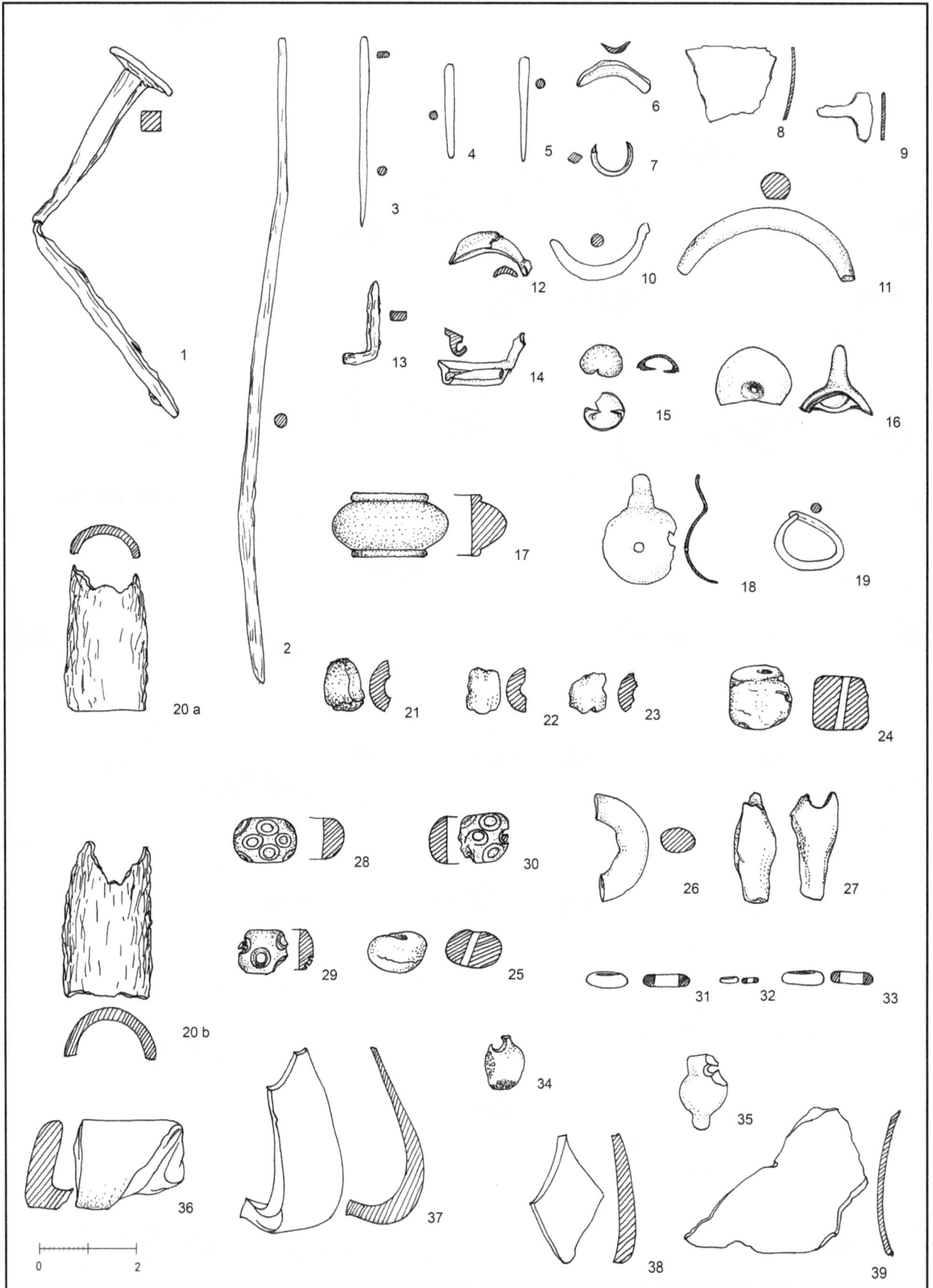

Pl. 24. Dragišić, grave 34. 1-2, 13, 20 iron; 3-12, 14-19 bronze; 21-27 amber; 28-39 glass

www.ingramcontent.com/pod-product-compliance
Lightning Source LLC
Chambersburg PA
CBHW061009030426
42334CB00033B/3427